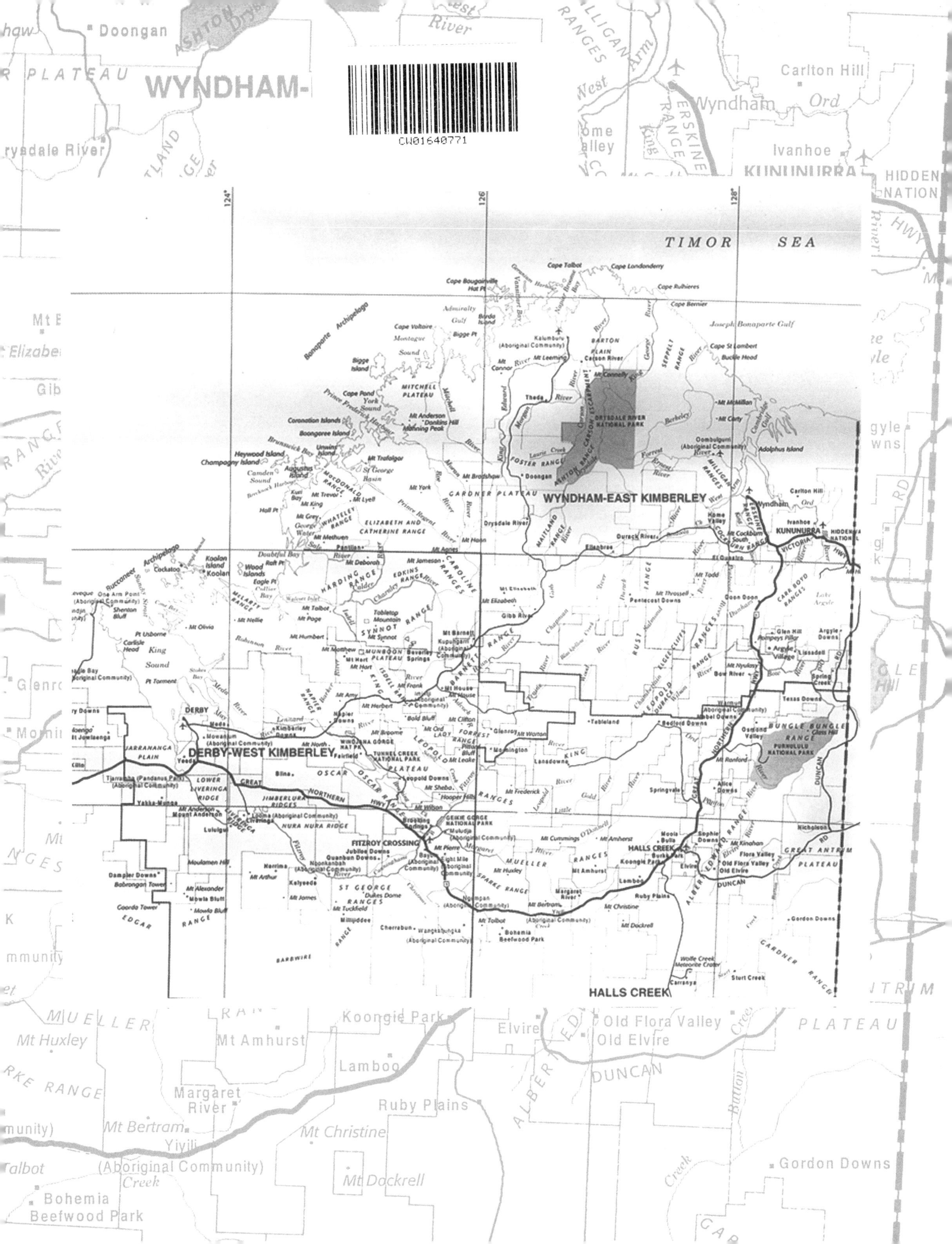

Doongan
WYNDHAM-
CW01640771
Carlton Hill
Wyndham
Ivanhoe
KUNUNURRA
TIMOR SEA
Cape Londonderry
Joseph Bonaparte Gulf
Bonaparte Archipelago
MITCHELL PLATEAU
DRYSDALE RIVER NATIONAL PARK
GARDNER PLATEAU
WYNDHAM-EAST KIMBERLEY
ELIZABETH AND CATHERINE RANGE
Drysdale River
Durack River
El Questro
Buccaneer Archipelago
King Sound
DERBY
DERBY-WEST KIMBERLEY
Gibb River
Doon Doon
Argyle Downs
BUNGLE BUNGLE RANGE
PURNULULU NATIONAL PARK
FITZROY CROSSING
HALLS CREEK
Mt Huxley
Mt Amhurst
Koongie Park
Lamboo
Margaret River
Ruby Plains
Mt Bertram
Yiyili
(Aboriginal Community)
Mt Christine
Mt Dockrell
Bohemia
Beefwood Park
Elvire
Old Flora Valley
Old Elvire
DUNCAN
PLATEAU
Gordon Downs

PIONEERS
of the
KIMBERLEY

THE MAGGIE LILLY STORY

by
Anne Marie Ingham

HALSTEAD PRESS

SYDNEY MM
Published by Halstead Press
19a Boundary Street,
Rushcutters Bay, New South Wales, 2011

 Typeset by Brevier Design, Kensington N.S.W. Printed in Melbourne by Brown Prior Anderson.

National Library cataloguing in publication entry

Ingham, Anne Marie
Pioneers of the Kimberley

ISBN 1 8875684 46 8

1. Lilly family.
2. Western Australia – Genealogy
3. Kimberley (W.A.) – History.
I.Title

929.2

Contents

Author's Note

For many years now I have had the pleasure of knowing Maggie Lilly. She was introduced to me by one of her great admirers, Roger Steel. Roger, prior to his term in the Northern Territory Parliament, lived and worked in the region and for some years managed Legune Station near Queens Gulf and Bullo River. Roger has a wealth of knowledge of the people and places in Maggie's story and it was he who suggested that I write. After many meetings with Maggie, an abundance of fun and laughter, taping sessions, and reading copious notes she jotted down in exercise books and scraps of paper, her remarkable life is at last recorded here.

Maggie is "living history" but her story begins with the brief account of two earlier lives, those of her mother Hannah and grandmother Sarah, pioneering women of Northern Australia who braved the vast wilderness of the country in the 1800s. From them Maggie inherited an independent spirit, enterprise and capacity to work and achieve against whatever odds Fate dealt out.

When Maggie Nicholson married Edmund James Lilljenqvist—Sam Lilly—they combined individual talents to create the mighty Bow River Station, a million acres in the wild and beautiful Kimberley. Neither was born to wealth and from earliest days they understood the only way they would achieve was by hard work and plenty of it. Every job, no matter how unpleasant or lowly, was tackled with energy and good humour. Sam's daughters adored him and recall his endless store of humorous anecdotes with which he'd lighten the atmosphere when things went wrong and tempers frayed. Although I never knew Sam and his great sense of fun, anyone who could distill humour from such earthy activities as driving his Dunny Cart will win my heart every time.

Sam became Shire President of the Halls Creek Shire and served the district for many years in that capacity. The physical demands of station life eventually took their toll and by the 1970s he had wearied of the struggle. As a prelude to retirement from the land, he bought a house in Wyndham. He had many other ideas he wished to pursue but time and waning strength did not permit. He enjoyed a brief period as host of the Six Mile Pub, a life which Maggie detested. He died in 1983 and Maggie moved to Kununurra which in her youth was nothing but a cattle camp on Ivanhoe Station. Having myself spent half a century on the land and been deeply involved with livestock, I can empathise both with Maggie's deep yearning for the station life and with Sam's disillusionment in the never-ending and unequal struggle it demands.

Although Maggie and her mother had few physical possessions and worked hard for every penny, there is a wealth of memory and memorabilia from which to piece together their lives. Carefully stored away in biscuit tins and albums are hundreds of photographs, letters, printed matter, newspaper cuttings and Hannah's green suede diary in which she records the birth and death of her little son Georgie. It is a strange feeling to hold the little book and turn the insect ravaged pages in which she made note of her joys and tragedy over a hundred years ago.

At 88 Maggie's eyesight for close work is giving problems but she can still see her beloved Kimberley Hills and like so many people raised in the bush she has a phenomenal memory of places and events down to the smallest detail.

Writing Maggie's story has been a fascinating endeavour, and no easy task reducing 88 extraordinary years to the pages of one small volume. To my great delight I found a quotation from Mark Twain which seemed remarkably apt for this biography. It reads:

> *Australian history is almost always picturesque; indeed it is so curious and strange that it is itself the chiefest novelty the country has to offer, and so it pushes the other novelties into second and third place. Australian history does not read like history...it is full of surprises and adventures, incongruities and contradictions, and incredibilities, but they are all true, they all happened.*

Anne Marie Ingham
"Caleula Springs" Belgravia, N.S.W.
2000

Foreword

As we move into the new millennium, the women who civilised the west are becoming distant figures in outback Kimberley history. At the time of publication of this book only a few of the senior women remain—Olive Quilty, Edna Quilty, Peg Underwood, Elizabeth Durack, Enid Durack and Maggie Lilly.

These women were household names in the middle of the century. They were renowned for their work ethic and their support for their husbands in their rugged outback pursuits.

They all had important things in common—their relationship with the Aboriginal women, and their concern for the welfare of their children.

In reference to the east Kimberley and Victoria River district, to my knowledge Maggie Lilly is the last of the outback pioneer women resident in the area. She has served the outback with spirit and determination. She is highly regarded by her peers and she deserves her place in history.

by Roger M. Steele
Northern Territory Government Advisor
and Former Government Minister

Where the Pelican Builds her Nest

The horses were ready, the rails were down,
But the riders lingered still —
One had a parting word to say,
And one had a pipe to fill.
Then they mounted, one with a granted prayer,
And one with a grief unguessed.
"We are going" they said, as they rode away,
"Where the pelican builds her nest!"

They had told us of pastures wide and green,
To be sought past the sunset's glow;
Of rifts in the ranges by opal lit;
And gold 'neath the river's flow.
And thirst and hunger were banished words
When they spoke of that unknown West;
No drought they feared, no flood they feared
Where the pelican builds her nest!

The creek at the fords was but fetlock deep
When we watched them crossing there;
The rains have replenished it thrice since then,
And thrice has the rock lain bare.
But the waters of Hope have flowed and fled,
And never from blue hill's breast
Come back—by the sun and the sands devoured —
Where the pelican builds her nest.

— Mary Hannay Foott
1846–1918

CHAPTER I

Little Maggie

THE DIM SHAPES of scattered buildings began to emerge and take on detail as piccaninny dawn chased away darkness, the dim light heralding yet another breathlessly hot and humid day of the wet season. Hannah Nicholson was on the verandah of one of the corrugated iron houses along Villiers Street in Derby, Western Australia, taking advantage of the soft early morning air. She sat on a stretcher bed with her back propped against the metal wall. By her side on the white cotton sheet lay a small dark haired baby. With a featherlight touch she stroked the baby's pale cheek. "That's right, my darling little Maggie, you sleep while it's nice and cool."

Hannah had never known a time of greater happiness. Two days earlier, on 25 February, 1912, she and Tom Sautelle had rejoiced at the birth of their daughter Margaret. There was no formal marriage; Maggie was "a love child" and never was the term so apt. The midwife had put the small bundle into Hannah's arms saying, "It's a beautiful brown eyed daughter you have, Mrs Nicholson." When she held the infant and studied the minute but perfect features, Hannah promised herself that wherever she was, no matter what hardship she had to bear she would keep this child close all her days.

Hannah was not young but she'd come through the pregnancy and birth well. Hardened by years of heavy physical work, she was strong and resilient. She knew the overworked general practitioner of Derby, Dr Adams, would call as soon as he was able and two days after the birth she felt no urgency to see him.

He arrived about mid-morning after he had attended to his more urgent cases and Hannah had taken Maggie inside. He stepped down from his buggy and tied the long reins to the near side front wheel to ensure his buggy and pair didn't move away. He lifted down his battered leather medical bag and ran up the steps onto the verandah. "Anyone home?"

The midwife, her face wreathed in a welcoming smile hurried to open the door. "Good morning Doctor, do come in. Just wait till you see our new baby!" She bustled ahead of him to Hannah's room. "I'll go and make some tea. I'm sure we'd all like a cuppa." He would have already been offered a cup of tea at every home on his round but another cup was always welcome.

Having made sure mother and daughter were well he smiled and said, "You've a fine little

Topsy there, Hannah"— Dr Adams always called girl babies Topsy —"and for a woman in her forties you're doing remarkably well. All the same, I think you ought to call it a day." Hannah laughed happily and assured him on the matter. Margaret Sautelle who was life's perfection to Tom and her would be their one and only! Two years previously she had given birth to their stillborn son and Dr Adams cautioned her then on the risks of childbirth after forty—though many women of the era bore children into their mature years. Men who spent the months of the dry season working far from home felt the same need of the comforting presence of their wives, whether their working lives were just beginning or almost over. There were many pregnancies in older women who must have despaired to find themselves once more "in the family way" after their husbands had been home a couple of months into the wet season. It has been said that a woman is never closer to death than when giving birth and until safely delivered they faced many risks. Dr Adams could only advise, attend and hope his patients had no complications.

He was the sole medical practitioner in the area, his nearest counterpart being in Darwin, over a thousand miles away over a rough dirt track negotiable only in the dry season. He had in his care some 450 people, 200 or so being residents of the town and the rest scattered throughout the Kimberley landscape on station properties and miners' camps. Sometimes his calls took days to make; telephones and radio were far in the future and the response to an urgent call was limited to the speed and endurance of a horse and his rider. Riding or driving, depending on the conditions of tracks to distant stations, he often found the patient was past help and the only duty he could perform was signing a death certificate.

Now Hannah was feeling well and blissfully happy. Little Maggie was thriving and the new parents glowed with pride. As Hannah looked down at the sleeping child she thought how very grateful she was. Life had dealt some bitter blows and it made her present joy and wonderment all the sweeter. As she gazed out across Derby's endless flat grey tidal reaches her mind slipped back across the years to other happy times, in childhood.

Her mother, Sarah Ann Chapman, born in England in 1840, had sailed in 1863 to the colonies, where she married a teamster, Jack Beasley of Bowen, Queensland on 12 September, 1864. Four children blessed their union; three boys, Harry, Jack, and Charley and one daughter, Hannah, born on 15 May, 1869 in Pentland, Queensland. Sarah was a horsewoman of great ability and she and the children often accompanied Jack on the dusty rutted tracks to far distant townships such as Cloncurry in western Queensland and north to Normanton near the Gulf of Carpentaria, delivering supplies. One trip of epic proportions took them as far as the gold mining township of Playford, less than two hundred miles south of Darwin.

As Hannah grew older, Sarah stayed at home and Hannah became her father's help and companion on the long dusty tracks. The wagon was loaded with all manner of goods for the remote stations of the north and west of Queensland. They mostly carried essential supplies and occasionally something for a station wife, lengths of material for a new dress, baby clothes, some longed for books perhaps. Hannah was as capable as any man attending to the myriad chores along the way. She would tail the spare stock by day, help harness and unharness the teams, hobble up, do the cooking in black cast iron camp ovens and see that their life on the track was as trouble free as possible. They brought their own dry essentials—tea, sugar, flour, rice, salt, dried fruit —and a supply of tinned items including cockey's joy (golden syrup, a real treat). They picked up fresh food along the way—goat's meat and milk and maybe some fresh beef if the station had killed on the day they delivered goods, sometimes a sack bulging with welcome fresh vegetables from the homestead garden. Meat, unless salted, could only be kept a day or two so Hannah or her father would shoot duck or kangaroo to augment their rations. Day in and day out for months on end the team plodded slowly toward its destination. Good days and bad, she had loved every minute.

MAGGIE LILLY'S GRANDMOTHER SARAH ANNE CHAPMAN WHO CAME TO AUSTRALIA FROM THE GENTLE LANDSCAPES OF THE LAKES DISTRICT IN ENGLAND IN 1863 AND MADE A NEW LIFE IN THE HARSH PIONEERING ENVIRONMENT OF THE NORTHERN TERRITORY.

Like her mother, she was a fine horsewoman and with three brothers to beat she would take her turn riding unmanageable horses. What fun that was. The boys would tie the horse's head against a post and blindfold it with a bag, tucking the edges under the cheek straps of the bridle. When the saddle was firmly girthed up Hannah would mount, settle herself and when ready tell the boys to let it go. Swiftly they would untie the rope and remove the blindfold. Whilst blindfolded the horse would not move an inch but with sight restored anything could happen, depending on the animal's temperament. Some horses that were difficult to mount gave no trouble once the rider was in the saddle. The uncertainty of the outcome fired Hannah's sense of adventure. She remembered the exultation and excitement of these challenges, staying atop the wildly bucking animal until it wearied of the fight and ceased its frenzied activity. With sides heaving and sweat building up under the saddle blanket the horse might walk a few paces and stand waiting to see what the rider wanted next. Once a horse was "ridden out" it rarely tried again in earnest; a few token bucks maybe but the big fight was usually over. A smile curved her lips as she thought how different her games had been from those played by town bred girls!

She had raced her brothers on foot at every opportunity and invariably beat them. The only boy who could outrun her was the son of another teamster they'd encounter and camp with. These rare and welcome meetings were a chance to exchange news, probably months old by then. In those vast spaces where a day's travel may only be a few miles, twenty at best, any news was welcome. For teamsters' wives who accompanied their men there was the chance to talk to another woman. Sitting on logs or upturned buckets they tended the fire and the food while the children revelled in the company of new playmates. Then the teams were harnessed, the wagons loaded and they were on their way once more. Sometimes they travelled together enjoying the sense of security it offered and when their ways parted they waved and called farewells until the bush hid them from view.

A vision of her mother swam before Hannah's gaze. By the time of Maggie's birth, Sarah was a very old lady living at Pine Creek. She had been an enterprising woman far ahead of her time. On the wagon trip to the Northern Territory with her husband she saw that a more profitable future for

(Photograph by courtesy of Northern Territory Library — Federal Parliament Collection.)

her family was possible around Playford, later to be called Pine Creek. Gold had been discovered in a number of places in the area back in 1873 and with the railway from Darwin to Playford soon to be completed Sarah was sure the district would flourish. It was a very long way from their home in north east Queensland but such things were of little consequence to the intrepid Sarah when she had set her sights on a goal.

In Playford, tenders were being invited for the licence of the Grove Hill Hotel and Sarah successfully applied, agreeing to a rental at thirty shilling per week, terminable at one month's notice. The terms seemed harsh but Sarah was certain she could meet her expenses and still run at a profit. According to the records the rent covered the building, the furnishings, lamps and fittings and a "nearly new billiard table" which would be a great drawcard for miners and stockmen. She believed Hannah would help her in the venture and there would be station work for the boys. The Beasley marriage had become a matter of form only by then and husband and wife decided to separate formally. Jack went on working with his team in Queensland whilst Sarah set about running her new business. She joined in the town's social activities and it is recorded that in August of 1887 she was the first woman to win a race in the Northern Territory, the Ladies Hack Race staged by the Goldfields Racing Club. Horseracing was an integral part of life in the district and her sons Jack and Charlie became deeply involved. Charlie became a prominent local jockey.

Life in Playford held no interest for son Harry who returned to north east Queensland. He went back to the teamster's life that he knew and liked best. From the Charters Towers area he worked with his bullock wagons as far south as Moree in New South Wales.

Eighteen year old Hannah met George Cook, a man eleven years her senior, and promptly fell in

THE TOWNSHIP OF PINE CREEK IN 1912, MUCH AS IT WOULD HAVE BEEN WHEN HANNAH RETURNED TO VISIT HER MOTHER SARAH. SARAH, MAGGIE LILLY'S GRANDMOTHER, WAS VERY MUCH INVOLVED IN THE COMMERCE OF THE TOWN WHICH WAS STILL A LUSTY FRONTIER MINING SETTLEMENT.

love. They were married in October 1887 and their daughter Annie was born at Grove Hill in June the following year. In February, 1890 they had a son, George.

Meanwhile Sarah having sold the Grove Hill licence lodged plans for a hotel, to be called the Cosmopolitan, and later applied for a new storekeeper's licence at Maude Creek in 1889.

It was an exciting time in the area. In January 1889 the township of Playford was gazetted. That was followed by Brocks Creek in April, and in October, the Darwin–Playford Railway line was opened covering a distance of "one hundred and forty five miles and thirty four chains". This new service was of enormous benefit to people living in the small clusters of homes in the mining villages and to the region as a whole. It was a relatively comfortable alternative form of transport to and from Darwin and meant faster delivery of goods and supplies—even during the wet when the roads were quagmires, untrafficable for months on end. Needless to say, Sarah was elated.

George Cook was well known locally and highly respected in racing circles. He had several good horses including a colt purported to be one of the best youngsters introduced to the district. With their mutual love of horses the young couple had much to interest them, and as a wife and the mother of George's two little children Hannah had been utterly content. Sadly Fate had other plans.

Hannah's eyes filled with tears as she recalled the day so long ago. When, at the age of twenty two, with a babe in her arms and a toddler clutching at her skirts, she had received the devastating news that her first love was dead. George had not been feeling particularly well for some weeks but it was nothing specific. On his thirty fourth birthday, he rode from their home at Mt Shoebridge to collect the mail at Howley, one of the many small mining settlements along the new railway line. On the homeward journey a companion, William Blamey, accompanied him. A few miles along

(Lilly collection)

HARRY BEASLEY, SARAH AND JACK'S SON AND BROTHER OF HANNAH, REMAINED IN QUEENSLAND AND WORKED HIS TEAM AS FAR SOUTH AS MOREE IN NEW SOUTH WALES IN THE 1890S.

the track George Cook "had a bit of a turn… a bit like a fit." Blamey settled him in the shade and eventually brought him around. George wanted to keep going but could not control his limbs well enough to mount his horse. Thoroughly alarmed, William Blamey rode back to Howley, borrowed a buggy and returned to the sick man as quickly as possible, but George was already dead, the cause unknown. He was buried in a lonely grave near Brock's Creek. Brock's Creek was a railside settlement which served several gold mines, including the richly yielding Zapopan, between Howley and Fountain Head. As often as she could manage, the young widow rode out to that lonely spot and wept for her lost love in the solitude and silence of the bush.

Remembering the early days, Hannah realised how fortunate her first twenty two years had been. In youth, she took her mother's competence, adaptability and resilience for granted, but with the accumulated wisdom of the years, she saw Sarah as a woman of vision and amazing enterprise. At twenty three Sarah had left behind her family and home in England, emigrating to a harsh unknown land half a world away, to begin a new life where heat, dust, flies, lack of water, vast empty spaces and few creature comforts were the order of the day. To her Australian daughter Hannah, who had always lived north of the Tropic of Capricorn, life in the English countryside belonged in the realms of storybooks and fairy tales. The soft rain, snow at Christmas time, deep fertile soil, soft green pastures, gentle brooks, castles and soft skies were so different from the land she knew.

Hannah loved to hear her mother talk of her beautiful homeland but Sarah would finish by saying "Make no mistake about it, lass, all the people on the ship coming out here thought the same as I did. We believed we'd have a better chance in a new country. Where I was born and in the rest of England for that matter, people sometimes lived in a tiny village all their lives and never ventured anywhere, not even a few miles from it. Go ten miles away and they'd think you were a foreigner!" Sarah had come from Penrith in the County of Cumberland. This far north west corner of England is known as the Lakes District and considered to be one of the most beautiful parts of the country, but Sarah was far too engrossed in her new independent and progressive style of life to express any regrets. "You young Beasleys know the thousands of miles we've travelled and there's always been a friendly greeting. There's room to move here in more ways than one; you can even go a long way up in the world if you've a mind to. In the Old Country if you were born a miner's son there was precious little you could do but be a miner yourself. Here, you can try your hand at anything and succeed, what's more!"

Sarah had taken Hannah, Annie and little George under her protective wing after George Cook's death. Her heart ached for her daughter and wished she could ease her grief but she could only offer her loving support and practical help. Time and Hannah's own resilience would have to do the rest. The days were fully occupied from first light until long after the kerosene lamps were lit and the little children fast asleep. The two women sat outside under the star studded canopy of night, relishing the last cup of tea whilst they discussed the day's business. Hannah marvelled at her mother's capacity for work and listened with fascination to her ideas and plans. Where, she wondered, did Sarah learn all this? Her grasp of financial matters and her intuition were amazing!

Hannah would also have thoroughly enjoyed the work, the challenge, the constant coming and going of the miners, white and Chinese, and the business of running an efficient store—but grief was her companion, twenty four hours of every day. Hannah maintained a pleasant manner to all, then every night she cried herself to sleep. Only Sarah, hearing the muffled sobs through the thin walls of the building understood the depth of her daughter's loss.

Try as she might to settle in to the life now offering, the sad young woman remained restless. A letter came from George Cook's sister, Caroline Lane, expressing her sympathy and inviting Hannah to visit her in Newcastle. Sarah hoped a trip away might help and encouraged Hannah to accept. Hannah wrote to Caroline suggesting a time and waited for the return letter many weeks later. Eventually it was arranged and she and her two small children journeyed by coach to the Queensland coast, then south by rail into New South Wales. She hoped to gain some comfort from close proximity to her husband's sister; maybe family similarity would help her feel some presence of George and ease the loss.

At her home in Newcastle, Caroline had been very kind. Though she was past middle age, she offered to take and raise little George until Hannah was "on her feet". It seemed a good idea to Hannah at the time. She accepted the offer, giving Caroline an unusual piece of jewellery in recompense. It was the shape of a map of Australia, made from Pine Creek gold and studded with gems. She would certainly manage more easily with only one child and little George would be cared for in comfort and security by his aunt for as long as necessary. Broken hearted, but believing it was for the best, Hannah parted with her small son, not knowing she would never see him again.

Hannah and daughter Annie set out by train on the long journey to Townsville, in north Queensland, where she would visit Harry before making her way back to Pine Creek. As the miles lengthened her despondency grew. She wondered, fretted and worried—had she really had made the right decision in leaving George with Caroline? At the end of her tedious journey a porter carried Hannah's sparse luggage onto the platform where she caught sight of Harry's lean form hurrying towards her. When Harry Beasley had last seen Hannah in Pine Creek, she was a lively single girl full of fun and vitality. It was something of a shock to him that day to find a sad young widow and mother for whom life had lost its light and laughter. He kissed his sister and then swept the delighted little Annie up in a bear hug. Harry, who was working around the district with his team of bullocks had found temporary lodgings for them in town and with Annie skipping ahead, Harry and Hannah picked up the baggage and made for the boarding house he had chosen.

Hannah was expecting to stay only a few days in Townsville but Fate decided it was time young Hannah Cook's life took on a new aspect. She was introduced to a young man named Joseph Michael Nicholson from Holbro, Denmark. The dashing Dane swept Hannah off her feet. A country girl, she would rarely if ever have come in contact with his type, the tall, handsome mannerly European who courted her with such Continental charm and paid her extravagant compliments in his broken English. There is no doubt that Joseph was also equally captivated by this beautiful and passionate young woman, so strong and capable beyond his wildest dreams or comprehension. They were married in Townsville in December, 1892.

The first year of their marriage was marred by the birth of a stillborn girl, but Joseph and Hannah rejoiced when their second child Maude Florina was born at Tandy Creek, near Charters Towers in October of 1894.

Hannah recalled the romance and excitement. She had been sure that after George's death life held no more joy. So sure! ... until she looked into the clear blue eyes of the young man from Denmark. Joseph Nicholson was lively, charming and gregarious. It had felt so good to be cherished once more and to know the joy of loving and being loved and to hold her small baby daughter in her arms. She yearned for her little son so far away in New South Wales, but the new infant eased the ache in her heart and at twenty five she vowed to put all her strength and reawakened passion into making her new marriage a success. The Nicholsons moved from station to station where Joseph would be employed as a stockman. Joseph never seemed to work for any length of time at any place and their path led westward to stations more remote. Hannah longed to be reunited with little George, to collect him from his aunt and resume life with her family in tact. However, apart from her intuitive certainty and fear that Joseph would shun the idea, there was the distance involved and the fact that there never seemed to be any money available. Pastoral wages were low and the constant moves took a toll of the finances. As they moved farther and farther into the inland her hopelessness increased.

Eventually, they found themselves in the Northern Territory, and heading for the Kimberley region where Joseph had secured a job on Go Go Station. They were able to spend a little time with Sarah before moving on. During Hannah's unexpectedly long absence Sarah had been widowed, had bought and sold several businesses, and recently acquired a racehorse. When mother and daughter were reunited there was much to talk about, including Sarah's plan to marry William George Ashton, a teamster many years younger than herself. Before the Nicholsons moved further westward Sarah had a little time to enjoy Hannah's two daughters. She was delighted with her grandchildren but she had doubts about Hannah's future happiness. She could see through Joseph's charm to his shortcomings easily enough and knew with a mother's heart that a troubled future awaited her daughter. There was nothing she could say or do; Hannah had made her choice and she'd have to make the best of whatever a future with Joseph Nicholson held.

When Joseph took up work in the Kimberley region of Western Australia Hannah decided that it was better for the two girls, Annie and Maude, to receive an education down south in Perth. At that time, life on the remote Kimberley cattle runs held a considerable element of danger and there were increasing rumours of the Aborigines' hostility to white settlers and the frequent spearing of livestock. When they reached Derby, there were serious accounts of trouble circulating in the little town and it confirmed Hannah's belief that the situation was too risky for small children. Joseph had no wish to place his little daughters' lives in jeopardy and agreed to Hannah's plans, but as a Roman Catholic he insisted they be enrolled at a convent. They booked passage on the next coastal vessel travelling to Perth. With immense relief Hannah felt the engines throb under her feet as the ship eased away from the jetty out into King's Sound toward the Indian Ocean on their southward journey.

For a long time she had stayed near to the convent, working as a cook, laundress or housekeeper until the little girls settled in there as boarders. Recalling it, Hannah shivered involuntarily. Even in the Derby heat her body remembered how it had been so dreadfully cold. She recalled the endless piles of laundry; washing, starching and ironing mountains of white linen which had to be finished in spotless order with frills and pin tucks ironed to perfection. How careful she had to be each time she put an iron back on the fuel stove to reheat and pick up a hot replacement. Quickly she would rub it on a cloth wrapped around a lump of beeswax; bottom, sides and back, to clean the iron. The tiniest cinder would smear a black mark on the snowy linen and back in the wash it would have to go. The laundry reeked of hot beeswax. It helped the iron glide over the fabric but forever after, hot beeswax reminded her of those endless hours of toil. It was thankless, backbreaking work but with care she could save a little money and pay the convent dues well ahead thus assuring her girls' future care and education.

There came a time when Hannah felt reasonably comfortable about leaving the girls entirely to the nuns' care. She was still reluctant but told herself they had each other and seemed quite happy under the convent regime. The nuns were delighted to discover that Maude Nicholson, young as she was, possessed an extraordinary gift for music. They promised to give her every encouragement.

Once again, Hannah was in an invidious position, trying to do what seemed right for all concerned. If she returned to the Kimberley—and she was, after all a married woman with a duty to rejoin her husband—it meant leaving her two little girls so very far away. Certainly, they were in good hands so with little joy and a lot of resignation she returned to Derby on a State Coastal Shipping Service vessel. Joseph had come in to town to await the ship's arrival. He had found plenty to entertain him in the hotels and was in no rush to leave for the station.

Much had happened since Hannah's departure several years' earlier. It had been a time of violence, massacres and bloodshed on both sides. Joseph told her of the uprising at Oobergooma where he had since found work as manager. For a time he was enrolled as a police constable to help subdue the hostile Aborigines. Right through the area the fighting strength of armed warriors was reinforced when ex-police trackers rejoined their tribal brothers against the whites. Fully trained in the use of firearms and having learnt the ways of the white settler, they were a formidable opposition though they had few arms. They killed policemen, stockmen and some Aborigines who worked for white settlers, and they speared many horses and countless cattle. The ex-police boy Pigeon (Jandamarra) was the ringleader. For more than five years he and his gang managed to evade the patrols, swearing to kill white men and cattle wherever they came across them. The plan for Oobergooma was to kill the whites, burn the homestead and drive the cattle into the hills.

Forewarned, a Constable Spong and his men met the advancing warriors on a river flat. A large number of warriors, resplendent in ochre war paint, carrying spears and chanting their battle cry, faced the mounted men who carried Winchester repeating rifles. They were dauntless in their attack but spears were no match for the rifles and the bloody battle of Oobergooma was soon over.

Pigeon was badly wounded and the white men thought he had been killed. He recovered however, and with his magnificent bush skills seemed invincible. Pigeon and his men continued their warfare against the encroach of the white man and his livestock, but at the age of twenty four, he was finally cornered and killed. Joseph Nicholson was one of a party of five white men and nine Aborigines who successfully tracked the elusive warrior. For their services the constables each received ten pounds reward and the trackers an outfit of clothes consisting of a pair of moleskin trousers, a shirt, hat and neckerchief valued at one pound.

As the story unfolded, Hannah realised how sensible she had been to take her daughters south to Perth. Discretion certainly had been the better part of valour!

Joseph assured her that the trouble was over now. With the despatch of Pigeon and his loyal warriors the fierce resistance was broken and life on the stations was once more relatively safe. Joseph couldn't remember what had happened to his ten pounds reward money and his wages. He had nothing left with which to buy personal items to take out to the station, so before leaving Hannah had to use her own hard won shillings to purchase some essentials. She wasn't surprised so much as bitterly disappointed and angry. It was not a good start to the resumption of their life together and already her resolution was weakening.

For some time before this Hannah had realised that Joseph's gregarious nature had a dark side. His lively charm at first blinded her to his underlying weakness. In the heady days of their romance and marriage she believed he had been hardly done by at his places of employment but gradually the realisation dawned that he was a vain, unreliable ne'er do well depending on his "gift of the gab" to see him through. He could not resist alcohol and any and every occasion was an excuse to drink. As time went by he became worse and was only safe from the habit when working out on a station at least a couple of days' ride to the nearest pub. From the moment he arrived in town all responsibilities were forgotten. Drinkers soon found the agreeable talkative Danish stockman an easy touch and flattery was the magic key to open his pockets. Time and again in the past his drunken misplaced generosity had left the family hopelessly short of money for even the most essential items. Frugal and hard working herself, she could not bear such foolishness and lack of responsibility in a man with a wife and family to support.

The ride out to Oobergooma was clear in her memory. The track, suitable only for horses and pack animals, much of it barely discernible, wound its way over 140 kilometres of the superb Kimberley wilderness. They crossed the May and Meda Rivers and journeyed through country inaccessible to wheeled vehicles. The isolation held no fears for Hannah. She would concentrate on picking up the threads of her marriage and attempt some sort of compromise in the relationship with a man whom she now truthfully acknowledged to herself she neither loved nor respected. She did however respect the marriage vows she had made and would do her best to honour them.

It took two days' steady riding to reach the station. The homestead was made of bush timber, tin and bark while the outbuildings were mostly bough shelters. Supplies could be brought in by boat from Derby, crossing Stokes Bay and coming up river past the vast swamplands, but such visits required the charter of a vessel and crew. With no other means of communication someone still had to ride to town to make the arrangements, so for much of the time household goods were limited to what could be brought in by teams of pack animals. For a teamster's daughter who had lived for months on the road with few possessions, this was of no concern. Hannah had learnt in her girlhood how to plan and order supplies to last for months at a time, and to manage well on the barest necessities.

Hannah had travelled to many stations where Joseph had jobs and arrival at Oobergooma was much the same as previous occasions. She lifted her bags from the packsaddles and carried them into the corrugated iron and bush timber dwelling. The station blacks looked over the new missus with mild curiosity and the head stockman brought Joseph up to date on station happenings and jobs to be done.

Away from town and sober, Joseph was pleasant enough and Hannah settled in to her wifely duties. She decided now that she was here she'd make the best of the situation. It was not long before she found she was pregnant. A couple of months prior to the birth she rode in to Derby for the delivery. This went smoothly enough and on 23 August Hannah gave birth to a son whom she named Georgie. She duly recorded his arrival in a small, green, suede covered diary. Weeks later, Joseph came to town with a string of pack horses to stock up with supplies and to take his wife and new son back to Oobergooma, to settle in well before the wet season began.

Joseph made up for lost time in the pubs but eventually they started for the station. One of the first things Hannah did on arriving back at Oobergooma was to have a stockman find and bring in a couple of freshly calved cows to be broken in for milking.

Attending to stock work Joseph was sometimes away from the homestead for weeks at a time. On one such occasion, Hannah had left Georgie asleep under the watchful eye of an old lubra, and was milking one of the cows. With her head resting against the cow's flank, fully engrossed in the business squirting frothing milk into a bucket, she was suddenly overcome by a strong premonition of danger.

With smooth movements she slid the bucket from under the cow's belly, stood and turned to find herself staring down the barrel of a rifle. One of the station blacks stood not a few feet from her, aiming point blank at her back, and was pulling the trigger as she turned. Miraculously it did not fire. Whether the hammer had been only on half cock or it was a misfire, she would never know, but of one thing she was certain, it would have been fatal. Spent shells were never thrown away but were always reloaded by the men or Hannah; everyone knew how to perform this chore and every so often one of these shells turned out to be a dud.

Caught in the act, the man ran towards the huts and Hannah started after him. He disappeared so Hannah went to the homestead and asked the lubras, who were all standing huddled together and very fearful, where he had gone. They indicated the men's quarters and the furious Hannah turned on her heel and headed in that direction.

She found him there still with the gun in his hand. Reaching for the weapon she said, "Give me that gun, Bobby. ***I'll*** fix it!" and fearlessly snatched it from him. She never saw him again. He knew well enough that he would now be a marked man after his unsuccessful attempt to kill a white woman. With the terrible end of the invincible Pigeon and all his followers still fresh in his mind, Bobby vanished into the bush before anyone could arrange a search party.

The Nicholson relationship, in spite of genuine effort on both sides, deteriorated steadily. Hannah could see that the drink and associated problems would eventually be their ruin and asked for a divorce, which Joseph as a Roman Catholic steadfastly refused to countenance.

When Georgie was about six months old and the smiling, gurgling joy of his mother's life, he was struck by fever. Hannah sat through the long night doing all she could make him comfortable, sponging the hot little body, fanning the humid air to make a small breeze and talking quietly to try to sooth him. In desperation she begged Joseph to ride to Derby and fetch the doctor. When he saw how desperately ill his little son was, he saddled a fresh horse and left immediately. The eighty miles over rough country would not be travelled in a day. Even if he could locate the doctor, he would have to procure a fresh horse and still he could not be back until the third or fourth day. It was late February and in the wet, so the journey would be even more difficult. Hannah just hoped and prayed that by some miracle the doctor would come in time and save the little boy's life.

As Joseph's horse covered mile after exhausting mile, bogged to the belly at times in soil turned to mud by the monsoonal rain, Hannah kept her lonely watch. Though willing with all her heart for the exhausted little body to keep fighting, she knew the odds were stacked against Georgie. He lost his battle with the fever and Hannah felt his life slip away as she held him. He was barely six months old. Exhausted by her long vigil she sat on the greenhide stretcher and held the small still form in her arms, unconscious of the appalling heat and humidity, heavy tears slipping down her cheeks to spill onto the baby's face and tiny chest. At last, stiff from sitting, she rose, and placing the little body on the bed, gently wrapped it in a cloth, carefully tucking a corner over the little face to protect it from the busy searching flies and other insects.

In spite of her anguish, she knew what she must do and there was no time to waste. She found one of the stockmen and asked him to dig a small grave, showing him where she wanted it. "That little fella Georgie, im bin die?" Hannah nodded. "Yes, Charlie, im bin die." She then went to the storage hut and searched for a box. She found what she was looking for quickly enough. All station supplies came in bags, well made boxes, tins or drums. She tipped out the remaining contents of a box and found a lid that fitted, picked up some nails and a hammer and returned to the homestead.

A body buried in the bush in those days was usually wrapped in its swag or several metres of Berkemyer, a canvas cloth bought by the roll for station supplies and from which swags were made. Securely bound in its canvas cocoon it was then consigned to the grave in a matter of hours. Hannah could not bear the thought of the heavy hard ground pressing down to crush little Georgie's frail form. At least the makeshift coffin would hold it away from him awhile. She folded a blanket in the bottom of the box and then lifted the pathetic bundle into her arms, pulling away the corner of the cloth for a last look at her beloved Georgie's pale little countenance. It took all her will power to place the child's body in the box, an act in which she acknowledged that he was indeed beyond anything her love could alter, and that they must part. With a heavy heart she placed the lid on top and reached for the nails. For a while she could go no further. Sobs racked her body. At last she managed to secure the lid firmly, wondering was there ever a more terrible task for a mother than this? Many a bush woman had faced the same ordeal but that was of little help or comfort at the time.

Charlie called from the door. "Hole bin dug Missus." Hannah managed to voice her thanks and with tears blinding her, picked up the box and carried it over to the freshly dug grave. Kneeling on the ground she picked up the box and lowered it carefully to rest on the earth beneath. With the aid of the opposite side she managed to straighten herself and for a long while remained kneeling. Then gently, so very gently, she took small handfuls of earth and sprinkled them on the box. It made hardly a sound and she continued in this way until her legs and back ached and her hands were sore from the gritty soil. With a shovel she completed the task. It could not be left half done for the dingoes to investigate. She knew what they would be capable of once they picked up the scent. A few flat rocks too heavy for the wild dogs to move were brought at her request and the little grave was complete. She tied a couple of sticks in the form of a cross and pushed the end into the ground.

In the following days she wandered disconsolately around the homestead paying many visits to the little mound of earth and the little green suede notebook received yet another pencilled entry, "Georgie died on 9th February."

Joseph Nicholson did not return for many a long day. With agreeable drinking mates in Derby he forgot the reason why he was there. By the time he rode up the track to Oobergooma, red eyed, haggard and somewhat shamefaced from his prolonged binge he found his little son long dead and his marriage a thing of the past. Any vestige of affection or respect Hannah felt for him had withered and died in the long days of isolation and grief. She left soon after, riding back to Derby

(Lilly collection)

Country general stores were remarkable for the variety of goods they carried. Adcock's in Derby was no exception. It supplied everything from boots to bullets, household needs to harness. Coastal steamers provided deliveries to replenish the stock. Orders were carried as sea mail to Perth, filled by the supplier and dispatched on the next ship with cargo space, the process taking at least a month. Patience and forward thinking were essential to shopper and storekeeper alike.

and who knew what? One thing she did know was Joseph Michael Nicholson would play no further part in her life, divorce or no divorce.

Hannah found lodgings in Derby, took on housekeeping, cooking and any other work which was offered, regularly sending money to the convent for the two girls' board and education. She wrote from time to time but visiting her daughters was beyond her means. Domestic service was very poorly paid in spite of the long hours it demanded and the energy expended.

The new century began and it brought Hannah more sadness. A letter eventually found its way to her from Caroline Lane informing her that her son, little George Cook, was dead by drowning in 1898, just eight years old. She remembered how closely she had held the toddler, beloved son of her beloved George Cook, comforting herself that surely, if anyone would cherish him as her own, it would be her late husband's sister. She also remembered the overwhelming reservations she had at the time and how ruthlessly she crushed them for what she believed was the better option for her son's future. Why, oh why, had she not listened to her intuition? She had had three Georges in her life, all of whom she had loved unreservedly and she had lost them all.

Derby was a very small town isolated by hundreds of miles from the nearest settlements. People relied heavily on neighbours for support. Everyone knew each other and each other's business. The events that brought Hannah back from Oobergooma were soon known to all and their hearts went out to the unfortunate wife of the drunkard, Joseph Nicholson. Due to some misfortune and losses caused by Joseph's incompetence, his reputation as a stockman also deteriorated.

For a long time the grief stricken Hannah worked long, hard hours, fell exhausted into bed each night to get up the next day and doggedly start again. However, unnoticed by Hannah, Time, The Great Healer was at work and very gradually she found her spirits returning. As each week passed, her awareness of the community around her increased and the kindly folk of Derby responded. The warmth of human kindness enveloped her, and the healing process began to work its quiet miracle.

There were two little girls to care for and educate and it was obvious that Joseph Nicholson could not be relied on for any support. The full burden until they left school lay firmly in her lap so Hannah worked with a will, making Annie and Maude's future her priority.

One day some time after Hannah had taken up residence in Clarendon Street, a serious young man in his late thirties came to town from his pastoral lease, Federal Downs, also in the Oobergooma area. He brought with him some interesting mineral specimens, later referred to in the Derby newspaper as tin ore, and was discussing the find with some residents when Hannah came by on her way to Adcock's Store. "Hannah," one called, "Come and meet Tom Sautelle. He's come in from Federal Downs, out your way."

Hannah had put Oobergooma behind her and it was no longer "out her way" but she hardly registered the tactless phrase. One look at Tom Sautelle and it was love at first sight. She recalled the day, the hour and the moment vividly! So did he. Romance bloomed and Hannah wrote to Joseph once more to request a divorce so she and her new love could marry. In spite of all that had happened, Joseph refused, repeating that as a Roman Catholic, his beliefs prevented it. Such piety from a man of Joseph's calibre cut no ice with Hannah. Tom and she decided they would take up life together and if the town disapproved, so be it. As it happened, the townspeople liked and respected Hannah and wished the couple well.

Unnoticed, the baby Maggie had woken and was staring up at her from the bed through unfocussed eyes, while sucking noisily on a tiny fist. The sound brought Hannah from her reverie. The sun, the temperature and the humidity had all risen whilst Hannah had travelled the long road of her memories. She blinked to clear her vision. So deep had been her meditation that she had registered neither sight nor sound until her maternal instinct alerted her to the baby's movements. "What a life eh, Maggie? My poor little boys all gone, your sister Annie has children older than you, your sister Maude is preparing to take her vows and become a nun and now your mother is living 'in sin' as they call it! and I'll tell you what, young lady, I've never been happier and your Daddy is someone worth living in sin for." Hannah chuckled and lifting the baby held her close, "It makes me so sad when I think of your two sisters growing up without a mother or a father but you, Maggie Sautelle Nicholson shall have a proper family and I will never leave you, as long as I live."

CHAPTER II

Growing up in Wyndham

FOR TWO AND A HALF YEARS after Maggie was born, Hannah Nicholson and Tom Sautelle lived in Derby. Tom, six years Hannah's junior, was a hardworking man devoted to the woman whom he regarded as his wife and to their small daughter, Maggie.

The year was 1915 and news reached Derby that a meatworks was to be built in Wyndham on the Cambridge Gulf to serve the growing cattle industry in the region. It was logical to assume that a generous range of opportunities would be open to willing workers. Rumour had it that it would be at least four years in the building and when complete it would need staff at all levels. Tom and Hannah felt it offered better potential than Derby and they planned to investigate.

Tom would travel overland and Hannah and Maggie would go by sea to Darwin. "It's high time," Tom said "that Maggie was presented to her grandmother Sarah and this is the ideal opportunity." It would take him some time to reach Wyndham with their few belongings but first he must buy a thoroughbrace or other sturdy vehicle and horses broken to harness for the journey. Hannah secured a passage on the *Bambora*, a coastal vessel due to call at Derby in a few days. She packed and made her farewells to the people of Derby. There were sad moments when she told good friends about their move but she assured them that if it didn't work out they'd be back on the very next ship!

Tom promised Hannah that by the time she and Maggie reached Wyndham after their stay in Darwin, he would have found a place for them to live and applied for a job. Much as Hannah longed to see her mother she felt deep misgivings about leaving Tom. She'd had enough sad partings in her life and the thought of leaving him for several weeks caused her much anguish. She also knew what risks a lone traveller faced in that remote country and her mind visualised all the unpleasant possibilities. Tom reminded her that he had spent his life in the bush, first in his home state of Queensland and then on his own and other runs in the Kimberley. He assured her he would take no unnecessary risks. In only a month or two they would be back together, beginning a new life in Wyndham!

Hannah began to procrastinate and suggested they all go together, by ship or in the wagon. Tom was firmly against this and pointed out that time was getting on for old Sarah and it was imperative that she should see her grandchild. Hannah had to admit the sense of his argument. She had not seen Sarah since her brief stay in Pine Creek when she, Joseph, Annie and baby Maude were on their way to the Kimberley region. Letters that took months to arrive were the only contact the two women had had through many years, eventful and interesting ones for Sarah, and for Hannah, hard and heartbreaking. Those communications kept both of them informed of life's events and reinforced their mutual affection, but always and especially in times of anguish Hannah had desperately longed for her mother's presence and support. Once the final decision was made, she couldn't wait to feel her mother's embrace and bridge the missing years.

The arrival and departure of a ship in a remote coastal township were always an occasion and everyone in Derby who was able would be at the jetty to greet it, meet passengers and collect goods. A horse drawn tram conveyed passengers and luggage between the ship and the town via the long jetty. A tidal variation of twenty nine feet necessitated a lengthy structure and governed arrival and departure times. Ships were left high and dry, resting on their keels for hours waiting for the rising tide to refloat them. Tom and Hannah had already made farewells to their close friends and the townsfolk, but many more were said as people gathered on the jetty.

"You'll be racing them all off their feet at Wyndham, Hannah!" they joked. In those days running races were popular. Families gathered for picnics and races were always part of the fun. Fathers, mothers, boys and girls all ran and Hannah Nicholson had established a reputation as a great runner by always winning the ladies' running race.

MARGARET SAUTELLE NICHOLSON, AT THE AGE OF THREE OR FOUR DURING THE FIRST YEARS IN WYNDHAM.

(Lilly collection)

The *Bambora* made ready to cast off. The engines began to throb, deckhands waited for stragglers to run up the gangplanks before they were removed and the ship's removable rails locked into place. Then water began to churn as the propellers rotated and the space between ship and jetty widened. Hannah held Maggie up so she could wave to her father, who waved back until the *Bambora* was well out into the Bay on its way into Kings Sound.

The emotion generated at ships' departures is profound. Tom, who had successfully maintained a cheerful manner until their parting, was not proof against the wave of ineffable sadness that overwhelms those left on the wharf. He stood as the stretch of water between the jetty and the ship widened until he could no longer see the waving figures. The packed horse tram had passed him, making its ponderous way back to town, friends and strangers alike waving and calling their good wishes for a safe arrival in Wyndham. Slowly and sadly he turned and began the long walk back to town along the jetty.

In a patch of shade Tom had left the packed

vehicle ready to begin his own long, solitary, tedious and, in spite of his assurances to Hannah, far from safe journey. He knew his solitary presence on the track to Wyndham would be scrutinised all the way by the silent black sentinels of the bush and he fervently hoped to encounter no hostile groups or individuals. His dogs would alert him at night to human presence nearby, but realistically, a lone traveller was hopelessly vulnerable and Tom knew it.

His vehicle was heavily loaded but there was no furniture. Tom would make items like beds when they had a place to live. Besides the few essential housekeeping items, he had three bags of grain for the horses and a battered tin trunk packed with six weeks' supply of dry rations—sugar, tea, flour etc. There was a box with a frying pan, billy can and camp oven, another box of essential tools, one with saddlery tools, twine and a side of leather for harness repairs, two saddles and several bridles and head stalls, hobbles, a blacksmith box with spare sets of shoes, hammer, pincers, rasp, horse shoe nails, and a pot of Stockholm tar for minor injuries, a tin of axle grease, several hessian bags which were useful for all sorts of things, two hessian nosebags, a couple of buckets made from kerosene tins and a can of kerosene. Most important of all were the two forty four gallon drums of water for dry spells and a smaller one for convenience. Without water everything else was futile. One could not know the state of creeks and waterholes along the way and how far apart they lay. At every opportunity his drums would be replenished. Although people travelled both ways on the track they were few and far between so he had to be totally self sufficient for six to eight weeks. Fellow travellers would be in the same situation as himself, depending on their rations to see them through.

He untied the horses, freed the long reins and leapt nimbly into the seat. A gentle shake of the reins and the horses were off at a steady trot, out of Derby and beginning their long trek to Wyndham. His two dogs ran beside the wagon and when he stopped to water and spell the horses, they also drank gratefully and flopped in the shade with lolling tongues to watch Tom as he lit a small fire of dry twigs. Quickly they reduced to glowing coals and he set a small billy can to the side to boil.

When the *Bambora* arrived in Darwin, Hannah and Maggie checked at the Palmerston jetty as to when the next Pine Creek train would run. Hannah bought herself a ticket but Maggie was small enough to travel free. After a night at a hotel, they boarded their train and settled in for a trip that would take them several hours although it was only about 140 miles to Pine Creek. There would be a long stop at Adelaide River where people could take refreshments and then a number of short stops as the train pulled in to little sidings where clusters of miners' cottages had been built. It heralded its arrival with the exquisitely haunting wail that only steam trains seem able to emit and warned of its impending departure with a fussy little "poop". Maggie stood on the carriage seat and watched the activity with fascination. At every stop, freight was taken on and supplies and mail bags unloaded. Wagons, buggies and horses were grouped in shady spots. On the day the train came through, people came from miles around.

At last they reached Pine Creek. The old engine *Sandfly* pulled in amid a cloud of black smoke and hissing steam. It was a scene of bustle as Sarah climbed down and lifted Maggie to the ground. Immediately they were embraced by Sarah and Charlie. Locals who knew of Hannah's arrival crowded in to greet her and exclaim over Maggie. It was an emotional reunion awash with tears saved over twenty years of separation. Unaware of the profound significance of the meeting, two and a half year old Maggie was more interested in some horses waiting patiently for their teamster to return. When Charlie felt the tiny hand reach his and tug him towards them he was glad of a diversion from the overflow of women's tears. He lifted Maggie who rubbed the horses' velvety muzzles and laughed as the great beasts gently blew and tried to nuzzle her tiny fingers. Then Uncle Charlie assured her they had horses she could pat and ride so she returned willingly to Hannah and the crowd near the train.

It was a big day for Pine Creek. People came hundreds of miles to meet the train and collect supplies. Katherine was to be the next township on the line but for the moment Pine Creek was the railway depot and its commerce benefitted considerably from the influx on the train days.

Sarah caught Charlie's eye and said, "Let's go home. Don't know about you girl, but I could do with a cuppa!" She pointed to a home not far from where they stood. "That's us there and that's the Jones' house across the road."

Sarah was charmed by her lively, dark eyed granddaughter whose colouring so resembled her own. Later in the day, the old lady's eyes twinkled with amusement when she saw Charlie wandering around the yard leading their buggy horse with a laughing triumphant toddler perched on its back. "She's your daughter alright" she told Hannah, "you all over again!" Hannah laughingly replied "There's many a time I see her grandmother in her, I can tell you! See how she has Charlie doing what he's told!"

Hannah and Maggie settled in to Sarah's home and during the weeks that followed the women exchanged their accounts of the missing years from 1895 to 1915.

Pine Creek had remained Sarah's home. In those years following her sale of the Grove Hill licence to another pioneer woman, Ellen Ryan, she bought and sold various businesses including a store in Maude Creek and an accommodation house in Edith Falls. She carved another notch for herself in the history of the Northern Territory by joining eighty one other newly enfranchised women of the Territory to enrol at "Springvale", Katherine, on the 1895 electoral roll to vote.

In 1899, some years after Jack Beasley's death, she had married teamster William Ashton, a man

THE STEAM LOCOMOTIVE, "SANDFLY" WHICH ARRIVED IN 1886 AND SERVED THE NORTHERN TERRITORY UNTIL 1950. MAGGIE AND HANNAH WOULD HAVE TRAVELLED BETWEEN DARWIN AND PINE CREEK ON THE TRAIN DRAWN BY SANDFLY WHEN VISITING HER MOTHER SARAH BEASLEY IN 1915.

(Lilly collection)

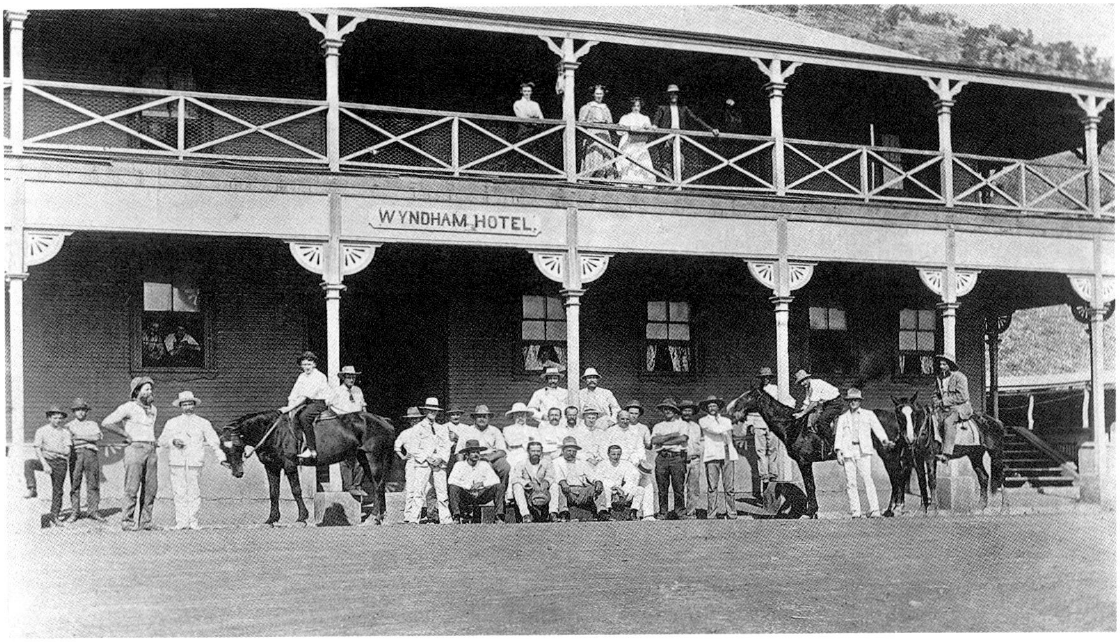

Wyndham Hotel early in the 1900s. In spite of its corrugated iron structure, the hotel was an imposing sight. The formally arranged men in tropical whites indicate some important occasion was being recorded photographically for posterity.

many years her junior. In 1904 she was again widowed. Ashton, who had chronic lung trouble, suffered a fit of coughing outside his home bringing on a severe haemorrhage, and his death occurred shortly after. From Sarah's account, Ashton's life seemed to be full of dramatic incidents. Prior to their marriage he was involved in a horrendous accident when his horses bolted with a wagon load of ore and the reins broke. The out of control team careered off, wrecking the wagon and killing a shafter, one of the horses nearest the driver, when the animal hit a large anthill. Ashton escaped injury and death by leaping free of the hurtling vehicle. A year or so after marrying Sarah he was charged with the murder of a Chinaman at Union Reefs, where a great many Chinese were working in the mines. In 1902 he and Sarah had camped at Union Reefs with two black boys and a lubra named Polly. After supper he became embroiled in a fight with a man named Ah Lip who later died. Ashton was committed for trial and a jury sworn in. According to Sarah and to the evidence of Leichhardt (one of the Aborigines), Ashton had become progressively more intoxicated, returning frequently to his wagon throughout the night for another drink. He constantly urged Leichhardt—"Go after him", meaning that he wanted Leichhardt to finish off the injured Chinaman. Ah Lip died of injuries inflicted by one or both of his assailants. Leichhardt blamed Ashton: "Prisoner make me kill him." The implication was that Ashton was too drunk to know what he was doing and therefore not responsible for the outcome. It proved to be one of the longest, most tedious cases on record, causing inconvenience to the jurymen, their families and others involved. For all that, it seems there was no verdict and Ashton was acquitted.

After his death Sarah remained much involved with the district, contributing her help wherever needed. She thrived on the rough and tumble life, the gold fever, the excitement when a mine struck it rich, the comings and goings of travellers, the fights, the occasional murder case. Life was rarely dull. There were no hospitals and many times Sarah and her friends risked their own lives to nurse the miners through epidemics that swept their camps. Her son Charlie tried to persuade her to retire to Darwin but it was a big wrench for the old lady to leave behind friends and colourful

MUCH ACTIVITY IN THE MAIN STREET OF OLD PORT WYNDHAM. THIS PHOTOGRAPH TAKEN ON 15TH APRIL, 1916 SHOWS PEARCE'S CAMEL TEAMS BEING LOADED FROM TWO DONKEY TEAMS WITH SUPPLIES FOR THE MOOLA BOOLA ESTATE MISSION. THE WYNDHAM HOTEL IS IN FULL VIEW WITH THE RESIDENCE OF THE MANAGER OF THE CONNER DURACK STORE AND THE STORE ITSELF IN THE BACKGROUND.

(From the collection of L. Hill)

memories bridging more than thirty years of life in a lusty frontier mining area. Darwin would seem dreadfully dull! Sarah was never lonely and never bored. Charlie was a very successful trainer and identity in racing circles and was often away with his horses at race meetings—but he knew Sarah was well attended to in his absence. The mateship of the bush would not have it otherwise.

Sarah had lost none of her resilience or sharpness of wit. The old lady listened to Hannah's story and it confirmed her earlier judgement of Joseph Nicholson's character. She had known the same grief at the loss of a child, her one year old daughter Elizabeth in 1877, but at the time she was not on her own. She had had Jack and the children to care for and friends to comfort her. Her heart ached anew when she pictured Hannah alone with her dead child at Oobergooooma Station. How she hoped that this new man in her daughter's life would be of a stronger calibre! Hannah in the course of conversation repeatedly assured her mother of Tom Sautelle's reliability. Yes, she admitted she did see him through the "eyes of love", a notoriously unreliable state from which to make a sound judgement. After fifteen hellish years of struggle she believed herself more able to accurately assess character and now in her late forties, less likely to make superficial judgements. The old lady shook her head...was there ever an age, she wondered, at which a woman ceased to be susceptible to a man's charms? She knew she was not destined to meet Tom and hoped with all her heart that her beloved Hannah had chosen well.

Tom was pleased with his horses. They hadn't worked together before but they pulled evenly and with a will. The grey had pulled the Derby tram at one stage of its career and was of excellent temperament. Tom smiled as he thought what a great mount he'd be to teach little Maggie to ride. He watched the road ahead of their pricked ears and calculated that even without misfortune of one sort or another it would take him weeks to reach Wyndham. It was only a matter of miles before the little used track deteriorated and the two horses were forced to picked their way slowly with the wheels rolling and bumping over the rough ground. Tom was a good man with horses and gentled them along, always checking that there were no loose shoes and no sores from rubbing harness. He regularly rested them. The wagon came in for the same careful scrutiny. He greased the axles well and checked the rims, spokes and hubs for any movement. If minor movements were not attended to, it was not long before the whole wheel would collapse; then only a wheelwright and a blacksmith's forge could reassemble the many pieces that went to make a wheel. Being forced to abandon the wagon and most of the contents through his own carelessness held no appeal for Tom.

Bushman though he was, accustomed to long periods of isolation and solitude, Tom was relieved when he eventually reached Wyndham. As the horses trotted into the port area he could hardly believe his eyes. Massive piles of building material lay on both sides of the road and a ship moored at the jetty was disgorging steel girders, pipes and corrugated iron. There were men looking at plans, measuring off distances and the whole place exuded a feeling of excitement. It certainly seemed as though the little town had a big future.

The locals, whose excitement at the district's new prospects knew no bounds, generously extended all the advice in the world. Known as Port Wyndham, the township, with its big store owned by Connor, Doherty and Durack, some shops run by Chinese families and a generous collection of hotels, huddled close to the port. On the flat ground near the jetty, the mighty meatworks would be erected. The right side of the road in to the port was dominated by the towering rock strewn Bastion and its fellow escarpments, and the mangrove covered tidal swamps edged so close in places to the base of the hills that there was little room for the road. Here and there in the folds of the hills a few buildings nestled among the rocky outcrops. Those who had time and energy to spare to climb the Bastion would be rewarded with a splendid vista of the Cambridge Gulf and the five rivers that flowed into the thirty mile long inlet.

Tom set up a camp on the common, hobbled and fed his horses and walked to the township to enquire about the housing situation. There were no houses to rent. You either built your own or

THE AFGHAN CEMETERY AT WYNDHAM.

(Lilly collection)

THE RAILWAY FROM THE MEATWORKS TO THE OLD TOWN OF PORT WYNDHAM. MAGGIE'S SCHOOL HOUSE IS THE WHITE ROOFED BUILDING DIRECTLY BEHIND THE POINT WHERE THE RAILS APPEAR TO CONVERGE. THE WYNDHAM HOTEL IS BEHIND THE CATTLE YARDS AND LEFT OF THE GOODS SHED.

camped. He found a block of cheap ground at the One-Mile Gully and began to plan a dwelling. In the hot climate, buildings could be very simple and inexpensive. Bush timber was used for uprights, hessian was stretched from pole to pole, nailed into place and then whitewashed. A material named Rubberoid that came in rolls was used for the roof. Cane grass was a free source of material for walls and verandah shelters. In a matter of days Tom had their dwelling completed. The onset of the Wet was only weeks away and outdoor endeavours were well nigh impossible once the rainy season began in earnest.

Wyndham people identified locations by the miles distance from the port. Because there was only one road in, everything was to be found easily somewhere along that one road. Tom learnt that there were pubs at the Three Mile and the Six Mile, that the Afghans at the Four Mile had a settlement with a bore, a mosque and their own cemetery. There was a store and boarding house at the Nine Mile and so on. The local cynics believed all the mileages were measured "by a greenhide rope on a wet day" as there was a wildly varying inaccuracy in the stated distances. Untanned leather or "greenhide" will stretch when wet and of course, Tom was as familiar as any other bushman with the proverbial "country mile".

Tom felt they'd made a good decision and couldn't wait for Hannah and Maggie to join him. It was exciting to be in a place where great things were about to happen. A letter from Hannah written care of the Post Office came giving Tom the name of the ship and the date of their arrival. He was at the jetty as the ship came up the Cambridge Gulf and berthed. He caught sight of them watching for him, and waved. The tiny figures waved back with great enthusiasm and as they drew nearer he could hardly contain his impatience. It seemed to take forever for the hawsers to be secured around the bollards and an eternity before the gangplanks were nudged into place and made fast.

Finally Hannah and Maggie were on the gangplank. Impatiently Tom waited at the bottom until people who preceded them stepped onto the jetty and he was able to reach out to help them off the shaky plank. Seconds later Hannah was in his arms and Maggie pressed in against the two. With much laughter and wiping away of happy tears they waited for a deck hand to trot agilely down the unstable gangplank with their two pieces of luggage. At that time, the tin trunk was the travelling case used by the majority of people. Vast cabin trunks, with fabric linings and drawers, were for the wealthy travellers but the lowly tin trunk served most people well enough. It had a handle at both ends and on the lid. It kept its contents safe and dry and in itself was not particularly heavy. Nuns when travelling many decades later still carried their entire possessions in one small black tin trunk.

Tom hoisted Hannah's brown, well worn trunk onto his shoulder and picked up Maggie's smaller one in his free hand, hooking his strong fingers into the wire handle on the lid. Maggie clutched her little bag containing presents from Grandma and Uncle Charlie and looked around for the horses.

She knew the animals Tom had looked at in Derby and immediately spotted the wagon amongst the other horse drawn vehicles waiting for the ship's arrival. She walked as fast as her diminutive legs would carry her to reach the waiting pair. Horses were her great love and she had ridden long before she could walk, winding her tiny hand around a short tuft of mane on the horse's wither, small legs stuck out almost at right angles across the animal's broad back. She knew no fear and since the first time Tom hoisted her onto the back of an old horse in Derby, Hannah and Tom had known this child would follow in their footsteps. Horses were in her blood.

It was no distance from the jetty to the One Mile Gully but Tom had wanted to drive his "girls" home in style. When he drew in the horses Hannah could see how busy he had been. She also was amazed at the activity in the port and it reassured her that they'd come to a place with a prosperous future, even if it was the hottest town in Australia! It was also a town without water and every drop had to be brought in a tank from a well at the Three Mile. A man in charge of the horse and cart carrying the tank went back and forth several times daily to fill a row of square tanks behind the Wyndham Hotel. It was a constant struggle to keep up the supply for the town and not a drop was ever wasted by the residents. It was used and reused and at last poured onto the vegetable garden or a struggling shrub.

It was not long before the family moved from the One Mile to the Seven Mile where Tom built a home from bush timber and corrugated iron. It was the first house there and Tom decided to dig a well. This proved a most difficult task involving blasting through notoriously hard rock known as blue diorite. Water in Wyndham, or the lack of it, was an ongoing problem. Until water was struck no one could predict the quality. More often than not it was brackish and often totally unusable. Good wells for no known reason would turn brackish and anyone who had access to quality water was indeed fortunate. Tom's well did provide drinkable water but not in any quantity.

Moving was not a difficult process as people had very few belongings in those days. Furniture was built from boxes, bush timber, sacking, flour bags and tins. Three or four kerosene boxes made a most efficient chest of drawers. The boxes were stacked one on top of the other. One side of the kerosene tin was removed and slid back into the box, cut side uppermost. With each box holding two tins which slid neatly into it, with the wire handle on the top of the can outermost, the household had a free, efficient and capacious chest of drawers.

A great deal of kerosene was used in lighting which assured a constant supply of the tins and boxes. Electricity was far off in the future. Light was from a kerosene lamp with a broad wick shielded by a glass funnel, or the more expensive model with a mantle which gave a beautiful soft

SUPPLIES FOR A FARAWAY STATION. OWNER OF CAMEL TEAMS, MR PEARCE, WITH HIS PARTNER O'LEARY AND DAUGHTER AT THE REAR OF THE CONNER DURACK STORE IN APRIL, 1916. THESE SUPPLIES ADDRESSED TO THE FARQUHARSONS HAVE YET TO TRAVEL HUNDREDS OF MILES BY CAMEL TRAIN TO INVERWAY STATION IN THE NORTHERN TERRITORY.

white light. The latter were made in a wide range from a very plain and inexpensive designs to the most elegant glass and embossed metal models. When the mantle made of a woven fabric had been used once, care had to be taken not to touch it as it would simply disintegrate. Too high a flame would send the mantle black in no time and the wick had to be turned down while the charred parts disappeared and the mantle recovered its translucent glow. However, with gentle treatment they lasted for months and were worth the effort. Other forms were the carbide lamp that gave off a brilliant light, and the slush lamp. This latter was made by rolling a stick of wood in a piece of rag and inserting it into a tin filled with fat. The stick acted as a wick and it was just a matter of topping up the tin with fat as it became available from cooking. It was a smoky form of lighting but free and easily achieved.

Shipping to the port had always been the source of fresh supplies but with the increase in population and the constant turnaround of vessels bringing building materials for the meatworks, goods were available on a more regular basis. "There'd be potatoes, pumpkin, onions and fruit, and", Maggie remembered with delight, "grapes packed in sawdust." These would be transported in the ship's coolrooms, but in Wyndham's unrelenting heat, without refrigeration or a supply of ice, nothing would keep more than a few days. However, householders who had a Coolgardie safe could certainly extend the life of fresh items briefly. The safe, which any handy person could construct, was simply a box with four slightly splaying legs to make the bottom fractionally larger than the top. The walls and door were made of fly proof mesh or hessian. A deep tin tray of water was set on the top. Lengths of cloth were cut to cover the four sides of the safe. The cloth was the readily available saddle serge or "collar check", a woollen fabric for counterlining horse collars. One end of each length of cloth was held in the tray on top by the weight of a brick or stone and the cloth hung down over the sides into another tray underneath. While ever there was water in both trays to keep the cloth wet, the evaporative cooling process continued. Meat would be wrapped at night and left out in the cool and then put back in the safe next morning.

Some meat was cut into very thin strips and dried or smoked. It could be eaten raw or reconstituted in water and cooked. However, salted meat was a staple of the diet as it keeps for a very long time. "It got very hard and dry after a while but once you soaked it, it was alright," Maggie recalls, but it was a constant struggle to provide palatable wholesome food. Many people kept goats so there was always milk available. Even the smallest babies can assimilate goats' milk without digestive problems. The male kids were castrated and, when grown sufficiently, slaughtered to provide an occasional variation in the diet of corned beef. Householders grew a few vegetables but with little water it was an uphill battle.

Most people's physical possessions were just the most essential items. There was neither the money nor the opportunity to acquire more. The Conner Doherty and Durack Store sold essentials and special requirements could be ordered by mail from stores in Perth and transported by ship—but people worked hard for a very meagre income and had to make do with the minimum. As much of the work for the men ceased in the wet, many households endured hardship, sometimes going months without income; during that time such things as home maintenance and harness repairs were attended to, ready for the start of the dry.

The Afghans spent the wet season in their settlement at the Four Mile. Their "ships of the desert" were no match for the boggy ground and sheeting rain so they rested over the few months whilst their masters caught up on repairs. "Old Zaman Shah," Maggie remembered "would come around and castrate the young male goats for anyone who wanted his services. He took care of slaughtering for the Afghans too." Each animal had to be despatched in the ritual Hallal ceremony. Whilst the Afghans lived, prospered and served the community as a whole, they lived a life apart, observing their demanding religious routines and never compromising their beliefs. Their strings of camels took goods from Wyndham to the high stations difficult to reach by other means—Kurungie,

(Lilly collection)

Maggies' father, Tom Sautelle, (centre) and workmates with steam locomotive, "Katie" at the Wyndham Meat-works about 1917.

THE COMPLETED STAR IN THE CROWN OF WYNDHAM, THE MIGHTY MEATWORKS IN 1919. THE MAIN BUILDINGS WERE SURROUNDED BY SMALLER BUILDINGS FOR STAFF ACCOMMODATION, RECREATION AND ADMINISTRATION. IN THE DRY SEASON THE POPULATION OF THE TOWN INCREASED BY MORE THAN 200 PEOPLE WHO STAFFED THE HUGE ENTERPRISE, PROCESSING CATTLE FOR EXPORT AS CHILLED BEEF.

Bedford Downs, Tableland, Greenvale and Elgie Cliff—and nothing was a trouble except pork products. Because pigs were unclean animals, they refused to carry bacon. Station people, longing for some nice tasty rashers, used to have the storekeepers wrap bacon in many coverings, place it in the centre of a pack and hope the Afghans were unaware of what they were carrying. If in the heat the bacon fat began to melt and drip out through the load, the whole pack would be discarded in utter disgust by the cameleer.

In Maggie's home, Tom would lay out hides and plan the best way to cut them to advantage. He would cut the leather into long thin strips from which he could plait whips. A kangaroo hide was cut differently from that of a bullock and the quality of the end product relied heavily on the meticulous use of the leather knife. If each strip was not straight edged and exactly the same width as its fellow strands, the quality of the plaiting suffered. From the intricate Turks head on the whip handle, down along the perfectly tapering fall to the tail, where the cotton cracker was attached, even tension was essential. It was indicative of Tom's consummate skill that he could command one guinea for a stock whip when a man's weekly wage was little more than that. A guinea was a shilling more than a pound, and was the unit used in paying for professional services and true craftsmanship.

Women sewed clothes by hand or with a treadle machine if they were lucky enough to have one and the younger children wore hand me downs. The Chinese tailoress, Cissy Lee Tong, made white tropical suits of linen or Assam silk for the men and other garments to order for those who could afford her services. Men's working clothes were made by Ah Show in a shop near the old hotel. Shoes were a rarity among town children who raced each other up and down the Bastion, their tough little feet impervious to rough razor sharp sandstone rocks strewn over its steep sides.

In the dry season, the men of the town including Tom travelled far and wide for work. Sometimes they only came back to their families for the duration of the wet. Some went as far away as cattle stations on the Gulf of Carpentaria. Tom worked at the meatworks when there was construction work going and carted wood with a horse and dray at other times. In those early years of Maggie's life there was no pressure on Hannah to work but she was always busy. She had a great capacity to care for others as well as a lively interest in the activities around her and it was not long before she was called to their homes to perform the duties of a midwife. In spite of the increased population of workers, and the advent of a hospital and nurses, Wyndham still had no doctor.

As Maggie grew, so did the huge complex of buildings that made up the Wyndham Meatworks. By the time she began school, it was one year off completion, a big enterprise by anyone's reckoning and destined to become the largest employer in the far north of Australia. It dominated the northern skyline, the town's economy and the lives of the residents, who, under this benevolent giant, were supplied with employment, a regular programme of entertainment, sporting venues and facilities hitherto undreamt of in those outposts of the Commonwealth.

While they were still at the One Mile Gully house, Tom had been offered a children's pony who accompanied them to the Seven Mile when they moved. "He was a Timor pony, creamy with a black mane and tail. His name was Possum and I spent more time walking behind him than on him." Maggie recalled. "Suddenly he'd have me on the ground and I never knew what had happened!" Like all children's ponies, Possum had developed a high degree of cunning; because of their size they are rarely thoroughly trained, ridden and disciplined by an adult. It doesn't take them long to find out that they can manage the child on their back to suit themselves. Once the bad habits are learnt, they become rogues for life.

Every so often Possum would get away and head for his previous home on Carlton Station. Yards and hobbles did not prevent his homeward flight. "He knew how to lie down and roll under the bottom bar of the cattle yards." Maggie laughs at the memory. "He was a good sulky pony though, and Mum drove him to some do at the Six Mile one day. She unharnessed him and put him in the yards there with the other visitors' horses. When it came time to go home there was no Possum; he'd escaped hours ago. We still drove the sulky home so someone must have loaned Mum another horse. There would have been no point in chasing Possum. He'd be a long way off by then; down the road, over the hills and across the Ord River to Carlton."

"He even used to swim the river with hobbles on and how he didn't get eaten I don't know! There were hundreds of crocodiles in those days! The manager at Carlton used to hold him for my father who always made him a plaited leather whip for his kindness. I know he made an awful lot of whips because of it, but one day Possum went and never came back. Don't know whether the crocks got him trying to swim the river or what but he was a real nuisance for everyone." By that time, his disappearance was a relief to all.

Maggie's father was a strict taskmaster and until she could ride at any pace bareback she was not allowed a saddle. Eventually Tom decided she had learnt well enough and cut her first "saddle" from a piece of leather which was held on with a surcingle, a broad strap which went over the leather pad and around the horse's belly. "I can't really think what use it was" Maggie exclaimed, but maybe Hannah was complaining about the washing! Clothing and legs get very grubby with a combination dust and horse sweat. Later she graduated to a light exercise saddle in time for her long fourteen mile a day ride to school and back.

The same year Maggie turned six and began school, the Great War ended. In November, 1918 the Armistice was signed and Australia took stock of its losses. With patriotic zeal young men had rushed to join up and fight; even the smallest communities gave of their best for a war on the other side of the world. From the outbreak of hostilities in 1914, Hannah was involved in Comforts Fund activities, collecting supplies for the men on active service. On her arrival in Wyndham she joined the townsfolk in their efforts. People had very little; nevertheless they gave what they could. In her letter to Hannah from Government House in Darwin, the wife of the Administrator, writing as elected President of the British Red Cross in the Northern Territory, was obviously aware of this and employed the greatest tact and restraint in her request for comforts.

Maggie's first school when she turned six was The Institute, then at the one room single teacher school in Wyndham. By then she was a very competent young horsewomen. Snowy, the huge gentle grey horse, took her to school each day and brought her home safely in the evening. Maggie craved more excitement than her mount was prepared to offer. "I got a tin with some hard lollies in it and would give it a good shake. It made him jump about the first few times and then he took no notice." In his previous career as a tram horse in Derby waiting on the jetty amid the bustle of shipping activity, Snowy had become accustomed to a cacophony of sounds and commotion and he knew perfectly well that his daily companion and charge, the diminutive child on his back, offered no threat. To Maggie's disappointment he proceeded to ignore her best efforts, and resumed his sedate demeanour.

However, it wasn't long before Snowy was returned to "men's work". Tom had acquired two heavy harness broken grey horses bred in the Northern Territory; Billy who bucked badly and Johnny Cake. With the docile Snowy to settle them and plenty of hard work to "take the sting out of them," they would make up a good team for wood carting. Maggie was to be found a replacement school horse.

One memorable day Johnny Cake was harnessed in the sulky and Tom decided to take Maggie with him in to the Port and across to Chimoulee. Not far from their destination disaster struck when the hame strap came undone. The metal hames, about two feet each in length, curved to fit the leather collar and joined by a few links of chain at their base, fell away and clattered to the ground. With them went the all important trace chains by which the vehicle is pulled. With a leg entangled in the fallen harness Johnny Cake became panic stricken, reared and plunged, tipping the vehicle and shattering one shaft. He then tried to bolt. Tom, with an iron grip on the reins leapt out of the sulky, missed his footing and was dragged along the stony road. He somehow regained his footing, gripping the reins hand over hand, and reached for the animal's head. Several times he was jabbed painfully by the point of the unbroken shaft as he fought to gain control of the horse's head. Tom was not a tall man and the big animal lifted him off the ground again and again as it struggled to break away, spurred into blind terror by the metal hames seesawing and clanking around and between his front legs. In his frantic efforts to stop a smash, Tom had lost sight of Maggie. If she'd been thrown forward and under the horses' hind legs she might be either trampled to death or run over by one of the wheels as they ground back, forth and sideways on the road as Johnny Cake tried to break away. Fortunately, two Afghans came along the road and with their timely assistance Tom was able to quieten and free the great trembling sweating animal. As he tried to soothe the horse the two men ducked nimbly beneath the animal's neck and unhooked the hames, now bent and caked with dirt, sweat and bits of skin and horse hair. "We take care of horse, you look to little Missie," one of the Afghans told Tom.

In an agony of fear for what he might find next, he passed the reins of the still snorting Johnny Cake to the men and steeled himself to look along the road. He saw no motionless crumpled bundle there and his eyes began to search along the rocky edges. A broken cry escaped him as he caught sight of a small figure standing well away from the roadside among the rocks. Bruised, battered and badly skinned on his arms and legs Tom stumbled over the rocks towards her. "I must have ridden the sulky until it turned over and threw me out on the rocks." Maggie can remember sobbing with the pain in her back as she struggled to stand up and walk a few paces further from the road to watch and wait until the violent activity ceased. As Tom swept her up into his arms she cried out. Gently and fearfully he lowered her to the ground as Maggie tearfully informed him "I hurt my back on the rock." Whilst the two Afghans led the horse away to a nearby yard, a passer-by from the Meatworks stopped to assist. Tom and Maggie were driven home to where a shocked Hannah took charge of the bedraggled pair and began to bathe and dress their injuries. Silently and grimly she listened to their description of the accident. She knew only too well what could have happened. "It's a wonder you weren't both killed!" Tom, his face drawn and grey from the aches of his own battered body looked quickly at his little daughter whose eyes, darker than usual from pain and fatigue gave him a wan smile. "You're a very brave girl Maggie," he said softly and gave silent thanks that Death had turned its back on them both that day.

Eighty years later slight pains echo faintly now and then to remind Maggie of that disastrous incident. "I think I must have suffered some internal damage when I hit the rock but it could have been so much worse. Poor Mum! What she must have felt when she saw the pair of us!" Tom, normally so meticulous in his care and use of harness must have agonised many a time over that small culprit, the hame strap with its loose buckle.

In her loving family relationship, Maggie's memory of the one and only time she was punished remains crystal clear in her memory. "I don't ever remember being punished for anything except one day after school I stayed back at the jetty to watch the cattle being loaded. It was so interesting I forgot about time. It was late when I got home and didn't I get the bridle reins around my legs! Dad said the horse had been away all day in the heat and it was cruel and thoughtless of me to keep him waiting so long for his feed and water." Tom's philosophy, like that of all good stockmen, was to see to the wellbeing of dependent animals first. He had always instilled this into his young daughter but just this once he felt she'd forgotten her priorities and she received a stern reminder.

Next door neighbours and Maggie's great friends were the Cole family. Their father Tom was a Kimberley drover and the first man to make a successful droving trip along the Canning Stock Route with 500 head of cattle and sixty horses taking six months to complete the journey. For twenty years his wife had accompanied him, travelling with the mobs. During that time she bore eight children most of whom had been raised out in the bush. Everything they had was carried in a buggy and pack saddles, including a piano accordion with which Mabel entertained her family and friends. She was a gifted musician and played superbly. Having lived as a child in Halls Creek and been educated by her mother, she decided her own children should receive a formal education, however brief, and decided to settle in Wyndham. As there were too many children for whom to provide mounts, Tom the eldest, uneducated as yet but a fully fledged stockman nevertheless, drove his three sisters, Ethel, Teeny and Polly to school in a sulky. The other four children Sandy, Harry, Charlie and Kathleen were still too young. The sulky was a considerably slower means of travel so Maggie would canter ahead some distance and wait for the Coles to catch up. If there was time to spare before school went in and after they'd freed the horses, the children would gather the fruit from a boab which grew next door. This tree bore particularly flavoursome fruit and the children munched on these with great relish. "The flavour of the flesh varies from tree to tree but the tarty tasting ones are the best. Right inside in the white pulp were the seeds and if you cracked them between rocks there'd be little kidney shaped nuts to eat. They're good bush tucker. The Aborigines

ground the white part for flour, or soaked them in water and ate the flesh with sugar. They would also throw the green fruit into the coals to roast."

Young Evelyn Coverley daily observed the children's arrival at the school from the top verandah of the Wyndham Hotel. Her comment about the time she first saw Snowy arrive with his tiny rider, "Little Maggie Nicholson looked like a pimple on a pumpkin", is well remembered. Now well over 100 years old and blind, Evelyn Coverley still laughs at the memory of the tiny child who had to devise ways of scrambling onto her huge, patient horse's back. The horses were unharnessed before school started and stood in what shade they could find to wait out the hours, shaking their heads and flicking their tails to ward off the clouds of flies in the furnace hot Wyndham temperatures. The children, a dozen or so, from kindergarten up to sixth class, traipsed into the schoolroom for the day's lessons, to sit on long wooden forms with the ink splashed desks in front of them whilst the teacher attempted to give attention to each child's individual needs.

It was a one teacher school. The teacher, whose residence adjoined the school, would be called upon occasionally to extend her teaching skills further and take into the class for a brief time an older boy whilst his drover or stockman father had reason to remain near the township. Young Tom Cole came into this category, a stripling, who had lived as a man doing a man's job in the stock camps. He would be expected to suffer excruciating and unaccustomed hours of confinement in the classroom, his long legs cramped under the small desk trying to make head or tail of reading and writing. Worse still, he was crowded around by inquisitive little children, six and eight year

Looking north toward Wyndham from the Telegraph Hill. Cattle were camped and watered here before the last leg of the journey to the Port.

olds who had a grasp on these mysteries whilst he, a man among men had not an inkling. As a result, the poor teacher's attention was further divided and the children left to their own devices made the most of it.

Maggie remembered a very fair boy named Johnny who constantly giggled, the sound of which drove the teacher to distraction. Young Tom Cole made the delightful discovery that he could easily make the boy giggle uncontrollably simply by pulling faces at him. This produced an instant and predictable reaction from the enraged teacher who wielded her stick unmercifully on the "giggler". There was no "sparing of the rod" in that classroom. "She used to beat him so hard and we'd beg Tom not to do it but he just kept on. It was awful really." Tom couldn't resist the fun and the poor boy couldn't help himself in spite of the sure and certain punishment he knew would follow.

Frequently the teacher excused herself from the class telling the children to be good while she went to "turn the cabbage". During these absences the children indulged in all manner of mischief including advancing the alarm clock which sat on the teacher's desk. Every time she went to her kitchen to minister to this mysterious cabbage the hands on the clock were moved forward. Morning tea time, lunch hour and home time took on a random quality to the point where the Cole children arrived home in their sulky one day just after lunch time. Their father was most irate. Why, he wanted to know, was he bothering with the time and expense of keeping a sulky horse on good feed for the long trip into town and out again five days of every week if the children's education took up so little time each day? Of course the children were found out when the parents questioned the teacher about the extraordinarily short school hours. Adjustments to the clock ceased, although the teacher's absences to attend to her cabbage continued frequently.

Patricia, a pupil at the school in those far off days recalled, "I grew up with the notion that the proper way to cook a cabbage was to immerse the whole vegetable in boiling water and as it rolled around, keep prodding it to get it cooked." Later it was discovered that each turn of the cabbage was a swig of gin!

After a while, Hannah, Tom and Maggie sold the Seven Mile house and moved to the Three Mile near the site of an old lemonade factory. The schoolteacher retired, alcoholic, unhinged and accompanied by an enormous number of cats. She moved into the Seven Mile house previously built and occupied by Tom and Hannah. She became the terror of the neighbourhood, threatening passers-by, banging her stick on the gate and shooting off her .22 rifle. "They took her away in the end but we never found out where. I don't think I learnt much at that school," Maggie considered, but like the rest of the children, she had a lot of fun. Her next school was at the Roads Board Office which later became the Council Hall until it was replaced in 1983.

Christmas of 1921 was a sad day. A telegram from Charlie to Hannah informed her of the death of their mother Sarah in Darwin, on 21 December at the age of 82. Despite her protests, Charlie had taken the ailing Sarah to Darwin to spend her last days close to a hospital and medical care. Hannah had not seen her mother since the visit in 1915 but regularly corresponded, always hoping that an opportunity and sufficient extra funds to permit another visit would come up. The passing of this great pioneer woman, her grandmother, meant very little to Maggie at the time but Hannah's grief was a shock to the little girl. She had not experienced anything like this before; her sturdy, cheerful mother weeping for the death of a stranger?—well a stranger to her, anyway. As the days went by and Hannah's mood lightened, the little girl's anxiety lessened. She couldn't bear to see her adored mother so sad!

Maggie's life was generally happy and continued on a reasonably even keel until she was about twelve. Tom worked hard for his family and was a good provider but it was about this time that his health began to break down. First he contracted malaria, a scourge of the Tropics which few people escaped in those days. The recurrent attacks varied in severity and quinine was the only treatment available.

Wyndham had recently acquired the services of Dr Adams who previously attended Hannah and Maggie in Derby. He visited Tom during his devastating bouts of the fever but there was little he could do but prescribe quinine and give Hannah advice on nursing the patient. Through the ensuing months, she cared for him, tenderly nursing him through the debilitating attacks ever hopeful their severity would lessen. Tom who had always taken his physical strength for granted began to find his body not quite up to many of the tasks required of him. With each bout he found himself weaker and could not understand why his work hardened body, always quick to heal in the past, was simply not responding in spite of dedicated care and increasing rest.

To Hannah's further distress Tom began to manifest symptoms which she took to be cancer of the stomach. He felt constantly nauseous, with a yellow cast to his skin, couldn't retain food and was in constant pain in the region of his abdomen. Before her eyes he deteriorated from a strong healthy muscular man to a stooped and frail figure who had to be admitted to the Wyndham Hospital for constant observation and professional nursing. Hannah was beside herself and asked Dr Adams what else could be done to help. Adams himself was powerless to do more, and suggested that maybe more comprehensive and up to date treatment was available in Perth.

In those days, sea trips were regarded as beneficial in their own right for recuperation after illness. Ocean liners were packed with people seeking improvement in their health through the rest, the fresh salt air and change of scenery. Perhaps that was the answer for Tom. A trip to Perth and back and whilst there to seek specialist medical help. Tom, in pain and growing weaker by the day was ready to try anything and agreed to take the trip. Hannah wanted with all her heart to go with him but he had been ill for many months and family finances were becoming stretched. She and Maggie would have to remain in Wyndham and wait out the weeks until Tom came home, hopefully somewhat restored and bringing with him a supply of whatever pharmaceutical marvels the Perth medicos prescribed.

It was a sad threesome who stood on the jetty where the S.S. *Kangaroo* was making ready for departure. It was time for the passengers to board. Hannah's arm was around Tom's waist supporting his now fragile skeletal form. Tom who found standing for any length of time impossible was relieved when they climbed the gangplank and went in search of his cabin. He held Maggie close and told her to take good care of her mother. He could hardly believe that their daughter was thirteen and on the threshold of womanhood. Suddenly, they heard the call "All non-passengers ashore". Wordlessly Hannah and Tom embraced and it was time to part. She told him to save his strength and rest on his bunk; she and Maggie would find their way off the ship. They hastened ashore and stood watching the vessel, their vision blurred by their streaming tears as it moved away from the jetty. Looking up they saw Tom leaning on the rail and waving. He'd valiantly struggled up on deck for a last farewell and it was not until the ship was far down the Gulf and Tom had long vanished from sight that the mother and daughter turned away and made for home.

Two days later, Hannah received a ship to shore telegram from the S.S. *Kangaroo* hand delivered from the Wyndham Post Office. It informed her that Tom Sautelle, aged fifty, had died at sea from recurrent malaria and gastro-hepatitis chronica on 18 May, 1925. She was devastated. It was impossible for her to assimilate the meaning of the dreadful words so clearly written on the flimsy paper she held in shaking hands. To the detached observer of Tom's physical decline, it was obvious he was a condemned man. She had nursed others and knew intuitively when their time was up but through the "eye of love" Hannah saw Tom returning, restored once more to resume their lives as before.

The ship reached Derby the following day and Tom was buried in the town cemetery. Albert Ah Chee and his family saw to the funeral arrangements and made sure flowers in abundance adorned the grave of their old friend. Hannah could only guess the day and hour of the burial. As Derby was a thousand kilometres away by the rough track Tom had traversed ten years previously and about the same by sea she could only be by the graveside in spirit. Deprived of that most important ritual, the final farewell of the funeral and burial, Hannah found it hard to accept that Tom was really dead. For a long time she felt sure that any day he would return on one of the coastal ships or she would hear the rattle of harness and the sound of horses' hoofs as he rode into the yard, tired and dusty after weeks on the track from Derby.

Telling Maggie of her father's death nearly broke Hannah's heart. It took time for her to accept that her beloved father who had sailed away on the boat only a couple of days ago would never be coming back to them. Hannah, holding her close, said they would "have to look after each other from now on just as he would want it."

The nurses at the Wyndham Hospital had given Maggie a threepenny piece they had found in Tom's bed and the little girl gratefully treasured the small silver coin as a last link with her beloved

IN 1925 IN DARWIN MAGGIE WAS KINDLY LENT HER MOUNT, A CHESTNUT MARE CALLED SYLVIE, BY THE OWNER OF THE VICTORIA HOTEL, A BEAUTIFUL STONE STRUCTURE WHICH IS STILL STANDING, IN THE HEART OF MODERN DARWIN. (LILLY COLLECTION)

father. Nearly seventy five years later that same "thripenny bit" remains a cherished part of Maggie's memorabilia.

It was imperative that Hannah find work and her first job after Tom's death was cooking at the Wyndham Hotel. This meant she would be able to have her meals there which was a big consideration. Maggie was accorded the same privilege when she offered to take the early morning teas around to houseguests each day. It made a substantial saving and she augmented their income by a further five shillings per week cleaning up the schoolyard.

Hannah was restless in her bereft state and in spite of the good job at the hotel she decided to go to Darwin. Sarah had died four years previously in 1921 but Charlie might come up from Pine Creek to meet her and although she was not as close to him as she was to Jack, he was her brother and it would be good to see him. Perhaps some comfort would lie in visiting Sarah's grave and they could talk of Sarah and old times. There was more happening in Darwin and perhaps this would act as a distraction.

The house at the Three Mile was sold prior to their departure and nothing remained to keep them in Wyndham. For Maggie the few days on the boat was quite an adventure and Darwin was new territory to explore. Hannah found a house close to the Parap School and each day Maggie joined other children as they passed the house. "We used to pass a place that had lots of peanuts growing in the front yard. We'd sneak in and pick up as many as we could before the man saw us." To the shout of "You kids get out of my bloody peanuts!" they ran like hares clutching the nuts against their tunics whilst their book filled leather satchels banged against their backs and they giggled with delight at their escape. On weekends she rode far and wide on a beautiful bay mare lent to her by the Darwin postmaster. As long as she had a horse she was content and many a happy hour she spent with the Knowles girls, who had horses, tearing around on the Darwin Racecourse.

For Hannah it turned out to be a desperately lonely interlude. She took a job as a barmaid at the historic Victoria Hotel in the centre of Darwin but at the end of each day she was exhausted, her feet ached abominably and she yearned for Tom. Past experience had shown hard work to be an excellent therapy for grief but this time it wasn't working. She began to realise Wyndham had long ago become her home town and she missed it. It seemed there was no escaping grief by going somewhere else so Hannah decided they'd go back to the community they knew so well, sad memories notwithstanding, and begin again.

Although Hannah had long ceased to worry about the fact that she and Tom were never able to marry, she felt it was one of life's bitter ironies when news reached her in Wyndham that Joseph Nicholson had died in the same year as Tom. He was found dead in his swag at Halls Creek, having lived his dissipated, spendthrift life just long enough to prevent Tom and Hannah making formal a union which had begun in love and devotion nearly twenty years before.

CHAPTER III

Life at the Nine Mile

WHEN HANNAH AND MAGGIE returned to Wyndham, Maggie went to school, now temporarily located at the Roads Board office, to finish the last school term in 1925. She was fourteen the following February and began work as soon as a job offered. "I went to work at the Six Mile Hotel. I was called a waitress," Maggie laughed, "but I did everything! I made the beds, cleaned the rooms, washed and ironed. In those days it was work; you had to get down on your knees and wash the floor." Without cleaners and floor polishers, the task was accomplished with a bucket of water, a scrubbing brush, a block of grey sandsoap and lots of elbow grease. "I even had to clean the silver on Sunday—it never ended!"

Meanwhile Hannah was working at the Wyndham pub and between the two, always accustomed to making every penny stretch as far as possible, they even managed to save a little. In what little time was left after her day at the Six Mile Hotel, Maggie looked after their goats; fed, yarded and milked them and did as many of the household chores as she could manage. By the time Hannah arrived home footsore from a long hard day in the hotel kitchen, there was little left to do but prepare a simple meal for the pair of them and put her aching legs and feet up for a rest.

However, people knowing Hannah's capability and capacity for work believed she could always manage to fit in another job. "We were living in a house on stilts at the Three Mile then and someone gave Mum a baby camel to rear. She called it called Lulu."

HANNAH NICHOLSON FEEDING LULU, THE BABY CAMEL SHE WAS GIVEN. LULU HAD A TASTE FOR UNUSUAL FOOD, ESPECIALLY THE LAUNDRY HANGING ON THE LINE AT THE THREE MILE HOTEL.

(Lilly collection)

Lulu sucked lustily on her bottle of goats' milk and captivated the heart of her new foster mother. The horses, however, were not the least impressed by the fluffy, fawn, infant that was nearly as tall as they were. Horses cannot abide camels. To them the odour is extremely offensive and they react violently even when the camels are a long way off. Most settle down but only after long acquaintance. Lulu was nobody's fool and having discovered that her presence resulted

JACKY NICHOLSON AND TENY THE MULE. TENY WAS FULLY GROWN BUT NO BIGGER THAN A DONKEY AND MAGGIE BOUGHT HER JUST AS A PET. JACKY HAD BEEN WITH HANNAH AND MAGGIE SEVERAL YEARS AND GROWN TALL AND STRONG. UNLIKE MANY OF HIS RACE WHO ARE SUPERB HORSEMEN, JACKY WAS NOT A "NATURAL." HE HAD PLENTY OF OPPORTUNITY TO PRACTISE RIDING, BUT AS MAGGIE SAID "POOR JACKIE, HE WAS NEVER ANY GOOD AT IT."

in some very entertaining behaviour from a creamy pony of Maggie's, she made the most of it. Shambling over to where the horse was tied, "she would plait her long legs in all directions and wave her neck around as if it was made of rubber." Showing no fear, Lulu would keep up the performance while the horse cavorted around at the end of the reins, snorting and showing the whites of his eyes. Finally he would sit on his haunches and pull back until the reins or bridle broke. Heaving and snorting the poor animal would trot away to the farthest corner of the yard. Lulu, thoroughly satisfied, would stand and gaze haughtily round, brown eyes under long lashes surveying her domain while she wondered what to do next.

Perhaps a visit to the neighbours? Lulu's other pastime was to saunter over to the clothes-line at the Three Mile Hotel and chew whatever was hanging out to dry. Tea towels, sheets or dainty underwear, it all went the same way. Proprietor and patrons howled for her blood when they surveyed the discoloured shreds of fabric hanging where freshly laundered garments and crisp white linen had once fluttered in the breeze. That form of intensely fascinating entertainment brought on Lulu's Waterloo. Hannah and Maggie could not afford to recompense the owners, so other arrangements had to be made.

She was banished to Gundigai, a house Hannnah had built and still owned but was not living in. Here they thought she would be well out of harm's way. Maggie tied her to a tree near a waterhole on a creek and twice a day she had to carry a bucket of goat's milk to the lonely, waiting youngster. However, the very next day when she took Lulu her milk, she found the baby camel had drowned. "The creek had come up and all I could see was a leg sticking up out of the water. She'd got her head and neck caught in the rope and down she went so that was the end of poor Lulu." Lulu's sudden demise brought a mixture of sadness and relief. They'd become very fond of the intelligent gangling orphan whose antics had brought many a laugh, but mother and daughter were overworked as it was and as Lulu grew they could ill afford the ever increasing quantities of sustenance she would require. Her capacity to travel long distances would also have increased, till every clothesline in Wyndham became "her oyster".

About this time Mrs Pearce at the Nine Mile Store and Boarding House offered Hannah the job of managing her establishment, with good living quarters as part of the arrangement. This suited Hannah very well and she accepted, but then Maggie had to board at the Six Mile Hotel. So Hannah suggested to Maggie that she leave the Six Mile and join her in running the Nine Mile. It became their home for many years. The work was just as constant and at times harder but mother and daughter were happier together and made an amicable and productive team.

"Mum always did the cooking and I tried to save her by doing the outside work. I chopped and carted wood to keep the stoves going. I even took the sanitary pan out into the bush." Had they been in town a council sanitary service truck would have called each week and removed what was delicately referred to as "night soil", replacing the used container with a fresh tar treated empty can. After this work people washed in phenol, a powerful disinfectant, and wood ash, to reduce the offensiveness. It was all part of life in unsewered towns and one of the less attractive features of "the good old days". It was always regarded as a job for the men in the family but as there were no men, it was Maggie's responsibility. "There was only Mum and me so I'd put it on a cart and bush it." They did not think they could ask any of men in the vicinity to perform this most personal and unpleasant task, least of all the guests who paid for their boarding house accommodation!

"I had a beautiful garden but to keep it watered I used to have to wind the buckets up on a windlass from the well. These were the old square kerosene tins." The tins held four gallons and depending on their use were cut down to half way or left with just the top cut out. The sharp edge was turned in and hammered, and two holes were punched in the sides an inch or so from the top. A length of no. 9 fencing wire, curved to form a handle threaded through the punched holes, was bent sharply to form a hook at each end. A six inch piece of old hose or pipe threaded over the wire handle made it easier on the carrier's hands.

Life in the outback could not have succeeded without the kerosene tin and the goat. "It took so many buckets to water everything! We had goats that had to be fed and watered and milked. Mum made butter from the goat cream after scalding the milk to get the cream to rise. She'd beat away for ages." Goats' milk is far more homogenised than cows' milk and extracting the cream is more difficult. Goat cream and butter are also disconcertingly white to anyone accustomed to the rich yellow of dairy butter. The flavour is distinctly different but a dash of yellow food colouring worked wonders.

"We hadn't been long at the Nine Mile when an old chap named Billy Madden came in from his station, Stonehenge, in the Bungles, with a little Aboriginal boy. His mother had abandoned him as a baby and the old man had raised him on goats' milk. He was a fat little fellow about six or seven and Billy asked Mum 'Will ya take him, Missus? It's no place for a little kid on his own out there with me.'" Stonehenge had no homestead. There was just a camp on Red Rock Creek where some of the lubras on the station looked after the boy when Billy was away. "So, Mum took him and raised him and he was one of the family. He always introduced himself as Jacky Nicholson, me as his sister Maggie and Mum was 'my Mum'." The little boy settled in with his new family and thrived on Hannah's cooking. "He had a very black skin and it shone."

Jackie was always Maggie's offsider. They built new yards for the goats, gathered wood, did all the outside chores, broke in horses and did the myriad tasks required by a high level of self sufficiency. "Jacky used to come nearly everywhere with me. He loved the open air pictures at the meatworks and if I was going, I'd take him. He'd go and sit somewhere on his own and people would talk to him and ask who he was, where did he come from? He'd assure them he wasn't alone, he was with his sister Maggie. I think they got a shock when they saw me."

"While we were at the Nine Mile I got my first cow." A man named Walter O'Connor had written to Maggie saying he had a little friend for her. "It was a little red heifer and lived with our goats for years." A drover offered Maggie another heifer on condition that she was able to catch it. "I made sure I caught it" laughed Maggie. "I had a very good camp horse at the time. Between us we got the heifer. Years later they went with us to the Bow but strangely, neither of them ever bred." Nevertheless they were the start of Maggie's long career in the cattle industry.

IN MAY 1931, MAGGIE LILLY CAPTURED A HISTORIC MOMENT ON HER BOX BROWNIE CAMERA. THE TWO RECORD BREAKING PLANES, SCOTTS MOTH AND THE ABEL TASMAN ON THE FLAT AT WYNDHAM.

(Lilly collection)

Drovers camped around this area with their plants and watered their stock at the well near the store. It was a busy part of Wyndham and rooms at the boarding house were in constant demand in the dry season. Hannah kept a good table with the home grown produce and in the season Maggie would ride out to the lagoons where the magpie geese were nesting. "I'd get a chaff bag and put two cuts in it and lay it across the horse's back behind the saddle. That gave me two big pockets, one either side. The geese make a nest out of the reeds by bending a clump of stalks over just above the water level and they'd keep at it until they get a round nest big enough to lay all their eggs in. I was light enough in those days to be able to step on the nest and collect the eggs. I'd slip them into the side pockets of the bag and go home with dozens. Mum used to make the most beautiful cakes. They'd fluff up and be bright yellow."

Maggie remembers the many "bag men" who frequented the outback in those days and congregated at the Nine Mile. It was said that a bag man was a swagman with a horse. Once they acquired some sort of wheeled vehicle they ceased to be referred to as bag men. They were loners who would have a riding horse, a packhorse and often a spare mount. Their worldly belongings were in the bags on their packsaddles. They would get seasonal trips with the drovers into Queensland, Western Australia or the Northern Territory. After the droving they would travel from station to station looking for work at £3 per week or set up camp by a creek to wait out the wet until the next droving season.

The Nine Mile collected its share of characters and one was a man named Harry Davidson of the 6th Rifles., 44th Battalion A.I.F. He had returned from the 1914-18 War physically unimpaired but mentally unstable. On good days he was a perfect gentleman but when his mind relocated itself to the battlefields of France, he became once more a soldier searching out the Hun. With great pride he wore his khaki army uniform, putties and tin helmet, and he always carried his loaded .303 rifle and his revolver. In his daily "tours on watch" he saw moving shadows as signs of the Huns'

(Lilly collection)

The great aviatrix herself. Amy Johnson in her plane at Darwin. Maggie saw her land in Wyndham and recalls the excitement of the townspeople. Note the spare propellor tied to the struts.

presence and stalked them, calling them to come out from behind sheds and trees, firing a few warning shots in their supposed direction. His addled mind recognised anyone in his vicinity as the Hun, to be shot and killed. One day he came into the yard at the Nine Mile, and seeing Maggie on the verandah doing needlework, he ran up the steps and grabbed her. With a tight hold on her arm he began to threaten her, shouting and waving his rifle and preparing to shoot. Maggie was terrified.

Hannah who was inside the house recognised Harry's voice and ran to see what the fuss was about. Her heart leapt with fear when she saw Harry holding Maggie with one hand and his loaded .303 rifle in the other. She knew that rushing out to remonstrate could inflame him further with dire consequences. So with great presence of mind and feigned casualness she called from the doorway "Oh, Harry, would you like a cup of tea? It's time for smoko."

Harry's mind snapped back instantly from the battlefield to the bush and his real surroundings. "Oh good morning Hannah. Thankyou, there's nothing I'd like better." He joined Hannah on the verandah for a yarn and a cuppa as though nothing had happened. Maggie with knees of jelly quietly disappeared into the house to pull herself together. She now had some inkling of how Hannah had felt at Oobergooma long ago staring down the muzzle of a rifle held by someone who had every intention of shooting her.

Accustomed as dwellers in those frontier towns were to lusty characters, people with a dubious past, wild drinkers and a wide variety of firearms, it was decided that at last poor Harry had become too dangerous to be left at large. He'd have to go. Maggie recalls the incident as though it were yesterday. "He gave Mum and me an awful fright. He was sent to Perth after that." Poor Harry, who had served his sovereign faithfully throughout the hostilities, lived out the rest of his tragic life in an institution for the insane.

Wyndham was the most convenient point for overseas aviators to land and refuel. "They'd all land on the marsh at the Three Mile and everyone in town went out to look at the planes. I remember Amy Johnson and Kingsford Smith and all the others. Scott's *Moth* and the *Abel Tasman*. They both broke records." The *Abel Tasman* pioneered the Europe–Batavia–Australia mail route in 1931. In the same year Scott's *Moth* set a new record for the flight from Australia to England. Maggie's little Box Brownie camera worked overtime and captured many rare historical moments. The films went to Darwin for developing so there was always a lengthy wait to see what had "come out". The camera was a simple little black box with a small lens, a tiny view finder, a little metal crank handle to wind on film, and a window the size of a five cent piece through which to check the number of the next section of film. There were no adjustments to make. It was simply a case of aim and press the button. It is thanks to Maggie's avid interest in anything that was going on and the extraordinary reliability of the little Box Brownie that such a variety of photographs records historical events in the region.

In 1929 after working hard at the Nine Mile, Hannah decided it was time to take Maggie on a trip to Perth to celebrate her seventeenth birthday. They had ten glorious days at sea on the *Koolinda*, relaxing and meeting people. The two hardworking women relished being waited upon by stewards, the luxury of beautifully prepared meals and idle hours to spend as they pleased. These voyages were a great treat for the people of the North as the only alternative was travel by land, fraught with difficulty and discomfort. People still rode horses and used horse drawn vehicles, but by 1929 many cars chugged, bumped and hissed along the dusty northern tracks. Cars could accomplish in an hour or so what would require a day in a horse drawn vehicle. Even so, the distances were enormous and it was no wonder that the Coastal Shipping Service was the popular choice.

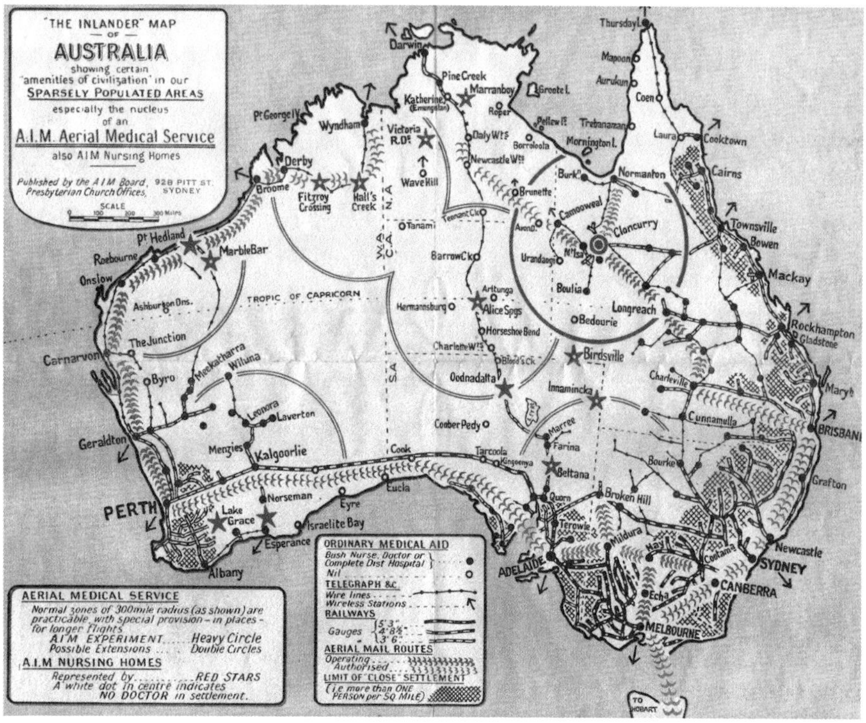

THIS MAP GIVES AN IDEA OF MEDICAL AND AIR SERVICES ACROSS THE CONTINENT IN 1929. THE SMALL AMOUNT OF HATCHING INDICATES AREAS WHERE THERE WAS MORE THAN ONE PERSON TO THE SQUARE MILE AND EMPHASISES THE ISOLATION OF PEOPLE IN THE OUTBACK. JOHN FLYNN, FOUNDER OF THE AUSTRALIAN INLAND MISSION SAW HIS "MANTLE OF SAFETY" FOR THEM SPREAD ACROSS 2,000,000 SQUARE MILES BY 1929. FLYNN DEVISED SIMPLE BUT EFFECTIVE METHODS OF AIR CONDITIONING IN HIS OUTBACK HOSPITALS BY BUILDING INTO THE DESIGN LARGE VENTILATION SHAFTS WHICH DREW FRESH BUT OVEN HOT AIR IN THROUGH COOLING WET CURTAINS WHICH WERE HUNG AT INTERVALS ALONG THE SHAFTS.

It was the first time Maggie had been to a city and her first meeting with her older sister, Annie, then 41. Annie had married Syd McCallum who had won a soldier settler's block after the 1914-18 War. By 1929 Annie and Syd had a large family, some of the children being older than Maggie. Unfortunately, Maggie never met Maude Nicholson, her other sister — a nun who had taken her final vows in 1923, and was 35 when Maggie visited Perth. She was described to Maggie as a small, gentle woman who had given her life to God, serving Him through her teaching and music. In her beautiful but severe habit she would have seemed a remote figure but no doubt Maggie would have enjoyed and cherished the brief encounter. No reason for the omission was ever offered.

"I suppose I should have asked Mum why I wasn't taken to meet her but I never thought to. I don't think we questioned parents about things so much in those days." There may have been a hesitancy on Hannah's part to confront Maude, a religious, with a half sister born out of wedlock, or perhaps the omission was due to visiting restrictions placed on the sisters of Maude's order. Neither party is alive to explain so the answer will never be known.

Over the last quarter of the twentieth century the rigid environment of the professed nun has gradually been relaxed. These days, she may live amongst the general community, no longer enveloped in a distinctive habit. Now she wears a small gold cross pinned to her blouse instead of the heavy string of wooden rosary beads and crucifix hanging from her wide black leather belt. She may eat in company and even stay with her family on visits. In 1929 however, even the most liberal orders maintained strict rules regarding visiting rights for the nuns. Perhaps Maude, later Mother Carmel, was subject to extremely stringent regulations and in obedience to the discipline sought no special dispensation to meet her young sister.

For Hannah it was a wonderful but extraordinary reunion. She had not seen her two daughters

THE M.V. *KOOLINDA* DINNER MENU FOR 20 JULY, 1930. FOR THE RESIDENTS OF THE REGION VISITS BY COASTAL SHIPS WITH THEIR SUPPLIES, NEWSPAPERS AND PASSENGERS PROVIDED CONTACT WITH THE OUTSIDE WORLD. FOR THE STATION WIVES WHO MAY NOT HAVE SEEN OR SPOKEN TO ANOTHER WHITE WOMAN IN MONTHS OR YEARS, A TRIP SOUTH BY SHIP WAS A TREAT BEYOND DESCRIPTION. DURING THE TEN DAY VOYAGE TO PERTH SOCIAL INTER-CHANGE WITH OTHER PASSENGERS ABOARD SHIP, THE FRESH MEAT, VEGETABLES AND FRUIT WERE ALL PART OF ANOTHER WORLD EXPERIENCED ON RARE OCCASIONS AND EVERY MOMENT OF IT TO BE SAVOURED. THERE WAS ALWAYS A CHANCE OF A ROUGH PASSAGE AND SEA SICKNESS COULD MAKE THE TRIP AN ORDEAL BUT THAT WAS TO BE ACCEPTED.

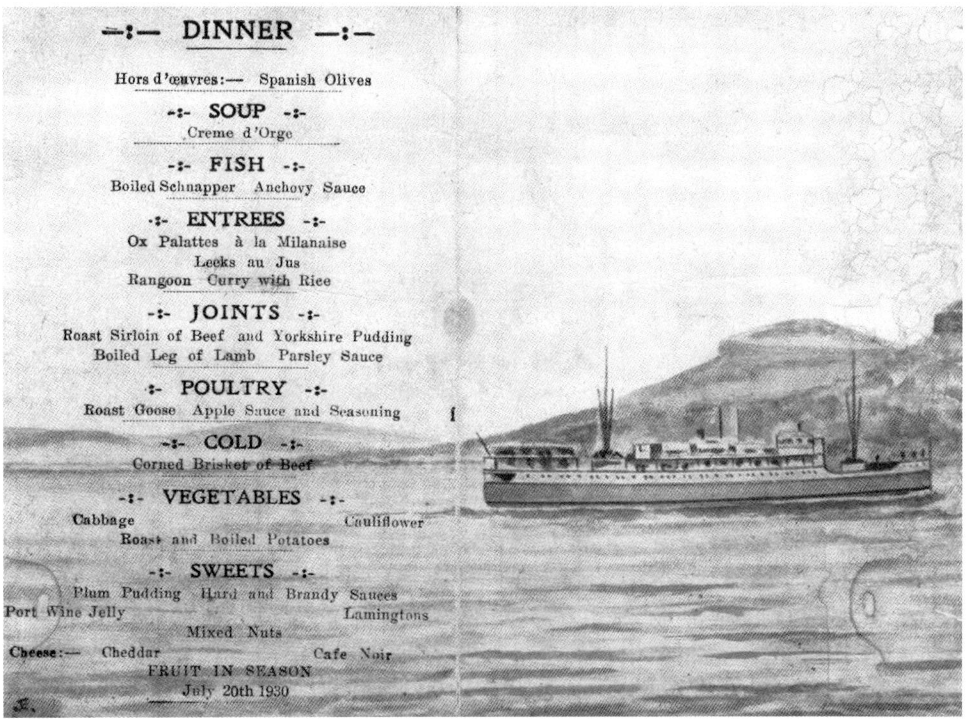

—:— DINNER —:—

Hors d'œuvres:— Spanish Olives

-:- SOUP -:-

Creme d'Orge

-:- FISH -:-

Boiled Schnapper Anchovy Sauce

-:- ENTREES -:-

Ox Palattes à la Milanaise

Leeks au Jus

Rangoon Curry with Rice

-:- JOINTS -:-

Roast Sirloin of Beef and Yorkshire Pudding

Boiled Leg of Lamb Parsley Sauce

-:- POULTRY -:-

Roast Goose Apple Sauce and Seasoning

-:- COLD -:-

Corned Brisket of Beef

-:- VEGETABLES -:-

Cabbage Cauliflower

Roast and Boiled Potatoes

-:- SWEETS -:-

Plum Pudding Hard and Brandy Sauces

Port Wine Jelly Lamingtons

Mixed Nuts

Cheese:— Cheddar Cafe Noir

FRUIT IN SEASON

July 20th 1930

for nearly thirty years and had missed so many important occasions in their lives. She could still only visualise them as the little girls she'd left behind. To meet them as middle aged women must have taken some mental adjustments. It had been a cruel deprivation, but from afar she had done her best under the circumstances life had dealt her and both daughters had made their way successfully according to their needs.

Maggie had a lovely time and was taken sightseeing around the city whilst Hannah caught up with the lost years of her older daughters and her McCallum grandchildren. Annie, whose face bore a strong resemblance to her long dead father George Cook, had inherited Hannah's sturdy figure. As mother and daughter talked, Annie confessed that making ends meet on their soldier settler block was becoming more difficult by the day. The great ignorance that existed among the people vested with the power to obtain and divide properties for soldier settlement is a heartbreaking fact of Australian history. The idea was good but the outcome was often tragic in many instances. Some were lucky but many were allotted land on which it was impossible to survive, let alone make a living. Having returned from "the war to end all wars" and been granted land of their own by a "grateful nation" many soldier settlers spent their lives struggling to survive and died worn out, broken men. The hardworking McCallums were stretched to the limits and Hannah suggested that a couple of her older grandchildren might like to spend some time with her in Wyndham.

The offer was gratefully accepted. Violet, only four years younger than Maggie, and her brother Ron agreed to join Hannah and Maggie. This was the happiest of inspirations on Hannah's part as Maggie and Violet — who didn't get on so very well with the rest of her siblings — began a friendship that lasted a lifetime. "She was a bit bossy with them but it didn't worry me and even though there was four years difference in our ages we were best friends from the start."

Not long after Hannah and Maggie returned home, Violet and Ron disembarked from the ship at Wyndham jetty and settled in immediately to their new surroundings. Hannah was at last able to enjoy at close hand some members of her long lost family. At last she could lavish upon them some of the love and care that had been their mother's due so long ago.

MAGGIE AT THE HEAD OF HER CHAMPION BASKETBALL TEAM AT THE WYNDHAM MEATWORKS COURTS IN THE LATE 1920S. TRENDY SPORTS SHOES WERE FAR IN THE FUTURE AND THE TOWN BOASTED NO SHOE SHOP. SUPPLIES CAME MAIL ORDER FROM PERTH AND BRISBANE SO THE GIRLS PLAYED IN WHATEVER THEY COULD FIND, INCLUDING, IN MAGGIE'S CASE, HIGH HEELS.

One thing that remained constant was the hard work needed to survive. Everyone pulled their weight in the recently extended family and somehow, the girls who did everything together found time to train entries for the next race meeting. Violet was a good rider so now Maggie had a pacemaker. With a companion most horses work better and extend their capacity. In those days, the formalities of pedigree, registration and studbook details did not exist for the runners at bush races. Some stations used blood horses as sires for their mares and so there was always the chance of picking up a horse which could turn out a winner. Maggie was possessed of an almost unerring eye for a fast horse and already she had had her share of winners. Race meetings and balls were the highlight of each year and brought people together from far flung stations and settlements. Maggie and Violet doubled their pleasure by always riding in the Ladies' Race and then being the sought after belles at the balls. No matter how hard people had to work, it all came to a standstill during race week.

MAGGIE AT SEVENTEEN. STUDIO PORTRAIT TAKEN ON HER VISIT TO PERTH WITH HANNAH IN 1929. "IT WAS THE FIRST TIME I HAD BEEN TO A BIG CITY." COMPARED TO WYNDHAM WITH ITS POPULATION OF ONE HUNDRED OR SO WHICH SWELLED TO FOUR HUNDRED IN THE DRY SEASON WHEN THE MEATWORKS WAS AT FULL CAPACITY, PERTH WOULD HAVE SEEMED VERY BIG.

It was not uncommon for neighbouring stations to muster cleanskin cattle from each other's properties and brand them as their own. It came under the "fair game" philosophy and as Maggie remembers, even the local policeman was not above augmenting his meat supply from time to time. "We did all sorts of things in those days and Jackie O'Neill, Violet and I used to go cattle duffing. We'd go out and pick up cleanskins on Ivanhoe Station and bring them back home. Can't say we got many but we did get some." Obviously it was a lot of fun; the cheek and the challenge meant far more than the acquisition of the cattle. Ivanhoe Station was one of the nearest to Wyndham and all in a day's ride.

Maggie, like her mother, was genuinely interested in people and totally involved in the activities of Wyndham. Bright, lively and at ease with everyone, she was a popular figure but was shy and somewhat embarrassed when dragooned into performing at the concerts on the stage in the hall at the meatworks. A concert could be an impromptu affair. People recited poetry, sang a song or played the harmonica — a very popular instrument among bushman with a gift for music; yarn telling was an integral part of the bushman's life and it was a rare person who was unable to make some sort of contribution. "We had some really good talent in Wyndham, including Mrs Tom Cole, who was Mabel Bridge. She was a wonderful musician." Maggie recalled one concert, "I had to do a silly sort of a dance and then they got a young man up to tell his story. He was a stockman who said he had been working on Spring Creek station on the Western Australian-Northern Territory border for Norman Finley." He complained about the food served to the men on Spring Creek. "An old goat died so we had to eat our way through that before we got anything else. Then an old cow died so that was dished up until it was all gone. Then the Chinese cook died. That's when I left."

As in all country towns, self help was obligatory. Amenities came through hard work by the people of the town and district, not from government largesse. The cottage hospital of Wyndham in 1930 needed an X-ray machine and a Popular Girl Contest was launched to raise the money. Maggie won hands down. Her efforts did indeed secure that much needed piece of equipment and she still has the letter of appreciation and the cherished gold wristlet watch presented to her nearly

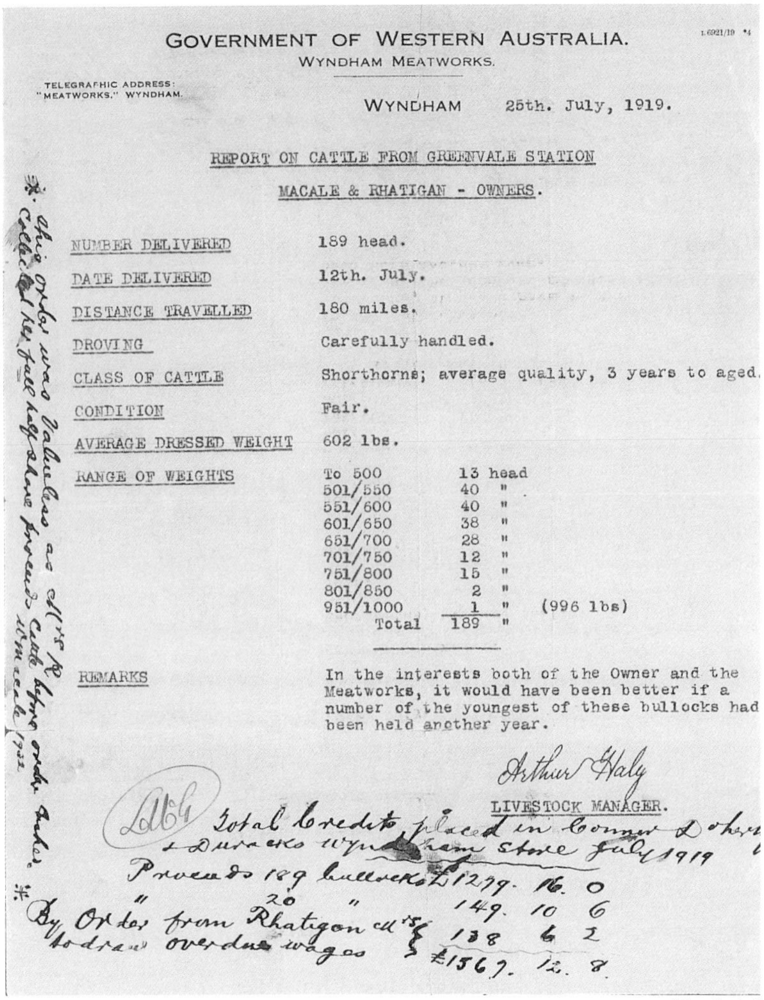

GOVERNMENT OF WESTERN AUSTRALIA.
WYNDHAM MEATWORKS.

TELEGRAPHIC ADDRESS: "MEATWORKS," WYNDHAM.

WYNDHAM 25th. July, 1919.

REPORT ON CATTLE FROM GREENVALE STATION

MACALE & RHATIGAN - OWNERS.

NUMBER DELIVERED	189 head.
DATE DELIVERED	12th. July.
DISTANCE TRAVELLED	180 miles.
DROVING	Carefully handled.
CLASS OF CATTLE	Shorthorns; average quality, 3 years to aged.
CONDITION	Fair.
AVERAGE DRESSED WEIGHT	602 lbs.

RANGE OF WEIGHTS

To 500	13 head	
501/550	40 "	
551/600	40 "	
601/650	38 "	
651/700	28 "	
701/750	12 "	
751/800	15 "	
801/850	2 "	
951/1000	1 "	(996 lbs)
Total	189 "	

REMARKS In the interests both of the Owner and the Meatworks, it would have been better if a number of the youngest of these bullocks had been held another year.

Arthur Haly
LIVESTOCK MANAGER.

Total Credits placed in Connor Doherty & Durracks Wyndham Store July 1919
Proceeds 189 bullocks £1279. 16. 0
" 20 " 149. 10 6
By Order from Rhatigan cheques to draw overdue wages 138 6 2
£1567. 12. 8

(Lilly collection)

A RARE DOCUMENT FROM THE WYNDHAM MEATWORKS IN 1919. IT PERTAINS TO RHATIGAN AND MACALE FROM WHOM THE LILLYS LATER BOUGHT TURKEY CREEK AND GREENVALE. THE MEATWORKS SUPPLIED PRACTICAL ADVICE AND ACTED AS A BANKING SERVICE AS WELL. A NOTE ON THE PAGE SUGGESTS SOME MISUNDERSTANDING BETWEEN KATE RHATIGAN AND WALTER MACALE ABOUT PROCEEDS.

seventy years ago. In 1930, when Australia was in the grip of the Great Depression a watch was a possession to be treasured. A gold watch was usually given as a mark of respect to an employee retiring after a lifetime's service. They were worn with great pride and represented a landmark in life. Such presentations have less significance for generations who have grown up amid the affluence of the last thirty years of the twentieth century.

The last camp for cattle coming in to Wyndham from the stations was Parry's Lagoon, some twelve miles from the meatworks. The land at the Nine Mile was a good spot to leave droving plants whilst delivery took place. Pack horses and donkeys, packs, spare horses and wheeled vehicles comprised the plants and there was no need for these to accompany the mob on the last leg of their journey. After delivery the men stayed around and camped with their plant, travelling in to the town for a little socialising. At the same time, accommodation at the Nine Mile was constantly in use and if Hannah's guests wished to go into town, they had to saddle up their mounts, ride in to Wyndham and back out again after dark. The mile pegs were inaccurate by anything up to a mile or two between pegs and their journey from the Nine Mile was closer to twelve or thirteen miles. After taking their leave of their boozy mates in the bright warm rowdy pubs, much the worse for wear themselves after a night on the grog they had at least two hours in the saddle whilst their horses picked their way along the track in pitch dark to the camp or the Nine Mile Store and Boarding House.

Hannah could see the potential for her next project — the Nicholson Taxi Service. A big T-model Ford with four cylinder side valve engine arrived from Perth. There was great excitement as it was swung out of the ship's hold in a massive rope net, and deposited gently on the jetty. The proud owner was granted a driver's licence and a taxi licence.

The taxi service achieved instant popularity. It was profitable but more than Hannah could handle. After a heavy day at the store and boarding house, cooking the midday meal over a hot fuel stove, and the forty kilometre round trip into town in the evening, she would then have to wait around until almost midnight to head for town. Longing to fall into a welcoming bed instead of having to go out again, she found herself bumping along the dusty, dark winding track to collect all the fares she taken to town earlier in the evening.

Hannah's passengers would disperse to the various pubs and for a few hours they would drink and catch up on news. A midnight tour of the local "watering holes" would locate her passengers,

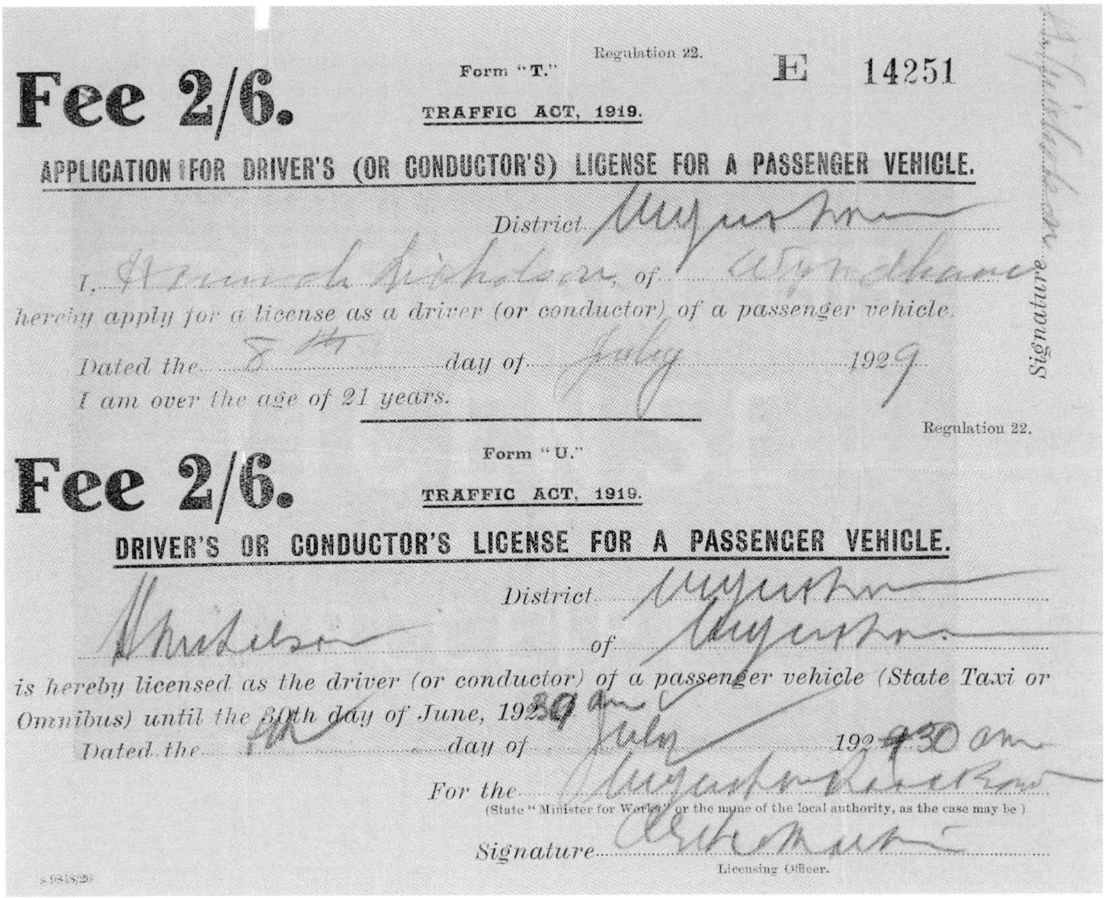

Regulation 22.

Form "T."

E 14251

Fee 2/6.

TRAFFIC ACT, 1919.

APPLICATION FOR DRIVER'S (OR CONDUCTOR'S) LICENSE FOR A PASSENGER VEHICLE.

District Wyndham

I, Hannah Nicholson *of* Wyndham

hereby apply for a license as a driver (or conductor) of a passenger vehicle.

Dated the 8th *day of* July *1929*

I am over the age of 21 years.

Signature

Regulation 22.

Form "U."

Fee 2/6.

TRAFFIC ACT, 1919.

DRIVER'S OR CONDUCTOR'S LICENSE FOR A PASSENGER VEHICLE.

District Wyndham

H Nicholson *of* Wyndham

is hereby licensed as the driver (or conductor) of a passenger vehicle (State Taxi or Omnibus) until the 30th day of June, 1930

Dated the 9th *day of* July *1929*

For the Wyndham Road Board

(State "Minister for Works," or the name of the local authority, as the case may be.)

Signature

Licensing Officer.

by then much the worse for wear and not always ready or willing to be taken home. The alternative was a twenty kilometre walk along a dark dusty track, but it was their choice. The legless ones would be loaded into the Ford with the dubious assistance of mates similarly affected by the night's indulgence, borne off to their waiting swags and decanted by Hannah at the drovers' camps around the Nine Mile or at the boarding house. "We charged thirty shillings to drive the drovers' boys into town from the Nine Mile and five pounds from Goose Hill to the Meatworks." This was far more than one man earned in a week but shared, it was well worth the expense. Maggie did a great deal of the driving too but at that point did not have a taxi licence.

One night a young man who'd been charged with cattle stealing but was out on bail asked Maggie to drive him into town. He suggested Tom Ronan should go with her for company. Tom Ronan was a bushman who later became a very successful writer Maggie drove him and Tom in, leaving Tom at the pub while she went to the pictures at the meatworks. They had to wait for the young man a few miles out of town. He had warned them his business might keep him late but they weren't reckoning on a wait till the early hours of the morning. Tom being a realist reckoned he'd be dead drunk and unlikely to turn up. He suggested they give him a miss. In fact he offered to hire her to drive him home.

Maggie was furious. "Maggie who was as straight in speech as in everything else told me in forthright unvarnished Australian that if I felt that way about it I could walk home." Having agreed

(Lilly collection)

GEORGE KINEVIN AND TOM FAY GRADING THE ROAD WHICH RAN FROM THE NINE MILE, ACROSS THE TWELVE MILE PLAIN, PAST GOOSE HILL AND ON TO HALLS CREEK. IT WAS MANY YEARS BEFORE MECHANISATION REPLACED THE TEAM OF THIRTY TWO HARDY, WILLING LITTLE DONKEYS AND THE EQUALLY HARDY MEN WHO WORKED WITH THEM. IN LATER YEARS WHEN THEY WERE NO LONGER A MAINSTAY IN TRANSPORT, DONKEYS RAN WILD AND PROLIFERATED. THEY WERE SHOT BY THE THOUSANDS AND, LIKE THE CAMELS, THEIR MAGNIFICENT CONTRIBUTION TO EARLY SETTLEMENT IN AUSTRALIA IS LITTLE KNOWN AND ALL BUT FORGOTTEN.

to a certain deal Maggie would stick to her side of the bargain, even though it did take her till nearly dawn to complete it. Tom Ronan and anyone else who had dealings with young Maggie Nicholson held her in high esteem and had profound respect.

"I'd have to cook and wash up on the nights Mum was using the taxi. I didn't mind the washing up so much but I couldn't cook. I suppose I gave the guests something. They didn't go hungry." In the face of Hannah's easy expertise gained over half a century Maggie experienced a certain feeling of inadequacy in the culinary arts and in any case she would rather have been anywhere but the kitchen.

A man from the township saw Hannah's dilemma with the taxi and suggested that she allow him to work as her driver, and house the vehicle in Wyndham where it would also be available for daytime work. Hannah, ever practical, could see a lot of sense in the proposal which would benefit more people and increase business. Now that she was well in her sixties and still working hard from the moment she put her feet on the ground at first light, to have those wearing night trips taken off her shoulders seemed a blessing. With some relief she agreed, although parting with her precious T-model didn't appeal much to a woman who had discovered the fun of having her own car. Not having to catch, harness and unharness a sulky horse was something of a luxury.

However, what should have been a lucrative and practical arrangement degenerated into disaster. Her trust was abused and when she recovered her vehicle it was damaged and neglected beyond belief. It was a disappointing end to a promising venture. George McHugh — whom Tom Ronan calls the "barefoot stockman" in one of his books, because of George's unusual habit of riding without boots — bought Hannah's battered but beloved Ford. George was head stockman at Argyle Station and many years later he wrote to Maggie, "That old Model T Ford of yours was the best Model T I owned. I sold her for twenty six pounds to Wave Hill Station." Hannah and Maggie had often wondered where it ended up.

Fortunately by then Maggie had acquired a second hand Chevrolet 4 Tabletop and became the family chauffer. First she'd had to learn how drive a vehicle with a regular gearbox and the mailman obliged letting her practise on his truck. "I drove it a couple of times then I used to carry the drovers' boys in from the Nine Mile and Goose Hill."

Hannah could not drive a manually geared vehicle. The old style mechanical gearbox, that relied on a clutch and worked properly only when the engine revs were synchronised with the gears, was too difficult. She had learnt on her T-model, which was advanced for its time being semi-automatic, and had one sump for gearbox and differential. Dropping the handbrake, which was between the two front seats, put the vehicle in gear and pulling it up disengaged the gears. The three pedals were foot brake, reverse and forward. The engine had to be started with a crank handle and this was not without considerable risk if it was cold. The old motor oils thickened and set as they cooled. Even when the vehicle was out of gear, the gears could be turned by the thick oil in the sump, moving the wheels forward and over the crank handle operator! It was a recommended safety precaution to jack up the rear wheels so they could spin until the oil in the sump warmed and thinned. But in Wyndham — purported to be the hottest town in Australia — the oil may never have set.

At nineteen, Maggie's life was full of activity. Since she had acquired the little Chev 4 Tabletop she could travel further and this enabled her to go bird catching for a short period each year. Loading the Chev with bird cages, nets, food and water, she and Violet would go out to the unexplored valleys south of Wyndham. They were repeatedly bogged in the sand on these excursions and only by laying corduroys of sticks and logs to give the little narrow wheeled Chev a grip could they get free. Near creeks and by ancient boab trees they would spread their nets and wait for their harvest. "We mostly caught finches. There were blood finches, Gouldians, black hearts, yellow beaks and double bars. Pink eyed doves too."

HANNAH AT THE WHEEL OF HER T MODEL TAXI. MAGGIE IS IN THE PASSENGER SEAT AND JACKIE ON THE FAR LEFT. LIKE HER MOTHER SARAH, HANNAH WAS A VERY ENTERPRISING WOMAN. HER TAXI SERVICE THRIVED WHEN FEW OWNED CARS AND MOST DROVE A HORSE DRAWN VEHICLE OR RODE.

There was only a short bird catching season each year. A man named George Reddel came up from Perth once a year to buy from the trappers. "I think we got about seven shillings and sixpence per dozen. Doesn't seem a lot but in those days you could buy a three course meal for two shillings and six pence." The tiny birds from their Kimberley homeland were destined to end up on the other side of the world. "George would take them all back to Perth and then go with them to London." The gloriously multi-coloured finches must have brightened many a heart and been an exotic touch in any bird fancier's aviary. There were no restrictions in those days. Few Australian people knew or cared about the wildlife in remote places and the export trade flourished. Many years later the valley and creek where Maggie and Violet hunted was named after her but at the time it was simply a vast beautiful pristine area of bush scarcely explored by white man.

In the dry season when the Meatworks was fully operational the little town of Wyndham's population swelled by anything up to three hundred people and in every pub on a Saturday night there would be a dance as well as the variety of entertainment offered by the Meatworks. Towards the end of the dry season the social activity became hectic. Finals in the sporting teams, dances, balls and the race cup meetings came in quick succession and Maggie was up to her neck in all of it.

Hannah saw to it that Maggie always had a nice dress for the balls and in spite of doing a man's work, Maggie never lost her femininity. At social events she was as smartly attired as anyone and with her ivory complexion, black wavy hair, dark eyes and slender body she was, in the slang of the day, "a real good sort". The fact that she had a lively personality and was a good all rounder meant she was always popular.

Young men from all around the district sought the favours of the young women of the town and neither Maggie nor Violet lacked eager escorts. Among Maggie's admirers was the young Charlie Schultz, who stayed at the Nine Mile on his rare trips to Wyndham from Humbert River Station. Although over 300 kilometres away by dirt track, Wyndham was his nearest centre of trade, Katherine being over 500 and Darwin 1,000 kilometres distant. Now famous as one of Australia's northern pioneers, Charlie was then in his early twenties, a lean young stripling who had been given sole responsibility for putting the wild, isolated and neglected Humbert River Station in order, ready for resale. Charlie's father had bought the station, that adjoined Victoria River Downs, for his oldest son, Billy, hoping it would keep him away from town and grog. It was a forlorn hope. Not long after, Billy was so seriously injured in a fall from his horse that he died a few days later and was buried on Victoria River Downs.

So daunted was young Charlie by the lonely and dangerous prospect of coping with the rundown station and its hostile blacks that he doubted he'd last the year. In fact he went on to spend most of his life there. Four years Maggie's senior, he admired her immensely but Maggie was prepared to offer friendship only, although that friendship remained constant for a lifetime. "There were lots of boys but I didn't want any of them. I was always nice to them but I had other interests and was always having to think up all sorts of polite ways of dodging them."

One was Tom Ronan who at that time worked as a drover and often stayed at the Nine Mile store and boarding house with Hannah and Maggie. Here he had a clean bed and three good meals a day for thirty shillings a week. Hannah would not tolerate liquor on the premises. Tom, like all his droving mates, enjoyed his rum. "Any jovial boarder who returned from town with a bottle of rum or whisky for the next morning would have it talked out of him, confiscated or even taken when he wasn't looking. It was always poured down the kitchen sink. Without being exactly a dipsomaniac, I was shocked to see good liquor so mistreated and the old lady and I had some awful rows about this." Tom could never have known of the years of anguish, deprivation and tragedy brought about by alcohol, that Hannah had suffered during her life with Joseph Nicholson. Even a whiff of grog on someone's breath would have instantly recalled heartbreaking memories.

Each year when the first mob came in from Victoria River Downs to the meatworks, a splendid booze-up was held at Goose Hill. Drinking and droving did not go together so after a month the men had built up an insatiable thirst by the time they delivered at Wyndham. The cattle passed within a mile of the Six Mile so it was a conveniently located watering hole for the drovers. In the light of Hannah's strongly held views on grog Tom was obliged to do his drinking there.

Amid all the excitement of the aviators and their record breaking flights to Wyndham, there was a disaster. Two Germans, Adolf Klausman and Hans Bertram, came down near Cape Bernier. They thought they were on Melville Island but instead they were on the mainland coast in an isolated and inhospitable location where they nearly lost their lives. Their Junkers Seaplane had been blown off course. They had no fuel and between them only a flask of coffee and a bar of chocolate.

A policeman named Gordon Marshall, who was in charge of the search party, came to visit Maggie the night after the news of the missing German aviators became public. At the time the police plant of horses was very low and extra mounts were essential. He sought Maggie's advice as she had the reputation for knowing the whereabouts of all the horses within thirty miles of Wyndham, and who owned them. "Tom Ronan was staying at the Nine Mile" Maggie recalls, "and the police asked him to join them in the search for the missing Germans." George Marshall offered Tom six pounds (120 shillings) per week for himself and his horses, of which Tom would pay Marshall one pound for his keep.

Tom Ronan was born to the bush. He knew and understood the country and his assistance proved invaluable. Maggie continued "He used to work with the VRD drovers so he took his three horses and joined up with the police plant which comprised horses, mules and a couple of trackers. They had to cross the King, Pentecost and Durack Rivers to get to Forest River, where Gordon Marshal was bringing in supplies by launch. After meeting up with him they packed the mules and went to Kalumburu. It was terrible country to pass through.".

Their Aboriginal guide, Eungeye, was mystified that the precipitous rocky ridges up which he could run so nimbly all but defeated the horsemen and their mules. The poor creatures floundered up the steep inclines, hooves searching for a tenuous foothold on the jagged ridges and any flase move could send them toppling, pulled off balance by their huge loads. At the top of the razorback ridges, Tom would rest the heaving, trembling animals whilst he made alterations to each one's harness. On the onward climb he had attached the breach band at the front of the back saddle to form a breast plate to prevent the pack from slipping down and over their rumps. Now, the breast plate was returned to the back of the saddle to resume its normal position as a breech strap and so prevent the pack from sliding over the animals' withers and neck on the nightmarish downward scramble. Tom watched their painful process with his heart in his mouth.

For man and beast it was excruciatingly hard work, except for one member of the party who took it all in from his elevated position on the pommel of Gordon Marshall's saddle. This was his pet Pekinese, a most incongruous little dog to be found among the tough cattle dogs and the mission trackers' mongrels. However the little dog turned out to be the best night watch dog of all.

The last ridge before the sea shore was too difficult for the horses and Tom stayed behind with them some three miles inland. Tom hated the country there. It was poor, stunted and inhospitable. Gordon Marshall and the others headed for the beach to reach the aviators who, according to the black's reports were "properly weak fella". By this time they were clinging to life by only a tenuous thread. Klausman lost his mind and raved through the nights. For the safety of all, especially his own, he had to be secured by chains. Bertram's mood changes wore everyone down. In his communicative periods Bertram explained that they had been navigating with the aid of an old school atlas and were blown off course in a storm. The plane had run out of fuel and come down on a beach which they believed to be Melville Island. They took a hammer and chisel to one of the floats on their Junkers aircraft until they freed part of it and used it as a boat to go in search of a village or sign of life. All they had for sustenance was a thermos of coffee and two bars of chocolate. They searched in vain and returned worn out and hungry. They had actually landed on one of the most remote, inhospitable sections of the Australian coastline. Discovery by the rescue party had snatched them from death's grasp at almost the last possible moment.

Their disappearance made headlines and there were constant updates in city newspapers. When they were rescued the account of their horrendous ordeal received widespread newspaper coverage. On his return to the Nine Mile, Tom described a sequence of dramatic events of the search and rescue to Maggie.

Wyndham is a little dot on the edge of nowhere as far as most of Australia is concerned. But one way and another it had its share of excitement. Heroism, record breaking aviation feats, drama and close acquaintance with people who achieved fame in various endeavours were all part of everyday life for Maggie. Tom Ronan tells the full story of the search for the missing aviators in his book *Once there was a Bagman*. A couple of years after the rescue Tom and some of the other participants were awarded the first class Order of the Deutchen Rosen Kreunze, by Marshalls von Beckendorf and von Hindenburg, and the Prince of Saxe Coburg Gotha.

After several years at the Nine Mile, Hannah and Maggie were informed by the owner, Mrs Pearce that she had decided to sell the business to people named Smith from Halls Creek. For a while this made no difference to Hannah and Maggie, and they continued to run the business for the new owner as competently and assiduously as they had for Mrs Pearce. However, there came the day when the Smiths decided they would like to take over. If they were not to be left without a roof over their heads, Hannah and the family had to begin an immediate search for new lodgings and there was not a moment to be lost.

Moving was nothing new. Maggie and Hannah took such domestic upheavals in their stride, but the Nine Mile had been their home longer than anywhere else and they would miss it, the comings and goings of their guests and the living it provided. Their constant hard work in the maintenance of the residence, business and gardens greatly benefitted the Smiths when they moved in. For those moving out the prospect was less inviting. Hannah and Maggie, Ron, Violet and Jackie would have to accept what they could find and start again.

Chapter IV

Enter Sammy Soapsuds

Lilly family lore believes that Carl Helmuth Liljenqvist, born in Sweden in 1860, came from a well to do and educated family. He chose a career at sea, served his time "before the mast", became a master mariner and was given the command of a sailing ship. The ship plied its trade between the Northern Hemisphere and Australia. He may well have continued in his chosen and successful profession for the rest of his life had fate not decreed otherwise.

On the second voyage to the Southern Hemisphere his ship was blown badly off course after rounding the Cape. Eventually with all supplies consumed and every last crumb eaten of rock hard weevilly ships' biscuits, the ship's company was starving to death. They began gnawing on pieces of the ship's hemp ropes. At last, the desperate weakened seamen brought the ship in to port, found a mooring and to a man, abandoned the ship.

Melbourne or Adelaide would be the most likely location but the family believes it was Sydney. No one is left to settle the matter and research has yet to reveal the answer. For a captain to abandon his ship was unthinkable and Carl carried the shame of his action all his life refusing to allude to it for many years. Consequently very little is known of the disastrous voyage.

He did however remain in shipping in the early years of his life in Australia. Research reveals that he was on the *Lavinia* (6/9/86), and the *Claymore* (5/11/86 and 24/12/86) but not in a position of command. These were sailing ships and coalers of the BB Line owned by Bickers. He is also recorded as having been a pilot on the Port River at Adelaide. It was possible for a seaman to hold such a position in those days without a master's ticket provided the company had sufficient faith in his proficiency. Now resting in a place of honour in the home of his granddaughter Alma, Carl's sextant has always been a cherished part of the family possessions and indicates the probable accuracy of the family's belief in his registration as a ship's master.

Carl married Elizabeth Anne Smith, a young woman of Scottish background, in Sydney in 1884. According to family records one of Carl's shipmates married Elizabeth's sister. By the time the Liljenqvists had been married ten years they had five children. When they decided to move to Adelaide the eldest girl, Nellie, for reasons unknown remained behind in Sydney. From South Australia they next moved westward to Perth with the four children Carl, Hulda, Agnes and Violet. They then travelled north to Derby by bullock wagon. This journey of about 3,000 kilometres must have taken some six months. A journey of such magnitude through weeks of solitude and across

A CHARACTERISTIC HILLY KIMBERLY LANDSCAPE.

waterless wastes carried with it many perils and few people at the time would have been able to warn them of the terrain or the risks. It would have been a great relief to all when they finally reached the little town of Derby. The cluster of tin shacks that comprised the town sat on a jutting point of land surrounded on both sides by tidal flats. Derby, the first official town and port in the Kimberley, was declared a township in 1883 and boasted the second highest tidal variation in the world—eleven meters, exceeded only by the Bay of Fundy in Canada. When the Liljenqvists arrived, the settlement was not twenty years old but already it had seen the inrush of miners to the Halls Creek gold rush. It was also the point of departure for export cattle from the Kimberley stations.

Here the Liljenqvists settled and had three more children, thus swelling the population of Derby considerably. To save people the difficulty of pronouncing the Swedish name of Liljenqvist the family shortened it to Lilly. It was never changed by deed poll but everyone accepted Lilly as the proper name. Another large family in Derby were the Roses and there was a saying that Derby was a town of lilies and roses.

Carl was a versatile man and one of his achievements was to build the Port Hotel on the main street. The family lived near Nobby's Well.

On 8 May, 1911 Dr Adams' list of house calls included a visit to a mother of a large family. Elizabeth Liljenqvist had given birth to a baby boy. After satisfying himself that the mother's condition was satisfactory, he turned his attention to the newest member of the household who was being bathed by the midwife. Dr Adams, who referred to all new baby girls as Topsy, called all

new baby boys Toby. But there was already a young Toby in the family, born the previous year, so observing the squirming lather covered infant in his first bath the doctor greeted the newborn with an off the cuff title, "Ah there, Sammy Soapsuds!" So Edwin James as he was later christened was always known as Sam and his older brother Valentine, born on St Valentine's Day, was always Toby.

Elizabeth's oldest child was twenty one when their seventh child Sam was born. The Liljenqvists had five children in ten years followed by a ten year break before Toby and Sam. Elizabeth, in her late forties, was faced with the task of rearing the two little boys and her last child, a daughter. By the time the three late arrivals were four or five, the rest of the family was grown up and Nellie, who had remained in the east and whom Sam never met, was married.

Young Sammy Soapsuds was born in a particularly difficult year for the people of Derby. The town was in the grip of famine. Derby was a very hazardous port and many foreign ships avoided the risk. Cargo for Derby was frequently dumped off at Broome. For a long time ships from Singapore left goods there expecting the coastal ship the *Koombana* to transfer them to Derby. The coastal shipping service called regularly at all the ports and masters of the foreign ships were more than relieved to leave it to "local" mariners to navigate their ships through the treacherous rips to Derby. The *Mindaroo* once entered Derby but, finding the cattle ship *Colac* at the jetty, turned and went on to Singapore before it could get caught by the falling tide. From Singapore it returned to Fremantle then sailed north to Broome where it finally dumped the Derby cargo.

On 18 February, 1911 the *Broome Chronicle* reported—

with an accumulation of Derby cargo at the Broome goods shed so great and the deterioration of perishable goods such as onions and potatoes etc. so dangerous to public health as well as causing no end of inconvenience to our busy shed, it is high time authorities stepped in and demanded that merchandise shall be carried on to its destinations and not allow our port to become the dumping ground for the convenience of passing ships.

What was the position of the Derby tradespeople and those dependent on them for their daily supplies? An actual famine existed. Flour had run out and the good people of the town were reduced to dog biscuits in lieu of bread and these also ran out. The local baker ceased operations for want of flour, the local coach builder could not build wagons on order or do any repairs and had to suspend operations. The storekeepers could not supply the most ordinary lines; whilst station people and those who travel by water to Derby to obtain their usual supplies—some travelling hundreds of miles—arrived only to find their journey was in vain as supplies had not come to hand. The vegetable supply of the town, both fresh and preserved was a thing of the past and the health of the people was consequently in jeopardy. In fact the whole place is in a state bordering on starvation.

Elizabeth Lilly, capable and resourceful though she was, had her work cut out to keep her large family nourished. She had added to her already full schedule by taking in boarders at the house at Nobbys Well to augment the family income and at that time of virtual famine any of the perennial jokes voiced on the hackneyed subject of boarding house cooking would have fallen very flat.

In 1912 the whole world knew of the sinking on 15 April of the White Star liner *Titanic*, with a loss of 1513 lives. A month earlier on 12 March of the same year, the coastal steamer and supply ship *Koombana* was lost with all lives and hardly anyone knew but the people of the Kimberley coast. She sank in a cyclone somewhere between Port Hedland and Broome and the wreck has never been found. It was a tragedy that in some way affected everyone in the region and Derby, Broome and Wyndham were devastated. In those towns where population was small, families were large and people's lives were closely entwined so many people on board, crew as well as passengers, were friends or family members. The embattled people of the region faced another period of shortage until the next coastal steamer was due.

With only a year between them the little boys were inseparable and grew up doing all the things boys could in a small coastal township. In the dry season thousands of cattle came in from the Kimberley runs. They were driven into huge yards and watered at Myalls Bore, where the longest cattle trough in the world was built to cater for the great mobs of thirsty beasts whose destination was either Singapore or Fremantle. The boys would watch the stockmen working the cattle and the loading of the bellowing unhappy animals who'd spent their lives in the wild hills of the Kimberley, hardly acquainted with mankind let alone the sea and the hot, noisy, strange smelling vessel into which they were being forced.

The busy waterfront was always full of interest. The ships' crews were made up from many races and the boys learnt of the large outside world beyond their isolated spot on the map. Fishing and boats occupied hours of their time and from their seafaring father they learnt to read the sea in all its moods and to understand the weather; vital information to both seamen and those who strove to work the land. Carl taught the family "If the weather is going to change it will do so three days after a full moon." Every generation of Lillys since has been raised to heed this advice "and by Golly," says Alma, "It works!"

Schooling in the one teacher school took up part of their growing years but it was a free style of life. They needed few clothes and went barefoot most of the time. People in Derby were just as poor

THE COASTAL STEAMER *KOOLAMA* AT BROOME, WITH THE TIDE OUT.

as those in Wyndham and lived by the same "waste not, want not" philosophy. If the boys wanted anything extra they had to earn it themselves. Consequently the boys devoted much attention to making pocket money. There always was someone who wanted a message run or chores done but there was too much competition. Little kids and girls could mostly do this and there had to be something better; a superior enterprise of their very own.

The boys discovered that the seamen who crewed on the ships were keen to buy cockatoos which they would teach to talk during off duty hours at sea. A cockatoo that was a good talker would be a highly prized and profitable possession and they were everywhere. They landed in their thousands in the boab trees along the main street, screeching and flapping and this sounded like the pocket money El Dorado they'd been looking for. It was catching the birds that required some thought. They had to travel for miles and climb one large tree after another, searching for young ones just on the verge of flight. Young birds were the most valued as they were easier to teach to talk but they took too much effort to obtain. This time and effort far outweighed the return that could be expected from the odd fledgling they may have managed to capture.

At last an answer presented itself. They'd appeal to the birds' stomachs! After scattering grain each day to attract the cockatoos, both the white and black of the species, rumours of the feast to be had at the Lillys' place spread around the bird population and ever larger numbers turned up each successive day for the free feed. Having gained the birds' attention the boys soaked the last feed prior to the next ship's expected arrival in alcohol they'd managed to procure by stealth from the

(Lilly collection)

THE LOCALS ALL TURNED OUT WHENEVER A PLANE LANDED IN WYNDHAM AND THIS AIRCRAFT, THE SOUTHERN CROSS FLOWN BY KINGSFORD SMITH WAS OF GREAT INTEREST. THE LITTLE GIRL ON THE LEFT IS KATHLEEN COLE, IN FRONT OF HER, JIM WEABER AND WITH BACK TURNED GEORGE KINEVAN, THE DRIVER OF THE COUNCIL'S ROAD GRADER. IN HIS CONTEMPLATIVE STANCE HE APPEARS TO BE SIZING UP THE PULLING POWER OF THE PLANE'S THREE ENGINES AS OPPOSED TO HIS TEAM OF DONKEYS!

house. The system was a great success. With intoxicated birds lying all over the place they simply had to pick out the young ones whose feathers had not yet grown and present themselves and their birds at the jetty when the next ship came into port. A little more lateral thinking and the boys came up with the potential for a greater profit. They systematically plucked the mature feathers from older birds whilst they were still dead drunk. To the sailors they all looked like young birds.

The trade thrived and the boys did very well. There were others engaged in the bird catching trade and one man caught a great many crows. Crows are superb talkers, great mimics and very intelligent. Having plucked the poor creatures of all their mature feathers he sold them to the sailors as young birds with a great future and potential conversational talent. Unfortunately, after being so badly treated and then offered the same food upon which the cockatoos thrived, the crows all died. The seamen, angry at the loss of money and perceived confidence trick refused to buy any more birds after that even though the cockatoos had given no problems. The Lilly enterprise came to a sudden end. The young entrepreneurs would have to think up a new lurk.

In those pre-radio, pre-television days when even books were hard to acquire on any scale, people had time for other hobbies and teaching birds to talk was a popular pastime. One bird of surpassing talent was the pride of the owners of the Continental Hotel in Broome. Sam often told the story of the priest from the Beagle Bay Mission who had come to town and walking round the back of the pub spotted the bird in his cage. He walked up and down in front of the bird's cage, endlessly repeating to the bird "Hello cocky! Hello cocky!" The bird sat on its perch in stony silence and ignored the priest. Finally, though, it had had as much as it could stand of this ridiculous creature talking at it and it replied, "Take a one way trip to Darwin, ya bastard!"

As they grew older the Lilly boys worked on properties around the area taking any jobs that were offering. Sam worked for a while on Ellendale Station. He could do anything required of him with perfect competence but he already knew that working with livestock would never be his first choice. He had an inventive mind and a passion for innovation. His opinion of life on Ellendale was not improved by the constant diet of mutton. Three times a day, seven days a week they were served mutton. Sam could never look a lamb chop in the eye again, no matter how it was served.

Sam had a great friend, Albert Ah Chee, who was as interested as Sam in things mechanical. All their spare moments were devoted to putting bits of machinery together. One day an old chap whose new car had, much to his disgust, broken down miles from town, told them "If you can get the bloody thing to start you can have it!" They walked for miles and miles and finally found it and got it going. They owned a motor car between them, a rarity for anyone in those days let alone two lads in their teens. In small towns there was no chance of the boys being apprenticed and becoming licensed motor mechanics. They learnt by trial and error aided by their remarkable flair and inventiveness in things mechanical. Albert, whose father was Chinese and whose mother was half Aboriginal, later Anglicised his name to Archer. Eventually he had his own garage in Derby and Sam probably would have liked to do something similar but his path led elsewhere. Nevertheless he used his mechanical expertise to great effect in other fields all through his life.

Both Toby and Sam found long term employment in Derby; Toby working for Adcock's General Store, and Sam at the Post Office where he remained for four years. The Post Office was a further boost to Sam's education and during that time he became a proficient Morse key operator. He and another operator were on duty at the Morse key on the night shift at the time the *Southern Cross*, Kingsford Smith's plane, went missing. It had been heading for Wyndham and in no time numerous aircraft were searching the area indicated in the plane's last radio signal. *Southern Cross* had come down in swampy ground some thirty kilometres from the main search area and a glimpse of the plane continued to elude searchers. It only carried food for the flight—sandwiches and a flask of coffee. Kingsford Smith had no emergency rations nor a rifle. Their radio would not transmit but now and then they received messages informing them that a search was well under way. Each day they expected to be discovered but it was to be twelve long days before relief came. The men were starving. Sam suspected that the whole thing had been staged as a publicity stunt and others at the time agreed. Although a court later found that it had not been a stunt at all, a degree of suspicion remained and Kingsford Smith and Charles Ulm were viewed with some disfavour in the public eye thereafter.

The incident cost the lives of two of Kingsford Smith's friends, who, on hearing of his disappearance hastily joined in the search. Keith Anderson and Bobby Hitchcock had taken off in Anderson's newly acquired Westland Widgeon, the *Kookaburra*. The tiny plane had a few mechanical problems but Anderson felt he could attend to these as they travelled, by landing every so many hours and making adjustments. At Alice Springs they took on fuel. Anderson, confident in his skill, ignored the suggestion that he leave behind some of the fuel and take spare water. They flew north following the Overland Telegraph Line, using the shadows cast by the poles as a guide. They landed near Wave Hill Station in the Northern Territory and made their mechanical adjustments. However they staked both tyres in their attempt to take off. Laboriously they managed to fit the spare tyre although they carried no tools for the task. The spare met with the same fate and with no puncture kit they were helpless. They had not a drop of water and both perished near the plane.

For a time after leaving the Post Office job Sam went to work for his brother in law George Lovell, carting to Freeneys oil boring plant, but neither Sam's nor Toby's time was fully absorbed by their regular jobs. So when the Council called for tenders for the operation of the sanitary service,

Toby and Sam put in their bid and won the contract. In those pre-sewerage days, people in towns were served by the sanitary cart which delivered an empty can to each household and disposed of the used one on a regular weekly basis. It was a job nobody wanted but someone had to do it. In a town of maybe sixty or eighty establishments, it required perhaps half a day a week and easily fitted in to the boys' regular work schedule. They bought a truck in partnership and began what was a relatively lucrative contract. Neither of the Lillys was burdened with false pride and both were blessed with great senses of humour; they took all the jibes in good part and wrung as many laughs from their new job as those who taunted them.

They became the dunny men of Derby with their dunny cart. Hundreds of funny stories, poems and riddles have been made up over the years about their line of work. Even books on the matter have been best sellers. One such riddle goes: "If a dunny cart had a bell on it what sound would the bell make?" Delivered in musical tones the answer is supposed to be "Dung!"

The work involved collecting a batch of clean tar treated cans from the council's sanitary section, then visiting every house and establishment in the town. The man jog trotted down to the outside dunny, usually located as far as possible from the house near the back fence. Here he opened a small door at the rear of the little building, dragged one can out, slammed the lid on it and replaced it with a fresh can. Making sure the lid was properly secured he would deftly sling it up on his shoulder and trot to the cart, dump it on the truck, collect another empty for delivery as the driver moved the truck along to the next house. People referred to the "out house" by such coy terms as the privy, little house, WC (which it was not as it had no water to justify the initials of water closet), and dub (short for WC). But by the general Australian public, always happy to shorten a name, the small and essential edifice was commonly and affectionately referred to as the dunny.

At Christmas time householders made it a practice to leave a present of some sort just prior to the last collection before the festive season. It could take any form including money or a few bottles of beer. One family had been given a live turkey for Christmas—a most generous gift in those hard times. With no place to keep the huge bird until it was time to kill and pluck it, the family locked it in the dunny. The dunny man must have been overwhelmed by the householder's apparent generosity. After the collection, when the man of the house with his sharpened axe went to get the turkey, it had vanished. They'd lost their Christmas dinner but in exchange they had a nice fresh pan.

The boys both did well, saving their earnings so each could follow his own star. For Toby, it was marriage and for Sam, a working trip around Australia.

Before Sam left, he presented his older brother with what must surely go down in the records as one of the most unique wedding presents a bride and groom have ever received. Sam set Toby up in business by giving him his own half share of the dunny cart.

CHAPTER V

Maggie and Sam

IN A SMALL SETTLEMENT such as Wyndham there was little of the district's activity that escaped the community's notice. Word that Goose Hill was untenanted soon reached Hannah's ears. Wyndham Meatworks owned the station and required a caretaker. Hannah applied and was readily accepted. Ron, Violet and Jackie gathered together all the four legged livestock, goats, horses and Teeny the dwarf mule and drove them across past Parrys Lagoon to their new home. Maggie and Hannah had a messy time catching the poultry, shoving them into sacks with holes cut in the hessian through which they'd pull a bird's head. Then the end would be tied so they couldn't escape and another bag full of squawking birds was slung onto the table top of the Chev 4. With relatively few household possessions it took only a few trips for the family to set up residence in the dirt floored house at Goose Hill.

Before the meatworks opened, Goose Hill had been the location for a stock inspector's residence and a dipping point for cattle bought by Connor, Doherty and Durack from the stations and destined for shipping to the Islands. From there the mobs walked the eight or nine miles to the Three Mile well and the huge trough where they took their last drink before going up and over the final steep hill down to the yards in front of the Police Station. From there a long race took them past the Wyndham Hotel and onto Anthon's landing jetty to board the waiting ship. Since the erection of the meatworks the order had changed and the historical Anthon's Landing was no longer the centre of activity. On the north side a series of holding paddocks, yards, drafting and forcing pens led to a long overhead race which syphoned the cattle straight onto the killing floor of the meatworks which produced huge quantities of chilled beef for export.

The meatworks which had enormous food requirements during the killing season had tried to establish a vegetable garden at Goose Hill but lack of a good watering system rendered the enterprise impractical. However, Goose Hill still carried stock and required maintenance to be carried out by a resident caretaker.

The newly ensconced family was required to maintain the fencing, oversee any stock and attend to repairs in exchange for their tenancy, but they still had to the find money on which to live. Fortunately long experience had developed their practical survival skills and they embarked on various pursuits to provide the necessary liquidity. Apart from Maggie's regular bird catching activities, eagle hawks presented another potential income. With their wing span of over two metres, these magnificent birds whose kingdom was the high bright sky over the Kimberley, soared and swooped with careless grace on the thermals whilst using their extraordinarily acute vision to watch for prey on the ground far beneath them. Then they would plummet earthward, grasp the prey in strong talons and be off in seconds. Unfortunately goat kids were high on the gastronomic preferences of these airborne raiders and for the many people who relied heavily on their goat herds for survival, the birds, always present in large numbers, were a constant menace. Consequently they attracted a generous bounty of two shillings and sixpence a head, literally "manna from Heaven"! Maggie recalls the scene: "Violet, Jackie and I would go out with the dogs and we'd get a few kangaroos. We'd drag the carcasses off to different spots and I'd poison them with red strychnine. Then we'd go round later and gather up the birds, cut their heads off and take them in to collect the money."

"There weren't many dingoes but they brought two pounds for each scalp, and that was a lot of money then. There was a bloke used to get them in the Northern Territory where they didn't have a bounty on them and he'd bring them into Western Australia and get someone to take them in for him to the police station in Wyndham. I did it once for him but I could have got into trouble. The old Sergeant knew what was going on and tried to get me to say. I didn't say, but never did it again. This man used to pinch horses along the way and one day he came out to Goose Hill and tried to give Violet a piebald mare. I said 'don't take that mare'. She would be very easily recognised. Anyway, he got caught just after that because of it." It is a mystery why someone with such entrepreneurial cunning would risk taking a pied animal in the first place as their distinctive markings immediately draw attention. Good stockmen of those days had prodigious memories for detail and could, from certain subtle characteristics often identify a horse's station of origin no matter how anonymous the colouring and before even looking at the brand which was the official language of ownership and origin. There was nothing esoteric about their skills. Their lives were dependent on horses so horses were an eternally popular subject for discussion. What stations were using what sires, what the progeny was like, the temperament, the country in which the animal was bred all added to a vast store of specialised knowledge essential in their particular livelihood. Many could neither read nor write but their consummate stockmanship was beyond question.

Maggie had grown up knowing all of the stockmen who came and went to Wyndham and was given many horses over the years by these men who admired the plucky youngster. She shared their love and enthusiasm for a good horse and especially a fast one. Many were good but one stood out from all the rest, her beloved Meeka, given her by Mr Weaber about 1929. He showed a consistent and remarkable turn of speed. He won her many races but mostly with male riders. She could only ride in the ladies' races. The restriction irked her constantly but another half century would have to pass before women jockeys were an accepted part of the racing scene. There was plenty of space out around Goose Hill to work her horses up for the race meetings and she and Violet tackled it with enthusiasm.

It was at this time that Hannah's brother Jack took a practical and benevolent interest in the Nicholson household. Strangely, Maggie had never met her Uncle Jack Beasley. For years he remained in Pine Creek training horses, then managed Alexandria Station on the Queensland border. Later, he had established for himself a sound reputation as a drover in the Northern Territory and was never short of contracts. He had always kept in touch with Hannah and Maggie and although he may have been thousands of kilometres away, relatively speaking he was "around". He always gave Hannah an idea of his movements and where to send a letter; if it missed him the station would send it on. It would find him sooner or later. From time to time, Hannah gave him an account of the happenings in the Nicholson household and when Jack heard that they'd moved yet again he decided it was high time his sister had a proper home.

He'd never married and had been a prudent man with his money. He had watched so many of his droving mates succumb to the traps of the track. After months away from alcohol and female company these lusty, lonely men made up for lost time. Some handed their wages cheque to the barman and told him to keep the grog coming until the money ran out. In seeking the company of the few available obliging women, black or white, they risked contracting the sexually transmitted "pox"—gonorrhoea—rife and incurable at that time. The outcome was an existence accompanied by pain, shortened life expectancy and if the disease attacked the brain, insanity and death. Jack Beasley, son of the canny, enterprising Sarah had no intention of ending up a penniless diseased wreck. He had other priorities, among which was assuring the wellbeing of his only sister. Hannah accepted his generous offer to buy her a home and the family acquired a dwelling with sheds and stables at the Three Mile.

Once again, the little Chev worked overtime, running back and forth moving house and the small domestic animals and birds. At the Three Mile and this time thanks to Jack Beasley, Hannah and Maggie had a home which was theirs for as long as they wanted it and with no conditions attached.

By then a pumping station had been built on the King River to supply waterless Wyndham. "There was a big deep hole they pumped from about twenty two miles from town and the pipe came across the marsh not far from the Five Mile. There was a standpipe there and we'd go down in the evening with the Chev. and fill up all the tins and buckets we could load on the back. We used that for ourselves." This was a treat after all the years of having to drink, cook, bathe and wash in water from indifferent to bad bores. When the water table lowered some became so bad that it was impossible to drink the water. "If you did drink it, it would make you sick."

At the Nicholson's new residence were sheds and rooms that were set up as a butchering business. Outside at the back was an area with a hoist to winch up a carcass for skinning and gutting, and rooms with benches for butchering. The family made use of the facilities and offered a service supplying householders with fresh meat delivered to their door. In the killing season from April to September they simply bought a body from the meatworks to fill the customers' beef orders. That was relatively straightforward but the during the wet it was far more difficult. They had to acquire suitable cattle themselves and that meant riding many miles to various stations, hoping the creeks and roads were negotiable, collecting the cattle and tailing them back to the Three Mile. "Then we had to tail them all day while they fed and yard them at night." Each week they would select the beast in the best condition then slaughter and quarter it. Between them they could heave the quarters onto the Chev and take them in to chill at the meatworks. Ron would collect the orders on the drive in and deliver them on the return trip. Maggie had hired from a small coolroom the meatworks with facilities to break down the carcasses and pack the orders.

"It was hard work, milking cows and goats, feeding pigs and tailing cattle we bought from various stations and there were times when they were very hard to buy." Tailing means driving the cattle on horseback. "We killed our own pigs and goats." Their carcasses also had to be run in to the meatworks as soon as possible and stored in the coolroom. "Meat only lasted a day once it came out so it had to be cooked quickly." Household refrigerators, kerosene or electric, had not yet become part of life in Wyndham and the old Coolgardie safe still offered the best there was. Maggie recalls the travelling involved in the enterprise, "In those days we had to travel every inch around every bend from the town around the One Mile Gully. The railway went straight to the works but we weren't allowed to drive on that so it was two or three miles further around for us. We went around every bend to the Works at around five miles per hour with potholes to a foot deep. In the wet season it was far worse. It was a lot of work for the bit of money we made."

Maggie divided her time between the newly acquired butcher shop, training her beloved horse, Meeka and the other lucrative but seasonal occupation of bird catching. Had she never caught a single bird the visits to the distant valleys were great treats in her hard working young life. However, each year they yielded to her quantities of their exquisite inhabitants which she housed, revelling in their beauty until it was time to sell them to George Reddell.

Once the meatworks opened for the new season and the employees poured back into Wyndham, social life under the aegis of the "Works" began. "I always had a nice dress to wear to the dances and whatever I needed but I never had any money. Mum always looked after that. When we wanted something we sent away to T.C. Burnie's in Brisbane or Boans in Perth." The firms sent out an annual illustrated catalogue that kept the recipients abreast of the latest fashions. The collection of tantalising glimpses of what people in the outside world were wearing was read from cover to cover time and again and once the exciting decisions were made an order was sent stating the article, the second choice, the size and colour. Sometimes catalogues even had tiny colour swatches of fabric glued near the dress illustrations and that made it all the more exciting, seeing the actual colour and feeling the texture.

Mail order took weeks. By the time the order travelled by sea to the far distant emporium in Perth or across Australia to the east coast capital of Queensland and the articles were packed and despatched to the farthest corner of the country the recipients had undergone a long period of anticipation. No alternative means of fashion shopping was available so they were accustomed the long wait and all the while the process carried with it an element of uncertainty. "Would the dress

EIGHTEEN YEAR OLD MAGGIE WITH HER BELOVED HORSE MEEKA AT WYNDHAM, 1930. ALTHOUGH MAGGIE TRAINED MEEKA SHE WAS ONLY PERMITTED TO RIDE IN "LADIES." ALTHOUGH FACILITIES WERE FEW AT BUSH RACE MEEETINGS EVERYONE DRESSED UP AND FOR THE WOMEN IT WAS A SPECIAL OCCASION TO WEAR THE LATEST FASHIONS.

WYNDHAM CUP RACE MEETING AND PATRONS IN 1930.

be as nice as it looked in the catalogue? Would they like the colour they'd chosen? Would it fit well and look nice on?" Mail order houses took the return of unsatisfactory goods as part of the transaction but no one really wanted to return the goods; it would take too long to get the replacement. The ordering of shoes involved supplying the size required and for safety, including a drawing of the feet. The foot was placed on a sheet of paper and carefully drawn around with a pencil. The stores took great trouble with the mail orders. They had a large and widespread clientele right across the country to places all over inland Australia. These bush bound people represented a substantial and valued portion of their business. The range they stocked went from the cheapest cotton dresses to beaded ball gowns. For the good seamstress, the catalogues provided endless inspiration and she could turn her family out in style at very little cost.

"I was always being given horses but a Mister Weaber gave me one I called Meeka. He was bred on Moola Bulla and he could go!" Very quickly Maggie realised that Meeka was in a class of his own and time and again he was to prove himself a champion.

Meeka had by now proved himself by winning many races for Maggie. The race clubs would occasionally include in their programme a ladies race or a ladies bracelet and she and Violet decided they'd try their luck at The Depot Races in 1933. This was a formidable challenge. First they had to ride the three hundred odd kilometres from Wyndham to The Depot, known these days as Timber Creek, which is on the upper tidal reaches of the Victoria River in the Northern Territory. They had to carry all their gear, feed, their own food and swags. They set out from Wyndham early in November to be there in comfortable time for the three day fixture on 15th to the 18th of the month and rode across country through the stations to their destination in the Northern Territory.

A young man Ned Delower known to his friends as "The Ghan" offered to accompany them. "He got this name because he had a bit of Afghan blood in him. He was a very nice young man and we were glad of his company." This route was no polite, gentle bridle track. Maggie recalls the trip, "We stayed at Station Homesteads where we could. One afternoon we got to Revolver Springs.

A HAPPY LAUGHING GROUP OF YOUNG WOMEN TAKING ADVANTAGE OF THE SHADE IN A BOUGH SHELTER AT THE DEPOT RACES IN 1932. ON THE GROUND FROM LEFT TO RIGHT ARE BETTY MALONEY, FLO MARTIN, (WHO PUBLISHED HER OWN BOOK *THREE FAMILIES OUTBACK* IN 1980), MAGGIE LILLY, VIOLET MCCALLUM AND, RIGHT OF TREE, MARY DURAK WHO LATER WROTE *KINGS IN THE CASTLES* — A RECORD OF HER FAMILY AND THEIR EPIC PIONEERING ENDEAVOURS.

There were dead bulls all around it and the whole surface of the water was covered in maggots. It took ages to clean it up before we could give the horses a drink. They clogged everything." The country is wild, mountainous, rocky and with creeks and rivers to cross; their final destination would offer them no cool comforting dip in the river to wash away the dust of travel. At The Depot the river was well populated with salt-water crocodiles sunning themselves on the banks or lurking in the shallows waiting for the next meal. "Ned just came along for the ride and to see the races but he was a great help to us girls. He managed stations later on up around Halls Creek."

Maggie, Violet, Ned and their horses arrived at the racecourse dusty, happy and unaffected by the baking humid heat of summer. Their friend Flo Martin who had come in from Victoria River Downs, referred to as "The Big Run", and managed at the time by her father, was already there with a warm welcome for the Wyndham girls. Flo wanted to know all about their epic ride and was glad they'd made the trip the rough trip without mishap. Their horses had been well shod before they left Wyndham so there were no loose or cast shoes, lameness or other damage to mar their arrival. The big paddock by the Victoria River was a scene of great activity. People who had travelled enormous distances were busy setting up their camps. Their trucks, wagons, pack mules and horses were loaded with whatever was needed for the stay and once "they'd set up house" it was time to visit other camps and enjoy this rare opportunity for company. The station women who may not have seen another white woman for months on end revelled in the chance to spend a few days with friends from far and wide. It was the high point of their year. It also was the onset of the wet and soon swollen rivers and impassable tracks would govern movement. It was time to distil every

(Lilly collection)

THE DEPOT RACES, 1933. CONTENDERS FOR THE LADIES BRACELET, L TO R: VIOLET MCCALLUM, MAGGIE'S NIECE, MAGGIE AND FRIEND FLO MARTIN. MAGGIE WON THE RACE ON HER BELOVED MEEKA AND LATER HER OTHER HORSE, GOLDEN GLORY WON THE VICTORIA RIVER TROPHY.

THE DEPOT RACES, 1933. THIS NEWSPAPER CUTTING IS AMONG MAGGIE'S MOST TREASURED MEMORABILIA. IT IS A JOURNALIST'S ACCOUNT OF THE VICTORIA RIVER JOCKEY CLUB MEETING AT THE DEPOT WHEN MAGGIE RODE MEEKA TO VICTORY IN THE LADIES BRACELET.

THE DEPOT RACES.

A Territory Meeting.

(By M.G.D.)

"Now the squatters and the cockies,
Drovers, trainers and their jockies,
Have gathered them together for a meeting on the flat."

"Victoria River Jockey Club, Annual Meeting, November 15 - 18," read the bright tangerine notices posted from Derby to Cloncurry, Darwin to Wyndham and Alice Springs. Not the most enviable of holiday places, the Victoria River Racecourse in tropical November. Spread on a red soil flat, dotted with ant hills and patches of withered grass, the hot winds sweep it from the desert, eddy and whirl on its sun-baked surface in dusty spirals laden with dead leaves, fallen bark and debris from the blacks' camps on the plain. But beyond the dusty flat, bending with blue-green languor through wild, purple ranges to the Timor Sea, is the mighty Victoria, home of alligators that laze in her mangrove mud. Boabs of majestic height and gigantic girth, fitting sentinels to the tropic grandeur of a great northern river, had burst into their November foliage and white blossoms that sent hints of perfume on warm gusts of wind.

Racing enthusiasts with pack mules and horses, trucks and motor cars gathered for the meeting with bushmen from far and near. There were drovers, station hands and camp cooks, dog trappers, eagle hawkers and wanderers of the endless, lonely tracks, shy stockmen from isolated holdings on the rim of the blacks' reserve, prospectors from Tanami and Tennant's Creek. Many, reticent and tongue-tied, came into contact with their fellow men scarcely more than once a year; others had stories to tell of comedy, tragedy and adventure out there among the wild cattle and the limestone gorges.

More in tone with their surroundings than the white community, the little groups of natives spread in the ample shade of the leafy nut woods, powerful half civilised primitives of the ranges; well clothed, politely spoken station hands "on holiday" with their lubras and fat brown piccaninnies, barracking for the horses of their home stations with the loyalty of school boys at their annual sports.

Race week is the time for stories, and 1933 a year of incident out there where the black man is feeling his power. Sun-tanned adventurers from the crew of the Maroubra told of deadly spears hurtling from the dense, jungle foliage of Arnhem Land.

"Spinifex Joe," just in from "no man's land," his pack saddles laden with dingo scalps, told of how his mate, Jim Nicholls, had left him, last "wet," for the bloodwood ridges where dogs were said to abound, how Jim was later found with a spear through his heart, his packs plundered and his rifle adorning a blackman's belt.

Charlie Patterson, who took a mob of cattle 1,800 miles, from Mistake Creek on the western border into Queensland, in the days of his youth, was there, too, with many a story of early droving treks, other race meetings, old mates dead and gone or just "missing" somewhere in the wilderness. Jim Maloney from Tennant's Creek, sanguine of its prospects, told of arid, dusty tracks and long waterless stages where many a lonely bag man has lain down his swag for a last long camp.

A mounted trooper from Timber Creek (two miles from the depot), in from a "nigger hunt" in the Moyle River country, told of a feverish chase from deserted camp to camp in search of the native murderers Tiger, Waddawurri and their band; of two native guides leading the police astray into a waterless region and fighting a tracker for his gun; of coming upon 70 head of stolen horses hidden in a gorge and of the half caste thief leaping to his horse for a wild ride to the Queensland border.

This year the depot races boasted 18 women against the half dozen or less of previous meetings. They were bush women for the most part, wives of the outback who had shared the isolation with their husbands and often long droving treks, cooking for the camp in impromptu kitchens on the hot, open plains. Admiring glances rested on Maggie and Violet, two girls scarcely out of their teens, who had ridden from Wyndham with packs and racers of their own. Someone had been rash enough to scorn the prowess of Golden Glory and Meeka, which the spirited Maggie had trained herself, and she had vowed she would ride 210 miles to the depot races to prove their worth.

The races were much the same as at any bush meeting—Flying Handicap, Stockman's Purse, Cup and Lady's Bracelet. The black boys' race, after many scratchings, dwindled down to two competitors, a dapper half-caste from Victoria River Downs, on a sleek bay mare, and Paddy of Newry, hatless and wild of hair, riding the black colt Friday. "Who's going to win the race?" Paddy was asked. "Me!" was the prompt reply, then, as a cautious afterthought, "S'posin' I no win, 'nother fella beat me." No fear of pulling in the black boys' race! Each is out for victory, spurs and whip in full play for the sheer joy of galloping and displaying the skill bred in them from years of wild riding over the plains on the heels of outlaw cattle. The half-caste wins! Some whisper that the bay was corn fed, against the rules of the race. There will be some little discussion on this score. Never was bush meeting complete without

Then the ladies' race! Maggie on her beloved Meeka, slim and brown and so much at home in her racing saddle, Violet on Speela, and Flo, of Victoria, most versatile of bush girls, who can fly an aeroplane and ride with any horseman in the country. The bushmen follow them with anxious eyes. Many have known the girls since their babyhood and watch with nervous excitement as they turn into the straight, with Speela in the lead. Past the judge's box Maggie spurs her mount to victory! Golden Glory won his laurels in the Victoria River Trophy, with the enterprising bush girl who had scorned the discomforts of the dusty track in bringing her horses to meet tried favourites of the Territory.

There was little sleep for the revellers during race week. The depot boasts a "dance hall" now, grass walls, bough roof and mud floor, erected by the jovial-hearted hostess of the guest house. Laughingly she tells of how she delved for mud in the mangroves by the river, trying to forget meanwhile the possibilities of lurking crocodiles. Her work, too, were the ant bed tennis court and the comfortable grass houses for the accommodation of the guests.

November in the Territory is not conducive to dancing, but dancing there was, to the strains of concertina, piano, and gramophone, the ladies in colourful evening dresses such as the depot had never seen before. Between dances, items were rendered by bushmen, gradually forgetting their shyness, songs that had kept the cattle quiet on the plains during the still night watches. Latent talents were discovered. Who knew that Laurie, the mustering cook, had "The Sentimental Bloke" by heart, and could reel off gems from Lawson, beloved of the stockman's heart?

By midnight, the dancing degenerated into a romp. Dingo howlings, weird and unearthly from the darkness, were dispelled before a bombardment of crackers, face powder fights ended by an irresponsible young stockman let loose with a tin of treacle. Weary merrymakers stole off at last with their swags, into the bush, to slumber undisturbed.

Only once a year, at the breaking of the wet, does such a gathering occur, an opportunity of meeting old friends and new, settling old scores and creating new ones. In the coming months when swampy plains and rushing rivers bring isolation to the scattered Northern settlements, there will be one bright week to look back upon, another such to plan for when November comes again and the depot is once more the Mecca of the North.

The races are over! Dingo scalpers, eagle hawkers, prospectors, are off to the wilds again, and the constable from Timber Creek back to the Moyle country of luscious ferns and running streams, and lurking danger. North, south, east and west, cars and trucks and packhorses are racing the threatening storm clouds of a dusty, northern sky.

ounce of fun and conversation to fuel their thoughts through the coming months when they were once more detached from the world and held prisoners in sodden isolated pockets of wilderness.

The Depot Race Meeting may only have been held in a paddock with a few bough shelters in a location hundreds of miles from anywhere and unknown to most of Australia but it was the great annual event for people within a several hundred kilometre radius. The attendance of women had swelled from six the previous year to eighteen in 1933 and they dressed with as much care and pleasure as did their city counterparts attending the Melbourne Cup.

The girls had a day or so to spell the horses before the big event and they made the most of every minute. Race day dawned bright and warm and excitement was in the air. Owners, jockeys and trainers bustled around, saddling up and giving instructions as entrants in each race lined up. There were several races on the card that day including the Ladies Race and The Depot Cup. Everyone was fascinated by the girl riders, these feminine creatures who had already ridden over three hundred kilometres and camped under the stars nearly every night. Once mounted on the excited horses they sat with ease and grace on the prancing animals as they lined up for the start. At a word and a wave from the official starter, they leapt forward and surged along the track, the girls each urging their mounts to greater effort. The overwhelming exhilaration of riding a race can only be fully comprehended by those who have participated and the three girls, Maggie Nicholson, Violet McCallum and Flo Martin moving at a thundering pace in a cloud of dust had no thoughts other than of being first past the post. Violet on Speela led for much of the distance but Meeka and Maggie were invincible. They won the Ladies Race and then Maggie rounded off the day's excitement when her other horse, Golden Glory won the Victoria River Trophy. It was a day to remember and the crowd loved her. She was carried shoulder high through the cheering racegoers for the presentation of her trophy. The dancing which always followed the day's racing went on well into the small hours but by midnight, to quote from a newspaper article by M.G.D., "the dancing had degenerated to a romp. Dingo howlings, weird and unearthly from the darkness, were dispelled before a bombardment of crackers, face powder fights and ended by an irresponsible young stockman let loose with a tin of treacle."

The Northern Standard reported the event of 29 December, 1933:

> *This meeting was a great success financially and socially. The Victoria River Jockey Club showed a profit of about 67 pounds on the race meeting although I am sorry to say the scratching pencil was used pretty freely. There was an attendance of from 80 to 100 people and the surrounding districts were represented. The Race Ball was held at the Victoria River Depot Store. Every night, Mrs James (the store's proprietress) kept the visitors dancing, singing and all sorts of games were played and the young lads gave what they called a Dingo Chorus which was the best imitation of a dingo pack howling ever heard here. It was really good and clever.*

The article offers a glimpse of life in one of the remotest corners of Australia at the time of the 1933 Race Meeting. Nothing remains of the James' Store or any of the other buildings by the river landing. They were all demolished many years ago and only a few stumps remain to indicate their location. Yet in reading the description of the celebrations, the girls in their elegant dresses, the lively young people who attended the event and rode in the races, the scene lives again in the mind's eye. For Maggie, the recollection of the sound of the music and laughter brings an aching nostalgia for the friends, many now long dead, and fun they shared so long ago. She still has a newspaper cutting about the fashion highlights—

> *The dresses worn at the Race Ball held at the Victoria River Depot were as follows: Mrs Shadforth—black Chantilly lace, Mrs Barnes, dainty floral georgette, Mrs James, old rose crepe de chine set off with amber beads; Mrs Fuller, pink lace with necklace and ear rings of jade; Mrs Walsh; white lace and georgette; Mrs C. George, old world frock of cream satin; Miss Maggie Nicholson, pale pink crepe de chine with diamond buckle; Miss McCallum, white satin with crystal beads; Miss Mackenzie, dark blue georgette; Miss Facey, white lace; Miss Martin, Floral marocain with pink tonings; Miss Lavinia James wore green satin with a shoulder spray of pink roses; Miss Maloney, striped silk with Peter Pan collar; Miss Durack, silk floral voile.* (Cutting from Lilly Collection)

Maggie discovered that Uncle Jack was at Victoria River Downs at the time and so after the races the girls arranged to paddock their horses at The Depot and get a ride to the station with old Jim

(Lilly collection)

A RARE HISTORIC PHOTOGRAPH OF THE DEPOT — LATER RENAMED TIMBER CREEK — TAKEN BY MAGGIE WHEN SHE AND VIOLET RODE FROM WYNDHAM TO THE DEPOT RACE MEETING IN 1933. AT THAT TIME IT WAS A BUSY RIVER PORT FROM WHICH SUPPLIES WERE DESPATCHED HUNDREDS OF MILES BY TRACK TO INLAND STATIONS LIKE VICTORIA RIVER DOWNS. THE VICTORIA RIVER WAS EXPLORED IN 1839 BY JOHN WICKHAM AND JOHN STOKES. BY 1880 VICTORIA RIVER DOWNS AND WAVE HILL WERE ESTABLISHED AS CATTLE LEASES AND CLOSE UPON THEIR TRACKS OTHER FAMOUS PIONEERS LIKE JOSEPH BRADSHAW AND THE DURACKS SECURED LEASES. THE PASTORALISTS NEEDED SUPPLIES AND FOR MAY YEARS THE DEPOT BECAME A HIVE OF ACTIVITY IN THE DRY SEASON. IN WORLD WAR II IT BECAME HEADQUARTERS OF THE NORTH AUSTRALIA OBSERVER UNIT.

Maloney in his truck. It was a momentous meeting for Maggie and her Uncle, a man who had always been an important part of her life through Hannah but until that moment a total stranger. Flo Martin had rejoined her mother and father and the girls enjoyed a few day's fun and hospitality at the famous station before heading for home. When they spoke of their departure to Uncle Jack he was most concerned. He could not bear to think of the girls riding alone through the hundreds of kilometres of wild country to Wyndham without a male escort. Their friend, Ned "The Ghan" had not accompanied them to Victoria River Downs and had begun to ride back to Wyndham as soon as The Depot Races were over. The wet weather was on its way too so he arranged to ride back with them. He left his droving plant consisting of his horses, packs, wagon and sundry items at Victoria River Downs. Maggie and Violet went back to The Depot and waited for Uncle Jack to follow a few days later. It was a long slow trip and a sad one for Uncle Jack. "We picked up our horses from The Depot and one day we had dinner at Desmond's Passage on Newry Station. Uncle Jack's red dog, Rowdy, picked up bait and died. The Ord was up so we had to spend a few days at the Four Mile tailing the horses of a day. Uncle Jack wouldn't hobble them of a daytime as there was so little feed, so I had to spend every day tailing the damned horses! We went on then to Carlton Station where the Manager Percy Pretlove and his brother Charley boated us over Heart's Crossing and we swam the horses."

It had all been a wonderful adventure but now it was back to everyday life and the butcher shop. Hannah, Ron and Jackie had managed on their own in the girls' absence but with the wet setting in it wouldn't be long before the reserves of chilled carcasses at the meatworks ran out and they'd be obliged to find their own beasts for slaughter. They had to find stations as close to town as possible because of the rising watercourses and places that had kept stock close to hand. Most properties covered over a thousand square miles and the stock roamed far beyond reach. Their only hope was to find someone with a mob of station killers excess to their needs. That narrowed their chances of success right down and so one way or another, supplying a beast or two each week and getting it into town was no small job.

Uncle Jack Beasley did not return to Victoria River Downs. He'd wearied of droving for a while and went out to Rosewood Station boundary riding. Now and then he provided some very welcome assistance in the butchering business by picking up a few head here and there to tide them over. Maggie may not have met her Uncle Jack until she was twenty one but he was worth waiting for. He was generous and very caring and helped in practical ways when he was able.

Christmas and the wet season came and went and a young man from Derby named Sam Liljenqvist arrived in Wyndham. He had arranged to work with a friend named Jack Shore also from Derby at Carlton and Ning Bing Station north east of Wyndham. Jack was a bore sinker who travelled with his boring plant wherever his services were required. Sam's reputation as a handy bloke to have around anything mechanical meant Jack was sure of a good offsider.

Sam and a friend name Jimmie who was an inspector of aircraft runways were staying at the Wyndham Hotel. When they arrived at the entrance of the dance hall Sam caught sight of a small dark haired girl standing with another pretty young woman in a dimly lit part of the foyer. Her dress was dark red, which enhanced her ivory complexion, wavy black hair and very dark eyes.

"Hey!" asked Sam, his attention focussed on the slight girl, "Who's that yella piece over there in the red dress?"

Had they been attending a papal blessing and Sam asked "Hey who's that old bloke over there in the white dress waving his arms about?" the response could hardly have been more embarrassed or incredulous. "She's no yella piece! Don't you *know* who that is? That's Maggie Nicholson!"

The term "yellow" referred to people of mixed blood, one half of the union always being Aboriginal. It was perfectly well understood and used by all. The other half could be white, Chinese, Malay, Japanese or any other race although the result of an Aboriginal Afghan union was specifically termed Black Afghan.

Unbeknownst to Sam and Jim the "yella piece" and her niece had spotted the two young men peering into the room. "The Wyndham hotel had a beautiful room for dances and Violet and I were standing there when we saw these two young men in their tropical whites staring into the room and we both said ooooh! They're nice!" They did not meet on that occasion but it wasn't long before their first encounter.

When work with the boring plant was finished Sam felt inclined to invest a little more of his time in getting to know Wyndham. He decided he would stay just a little longer if another job presented itself in the coming days. It did and it was something he knew all about already. Wyndham Shire Council needed a contractor to run the sanitary service. Sam rarely worked for wages. He preferred to contract. He could accomplish the requirements of the contract according to his own dictates; he could work harder and faster, complete the job and get on with whatever else he had in hand. The new contract was not a position for which people would queue, no matter how desperately they wanted a job. However, it was an essential service that the Council simply had to supply and Sam could afford to calculate his tender on a higher scale. It was accepted on the spot by a relieved Council and once again Sam became the Dunny Man. Wyndham was very small and the run took only a portion of one day a week. The system in Wyndham at the time was to empty the cans from a small jetty straight into the Cambridge Gulf. As the Cambridge Gulf was deep, tidal and therefore salty, and well populated with crocodiles, the addition of the weekly collection of nightsoil was not regarded as a health hazard to the town dwellers. The only people at risk were those who liked to drink salt water or swim with crocs, although Maggie recalls a character named Tommy who was being chased by the police did take the risk. He climbed over Gee Hong Yets' fence

(Lilly collection)

NEWLY WEDS, MR AND MRS SAM LILLY. THE BRIDAL GROUP POSES IN FRONT OF THE MISSION HALL. THE NEW MRS LILLY AND HER MATRON OF HONOUR ALMA HUDDLESTONE LOOK FRESH AND GLAMOROUS IN THEIR FINERY. HOWEVER IN THE SEPTEMBER SUN THE GROOM AND HIS BEST MAN WERE NO DOUBT SWELTERING. SUITS WERE MADE OF HEAVY WOOL SERGE OR WORSTED AND TO MEN WHO SPENT LIFE IN COTTON SHIRTS, SUCH FORMALITY WAS INDEED A LABOUR OF LOVE.

and jumped into the Gulf. When he surfaced in the green murky water he cheekily invited his pursuers standing frustrated and ineffectual on the jetty to "Come in and get me!" It was a foolhardy gesture of defiance as there was always a swarm of crocodiles competing for space at the outlet of the meatworks' blood drain just yards away. It was a lucky day for Tom because the crocodiles had already dined well. They ignored the splashing figure which at another time would have brought a frenzied rush from the banks and shallows.

Sam completed the council contract swiftly and efficiently each week and spent the rest of the time playing pool. Years later he was to admit that he made a lot more from playing pool than the working for the sanitary department.

Sam's job didn't render his company unwelcome to the young women of the town, although Maggie was not impressed. To this day, she refers to it as "that job".

By then, Sam had spent a lot longer in Wyndham than he had intended. "He loved the girls and even had a whirl with my niece Violet!" Maggie laughed at the memory "and after all that he picked me! I couldn't believe it! I never let him get away with what he said about 'the yella piece' though! He didn't know I knew and when I told him he was so embarrassed! I just laughed and said 'You ought to be used to yella fellas. There's a whole lot of your friends in Derby are yella fellas'."

Maggie expressed surprise that Sam choose her from all the other girls. The few locals girls were joined by many more when the staff arrived from down south in the killing season, so for part of the year there was quite a choice of young females for local hopefuls to savour. Sam however, in spite of his whirls with the other girls was totally captivated by the ebony haired Maggie who laughed and teased him about his tactlessness; this slender feminine creature who from early teens had done a man's job and never gave it a second thought. In a town where men outnumbered women many times over, Sam had watched the young and the not so young pursuing Maggie and vying for her favours. Maggie was held in high esteem by all, but he was impressed by the manner she adopted; how she treated them with an even hand as she cleverly and with kindly good humour parried their constant overtures. Well, thought the young man from Derby, they could live in hope and court her all they liked, but it won't do them any good. He, Sam Liljenqvist, the new talent in town, was about shoulder his way through the mob to a rails position and make a winning run.

However, the conquest was not so difficult. The first night Maggie saw Sam dressed in his tropical whites at the Wyndham Hotel dance she was attracted to him. Later when they met she knew instantly that she could relax her guard and enjoy his company. He was interesting and fun. She loved his laconic sense of humour that was never far from the surface. Although he could discuss livestock, Maggie's favourite topic of conversation, and had had some practice working with them, his experiences were very different from her own. He had a vast store of mechanical knowledge, had been taught a great deal by his seafaring father and he'd spent four years working in a post office. His broad outlook, varied experiences and inventive mind put him in a class apart from any of the other young men of her acquaintance. She was conscious that her own schooling had been limited by comparison, but it was of no concern to Sam. Maggie Nicholson was the girl for him and being a very direct young man who spoke his mind, he left her in no doubt about his sentiments very early in their acquaintance.

On Sam's proposed journey of discovery around Australia, a thousand kilometres from his Derby home, Wyndham was only the first leg and it was destined to be the last. The rest of Australia suddenly lost its allure.

Once Sam proposed and Maggie accepted it was a very brief courtship. Maggie had turned twenty three in February and Sam twenty four in June. They were very much in love and ready to make a lifetime commitment.

It was obvious to Violet that her best friend and aunt, Maggie, had lost her heart to Sam and she knew before they did that it wouldn't be very long before the wedding bells rang out. Violet had had a wonderful four years, a blend of hard work, amazing experiences and great fun but it was time to go. Maggie's life had other interests and priorities now and as Wyndham held no romantic interest to encourage Violet there was no reason to delay her departure. Ron who went with a drover when he wasn't at the butcher shop had acquired a car and so he and Violet motored all the way home to the McCallum family farm. "We were so close. Best friends ever. Violet did all my wedding shopping for me."

It was not long before Violet's own marriage took place and a family soon followed.

Maggie and Sam were married on 28 September, 1935 by Reverend A. Bell of the Methodist Inland Mission, at the Mission House in Wyndham. The wedding party numbered six with Maggie's friend Alma and her husband Jack Huddlestone the matron of honour and best man respectively, Hannah who, as mother of the bride, gave Maggie away, and the officiating minister.

Maggie's friend of many years, Charlie Schultz, had never been in the running but when in later years he became a family man his daughter Donna revealed, "Whenever Maggie's name came up, Dad would say 'Huh! She could have had **me** but she chose the Dunny Man instead!"

Chapter VI

Buying the Bow

Following the simple marriage ceremony Maggie and Sam returned to the house at the Three Mile. No honeymoon marked the beginning of the Lillys' wedded bliss; it was business as usual. Hannah cooked, Maggie ran the butcher shop and Sam continued with his contracting.

In 1935, Australia was still in the grip of the Great Depression and few people, apart from the wealthy, were in a position to regard the honeymoon as an essential part of the wedding arrangements. In closely populated regions, a weekend at a boarding house in the mountains or at the seaside may have been possible—but for Maggie and Sam in Wyndham the nearest towns, Darwin and Derby, were a thousand kilometres away. They had each other and a lust for life and were sensible enough to make the most of what already lay within their grasp. They were young, strong and ambitious and when they combined their considerable skills, the only way was "up".

Sam contracted to build Wyndham's first airstrip in 1936. Although the area chosen was generally flat it was full of dips and humps so the task for Sam and his men was to flatten the humps and fill the holes. For years planes had been landing on the marsh without mishap, but aircraft were becoming heavier, faster and more sophisticated and a proper airstrip was essential. With an old truck to carry their tools and take earth from the high spots to dump in the hollows, they were at least partly mechanised. The actual levelling was all done with pick and shovel. Sam was as lean as a greyhound and his reputation of being a tireless worker was by then well entrenched.

The next job was the repairs of Highway No. 1 into Wyndham. Highway No. 1 was a narrow dirt track that crossed watercourses and flats that were either swamped or under water in the wet. The mobs of cattle that moved through the same area in the dry season did no harm to the road but the vehicular traffic constantly spread the gravel right off the track. The surface required constant attention. The new work designed to keep the gravel on the road entailed the creation of a raised edge on each side. This could only be achieved by the blasting and carting of local rock which when chipped into blocks was tightly wedged in place to form solid stone barriers on both sides. The workmanship was meticulous. In 1937 traffic along Highway No. 1 only consisted of wagons, cars, and a few trucks. However, in years to come, convoys of Army trucks, increased numbers of private cars and trucks and finally—the mighty juggernauts of transport—the road trains, taking cattle to the meatworks, thundered along between the carefully laid stone blocks. More than sixty years later

(Lilly collection)

ABOVE: HOME, SWEET HOME FOR THE YOUNG NEWLYWEDS WAS A BUNGALOW AT THE THREE MILE. THE PRACTICE OF THE TIME WAS TO HAVE A VERANDAH ON ALL FOUR SIDES AND CLOSE THE VERANDAH ON THE CORNERS WHEN AN EXTRA ROOM WAS REQUIRED.

BELOW: LOOKING WEST ALONG THE OLD HIGHWAY NO 1 TO WYNDHAM. UNTIL RECENT TIMES THIS WAS STILL THE MAIN ROAD. IT IS A TRIBUTE TO THE MEN, INCLUDING SAM LILLY, WHO WITH PICKS AND SHOVELS BUILT AND MAINTAINED THE ROAD DURING THE WAR. IT HAS ENDURED HALF A CENTURY OF PUNISHING WEAR AND TEAR FROM ROAD TRAINS AND OTHER VEHICLES AND FLOODED GROUND IN THE WET SEASON. BEFORE ROAD TRAINS WERE INTRODUCED CATTLE WERE DRIVEN ALONG THIS ROUTE FROM THE KIMBERLEY STATIONS TO WYNDHAM.

the long white lines of rocks still lie firmly in position, a lasting tribute to the skill of the men who undertook the roadwork.

At first Sam drove the Main Roads truck and then later contracted with his own vehicle, assisted by a driver, Con Ahearn, and Dick McKellar as overseer. Maggie had good reason to remember two of the other men in the work party One was Mick Kelly, the "Nip" so named for his constant habit of "always trying to borrow a couple of bob" and Charlie Scott, who came to her one day with an empty tomato sauce bottle and asked her to fill it with methylated spirits. Not long after Sam found the two leglessly drunk. "I didn't think anything of it when Charlie asked. Just thought he must have needed it for something." Maggie laughed "and wasn't Sam mad at me! He'd get no work out of them till they sobered up."

"Don't you ever give them anything!" he told me " ***No*** metho, ***no*** lemon essence and ***no*** brake fluid! They'll get blind on any of it!"

(Post cards produced in the latter 1990s have been shown to Maggie, crediting the stonework to Chinese labourers and others. "For God sakes," she exclaimed, thoroughly exasperated by such misinformation, "who else will they come up with next!? Sam and the boys built it. Not the Chinese! Or anyone else either!")

With Sam working so hard on the road maintenance he could spare little time, energy or enthusiasm for the butcher shop. One trip for cattle he and Maggie had to make was out as far as Dunham River. It took a whole week by the time they had ridden out with pack horses and tailed their cattle back to the yards near the Three Mile. Following that were the long days spent watching them while they fed and yarding them each night. With Sam's contract they were better off without the butchery and to Maggie and Sam's relief and delight she managed to sell it to an interested party for £450—a large amount of money.

Now Maggie was able to give Hannah more assistance much to the old lady's relief. Hannah was cooking for and looking after a houseful of eight, because the men who worked with Sam also boarded with them. Not only was Hannah keeping up the food to the hungry men, she washed their clothes as well. The copper worked overtime boiling up the roadworkers' dusty pants and shirts, and when Hannah climbed into bed and blew out the lamp each night she wondered if there could ever be an end to work.

The house, according to Maggie, "had verandahs all round and the corners of the verandahs were boxed in to make rooms. The men slept in their swags on the verandah. It was a funny old place. There were all the butcher's rooms and sheds out the back where the shower room was and the lavatory was right out the back and over the fence!"

By 1937 the young Lillys felt financially able to contemplate buying some land. They approached Kate Rhatigan, a well known pioneer of the region, and her son Jack. Kate, then in her sixties, owned the Turkey Creek store, residence and small lease, which Maggie bought. Jack held four twenty acre blocks and some three hundred thousand acres leasehold, but needed two more years to sort out his stock and affairs. He had a partnership with Walter Macale of Greenvale.

Kate Rhatigan had come with her husband Mick, formerly an East Kimberley police constable, to take up a new job in Turkey Creek. In 1897 the telegraph station there was completed and Mick became the linesman until his death in 1920. The area around Turkey Creek, even though it had a Police presence prior to 1910, was the scene of various attacks and killings and no place for the faint hearted. In the 1915 Mistake Creek massacre eight Aborigines—adults and children—were killed and others were wounded in an attack just three miles though the hills from Turkey Creek. Two of

Mick Rhatigan's men, Carogbiddy, known as Nipper, and Joe Winn, a Darwin Aborigine, were blamed and rumour had it that Jack Rhatigan was also involved. It was believed to be a grudge attack as the victims included Nellie, Joe Winn's former woman, and her new man Hopples. On the strength of the rumour, Jack Rhatigan was charged in company with Nipper and Winn. However investigations established that there were no grounds for implicating him and the case against him was dismissed. Winn tried to escape on a horse of Jack's and was shot dead by a police tracker, Sandy. Nipper was sent south to end his days in Perth. He worked in the Police stables and died of tuberculosis in hospital in 1918.

Kate spoke about the early days when wild blacks stalked around the house while her husband was away and how she had to stand and watch while they speared her goats down on the creek. In spite of dramatic incidents like this, the courageous widow Kate who had raised her own family and several Aboriginal children at Turkey Creek chose to remain on her own in this isolated outpost until the young Lillys took over.

In the two years until 1939, when Jack Rhatigan was ready to relinquish his Turkey Creek block, the young Lillys took on other work.

The pumping station at Wyndham needed wood to run the steam driven pump and Sam agreed with the station's wood contractor Billy Flinders to supply one hundred cords of wood. Maggie and Sam loaded the truck and set up camp in a section of bush with a good supply of timber. "It didn't seem to matter whether the wood was green or dry," recalls Maggie—"but it was all done with an axe. Sam didn't have to cart it though. Billy did that. Cords were bundles of wood and when I'd finished at the camp and made the bread, I'd help stack and count the cords."

Uncle Jack Beasley had several droving trips to complete and suggested Maggie and Sam would like to work for him. These trips were from Kimberley stations to Wyndham and although considerably shorter than the epic drives eastward from places like Mistake Creek and Wave Hill Stations into Queensland, they still involved the same management. A string of pack horses, mules or donkeys carried the rations, camp ovens, shoeing tools and spare shoes. Spare horses were essential in case of lameness, saddle sores etc. and there had to be spares of any other item that might be needed. It was too late when an essential item was missing hundreds of miles from a source of supply. Someone had to be the cook and often the cook had to take a turn as a ringer with everyone else on the two hour night watches. The cook also had to be up early to feed everyone and late to bed as well, keeping the fire well stoked, with hot coffee on the side for the night watcher. For their extra hours of duty the cook was usually paid a little better and they earned every penny.

Sam was fond of telling the story of a drover who had an old black ringer who couldn't tell the time and so couldn't gauge his two hours night watch properly. To solve the problem the drover pointed to a star. "You watchem that star. When that fella star catchem up with moon, you come wakem me." At first light he awoke the Boss who wanted to know where he'd been all night. "Oh Boss, I bin watchem that star, he bin chasin' up moon, chasin' up moon. Oh Christ, all night he bin chasin' up moon but he can't catchem!" The poor old stockman and his weary horse had been ringing the cattle all night long.

On one trip they brought in 500 speyed cows from Rosewood to Wyndham. On another trip they lost a hundred head from tick fever or "redwater", which is spread by tick borne parasites and named from the quantity of dissolved blood cells in the urine turning it red or brown. An infected mob cannot be moved until all symptoms of the disease have disappeared. This requires at least a week by which time the susceptible animals have died and others less affected are showing signs of recovery. In many areas the cattle have built up an immunity but this mob had come from a station where the animals had not had the previous contact needed to develop a resistance to the devastating parasites.

"We were camped with one night with a mob of six hundred bullocks coming in from Go Go on the Fitzroy and we heard shots." Rifle shots in the night for unknown reasons were unnerving enough for anyone in such remote parts but they could have set the bullocks rushing as well. "Didn't know what was happening until next morning old Eddie Fogharty came over. They were back behind us with a mob and had a cow camel with them." Cow camels do not come in season—the bull does, and goes in search of females. During the night a big bull camel in season came into the camp in pursuit of Fogerty's cow. At such a time the males are extremely aggressive and dangerous. "The old fellow took a fire stick to him to chase him away but ended up having to fire shots at him."

By the time they were a few days walk to Wyndham the bullocks were footsore and some quite lame. They brought the bullocks in on the west side over the Coburn Ranges and there was only one place to come down and that was near the Wyndham Prison Bottle Tree. This was a tree where the police used to restrain prisoners when bringing them in to Wyndham under escort. It is said they were lowered through a hole in the top of the trunk and fetched out next day on a rope ladder if they had not managed to escape in the night.

The hill was so steep that Sam and the other men had to link arms behind to push the lame bullocks over the edge of the rocky slope before they'd pick their way painfully over the rocks to the bottom. Meanwhile Maggie kept a worried eye on the pack donkeys. "The packs were slipping so far forward I thought it could bring the donkeys down. The one with the meat bucket had it right over his withers." They camped that night at the foot of the hill and after that the terrain was relatively easier but still hard on the footsore bullocks.

In 1939 when the Rhatigans were ready to hand the properties over it took two weeks for Sam and Maggie complete their to move to Turkey Creek. Hannah stayed behind at the Eight Mile bore with Jacky and watched the stock while Sam and Maggie moved house in the truck. Then they drove their horses, goats and cattle home with the aid of two lubras and their husbands. Typically, the old house was built of iron and bush timber. The dining room boasted a cement floor. The remainder had dirt floors. To avoid ending up choked by dust, "you had to splash a bit of water around before you swept them," according to Maggie.

While Hannah dealt with household matters in the wet and the dry, Maggie helped Sam. Most of the stockmen were Aborigines and if Sam was away with the men, Maggie and the Aboriginal girls tackled the other jobs. "I always took the girls who had no kids. They built yards, and broke in fresh horses ready for the next season. One year we had a fire in the bull paddock. The fence posts were snappy gum and very hard but many were smouldering at the base and would have kept going till they burnt right away. We had hardly any water so the girls and I got mouthfuls of water and sprayed it on the burning bits. It worked very well and we didn't lose any of the fence."

Uncle Jack gave Maggie and Sam his droving plant and in 1941 and 1942 they made two trips with cattle from Louisa Downs to the Wyndham Meatworks.

Next Sam contracted to supply eight foot posts for the Mabel Downs Stockyards. This was a big job by anyone's reckoning. Any set of yards in that region required the capacity to hold many hundreds of cattle at any one time. At ten shillings per post, the final total was an impressive sum but in the locating, cutting, loading, carting and unloading Sam earned every penny of his money.

Next he built the bronco yards at MacKenzie Springs for three pounds per week. He had to dig the postholes for the uprights. There was no such luxury as a tractor mounted posthole digger then; it was all laborious crowbar and shovel work. Firstly the layout and size of the yards had to be settled upon; then the holding yards, the long race, forcing pens and so on were all measured out. Distances between posts were marked and the backbreaking digging began. Sam worked all the daylight hours.

When there was a break in the work at Turkey Creek Maggie left Hannah in charge and took three mares accompanied by their foals, riding one and using the others as pack horses, and rode to MacKenzie Springs stopping at Tickalara on the way. Jack and Alma Huddlestone, Sam and Maggie's best man and matron of honour, were at Tickalara where Jack was manager. This made a nice break for Maggie. There were no telephones so the two young women had plenty to catch up on. Sam, working alone, had to look after his food as well so when Maggie arrived to relieve him of this tiresome but necessary chore for a few days it was a welcome break. It was from all these contracts involving such grindingly hard work and the year's muster from Turkey Creek that Sam and Maggie built up their capital.

Throughout the War years, 1939 to 1945, Maggie and Sam lived at Turkey Creek. The meatworks in Wyndham had been closed down for the duration and cattle from the property had to be sent eastward. The fats went to Katherine Meatworks and the stores, which were unfinished and not ready for the prime meat market, went to Mistake Creek Station.

It was during the early months of 1942 that Northern Australia suffered most from the Japanese bombing. The coastal trader *Koolama* was heading north toward Wyndham when she was attacked and damaged on 20 February by Japanese bombers some thirty kilometres from Cape Ruhliers. In a small cove the passengers were put ashore from the lifeboats, with food supplies recovered from the cargo. Distress calls from the stricken ship reached Drysdale Mission some 160 kilometres distant and Father Seraphim Sanz set out from the Mission in a lugger with four Aboriginal trackers to search for the marooned passengers. The women, one with a small baby, and the injured were taken back to the Mission in the lugger. Ninety three men, led by the Aboriginal trackers and accompanied by Father Sanz, walked across country. They crossed the swollen Drysdale River and suffering abominably in the heat reached the Mission five days later. One man died—the second officer who collapsed and died from a brain haemorrhage whilst walking with Father Sanz. A skeleton crew handled the badly holed ship with her severely damaged steering gear and she limped into Wyndham ten days later. Once at the jetty, pumps were employed to keep her afloat. However, during another raid when the Japanese flew in to bomb the fuel dump at the aerodrome, the men working on the *Koolama* were forced to run for cover and when they returned she had sunk and lay on her side tipped over by a heavy load of steel stacked on deck. Now in her once hospitable staterooms and cabins, repositories for so many memories of the people of the Kimberley, the green murky waters of the Cambridge Gulf rose and fell with the tide. Her great bulk effectively rendered the Wyndham jetty useless and no more large shipping came to the town until the end of the War. When the government owned meatworks reopened in 1946 the 3,000 tonne hulk was eventually towed a few hundred yards distant to lie among the mangroves, where at the turn of the century, part of the superstructure is still visible at low tide. It was a sad and ignominious end to a ship that for years had been a lifeline for the people of the Kimberley. According to Lieut. Commander Tsunaaki Yonehara who gave the order to bomb, she would never have been attacked had she not had been armed with a Vickers machine gun mounted fore and aft. One local legend has it that someone on the deck took a pot shot at the Japanese plane with a .303 and it was then that the pilot turned back and attacked.

Broome was badly bombed by the Japanese on 3 March, 1942. On the previous day a Japanese reconnaissance aircraft was spotted very high in the sky over the township and another unidentified aircraft was regarded by sky watchers as suspicious. Broome had been designated an evacuation centre but facilities were inadequate for the numbers of planes and people being landed there before being sent south to safety. At the time there were several aircraft and a large fuel dump on the Broome airstrip and three Dutch flying boats moored in the bay. Through the night they were joined by another thirteen flying boats carrying Dutch refugees, mostly women and children from Java. The authorities were deeply concerned about the brief visit of the Japanese planes and tried to speed up their departure. Crews using pearling luggers spent the whole night refuelling the flying boats and their captains were advised to take off as soon as possible at dawn. Unfortunately tidal conditions were unfavourable and not all the aircraft were refuelled by the morning. They were still in Roebuck Bay at 9.30 am when ten Japanese aircraft—nine Zeros and one reconnaissance plane—swept in over Broome. Some of the group concentrated on bombing the airstrip and fuel dump, others provided cover and the remainder made for the moored flying boats, strafing them until every one of them was on fire. Women and children still aboard were incinerated and those who had jumped out were either burnt to death by the burning fuel spreading over the water or hit by the rain of bullets. Those in the water tried to help each other and some brave rescues were attempted but the water was full of the dead and dying. No one had counted the people who had gone ashore earlier, no one knew how many lost their lives on the burnt aircraft and no one could know how many were lost in the water. Many were thought to have been taken by sharks that abounded in the area. A mass grave was dug for the bodies recovered and authorities could only guess at the loss. The figure they arrived at was around seventy. When the Japanese pilots were satisfied they had completed their task and the people of Broome were trying to deal with the carnage in the water that they had caused, the planes regrouped and flew in V formation over the Japanese Cemetery before leaving for their base in Koepang. The pilots said later that they had no knowledge that there were people on the flying boats and nor did they attack the women and children in the water, but the outcome could hardly have been worse if they had.

Prior to the attack on 3 March all white women and children from Darwin, Broome, Wyndham and Derby had been evacuated to the South. Maggie, Hannah and some of the station wives chose to stay but they were not permitted to come into town.

The station people had to buy supplies in Broome, as Wyndham was no longer an active port. This was no ordinary shopping excursion. They would be on the road for the best part of a week and travel over one thousand kilometres each way over a track through station properties. "We camped along the way, but the gates! There were so many and of course, I was the gate opener!" Maggie laughs at what seems to be the lot of the wife of a man on the land. It is not until the children can reach and wrestle with tricky gate chains and are strong enough to lift and carry sagging gates that she can finally sit comfortably and watch someone else doing it.

Travelling at any speed on the narrow track was out of the question. They carried their swags and plenty of food and water for their needs on the trip to Broome. It was essential to allow for hold ups and mishaps. They would purchase a substantial quantity food stores, especially if the trip was just prior to the onset of the wet. Once the rivers were up there'd be no trips to Broome for at least four or five months. On the return trip the truck would be even slower with its cumbersome load of station supplies but they would be lucky if they came home with everything they wanted. Wartime conditions played havoc with supply routes but like everyone else they managed. Hannah, nearly seventy now, was managing at the Turkey Creek homestead and Jacky Nicholson, now married to Peggy (a sister of Tim Timms), was looking after the stock in their absence. Hannah knew they could be absent for many days and she had the station women close by. In the little cluster of buildings that comprised Turkey Creek there were people upon whom she could always rely if she needed help. At the police station was Bill Bunt and his wife; there was also the post office, and when the solitary hours grew long there was always someone to have a yarn with.

Maggie, being a woman, was not allowed into Broome, so Sam used to approach the servicemen there. "When we got nearly there, Sam would leave me behind in the bush and go on into town. The men would greet Sam and say, 'G'day Sam, how's your wife? Oh, by the way, the general is away all day today.' Sam would come back and pick me up and we'd have a nice day's shopping and lunch at the pub." The day in town brought them up to date with all the news that would take months, if ever to reach them at Turkey Creek. Once the truck was loaded and everything tied down they turned for home.

Maggie remembered one trip when she and her matron of honour, Alma Huddlestone, sneaked a visit to Derby. "Don't now what we thought we were doing there. There was no shipping so no shopping much. We'd had lunch and we were standing outside the pub reading the notices on the wall and waiting for Sam when we heard these two men talking. "They were saying 'as soon as you spot the two of them put them under close arrest'. Well! God save us! Didn't we get a fright! We felt so guilty. We weren't supposed to be there anyway and we thought they were talking about us!" Fortunately, it was not Maggie and Alma they were looking for but two servicemen who had gone AWOL (absent without leave). The two men were standing at the end of the jetty and as the girls watched they were quickly apprehended and marched off under guard. When Sam finally emerged from the pub fully expecting to be asked what took him so long, he was greeted by the two young women who were still getting over their fright, exclaiming "We thought we were going to be arrested and put in gaol!"

1945 was a momentous year for Australia with the end of World War II, and a year of changes for Maggie and Sam. In February their first child was due. About this time with a baby on the way Sam and Maggie decided to change their name from Liljenqvist to Lilly by deed poll. The name they had lived with for years as a diminutive became official.

A few weeks ahead, Maggie travelled all the way to Perth to await the birth. She had to attend the outpatients department on a regular basis but there was no place available near the King Edward Memorial Hospital where her confinement would take place. She had to stay in a suburb far away from the Hospital and her plight precipitated a wave of consternation among staff. Matron A. Walsh addressed a gathering of interested women on the matter which was followed a meeting of the House Wives Association. Representatives from thirteen organisations were invited. The meeting formed a committee comprising leaders from women's organisations and one man, J.J.E. Archdeacon from the Infant Health Association, to investigate the possibilities of providing a new building near the Hospital capable of accommodating at least twenty five women.

On 2 February, 1945 a daughter, Maureen, was born to the Lillys. Maggie returned to her beloved Kimberley leaving behind her the beginnings a new era in hospital care accommodation for the country women of Western Australia.

(Maureen Coulthard collection)

ABOVE: STATION HOMESTEADS ARE OFTEN VISUALISED AS GRACIOUS AND SPACIOUS OLD STRUCTURES TELLING OF PAST WEALTH AND PIONEERING ACHIEVEMENT. HOWEVER IN REALITY THEY COME IN ALL SHAPES AND SIZES, MORE OFTEN IN HUMBLE FORM. SAM LILLY (CENTRE) LEANS ON A BUSH TIMBER POST OF THE CORRUGATED IRON GREENVALE HOMESTEAD TALKING WITH TWO MEN FROM THE AGRICULTURAL DEPARTMENT.

BELOW: THE FIRST BOW RIVER HOMESTEAD WAS BUILT BY SAM AND MAGGIE LILLY FROM MUCH OF THE MATERIAL, ROOFING IRON AND TIMBER, SALVAGED FROM THE OLD TURKEY CREEK STORE.

(Lilly collection)

At Turkey Creek the residents decided it was about time an aircraft runway was cleared and everyone set to with whatever equipment they could muster. Sam drove a drag from steel welded into a V shape drawn by a donkey team, which he'd made to clear tracks on the station. Others heaved rocks and other unwanted material onto old trucks and wagons. With picks, shovels, energy and enthusiasm a landing strip soon took shape. This meant an end to the long wait for mail that came in a truck every couple of weeks in the dry. In the wet it had been a six weeks round trip for a man with a pack horse if they were lucky. Connellan Airways, aviation pioneers of the North, responded to this achievement by beginning a once a week mail service. Another wonderful outcome from all the endeavour was that the Flying Doctor could also land there. This uniquely Australian service, first envisaged by Rev John Flynn as "a mantle of safety" over the outback, could now include another isolated community on its map. For urgent cases it meant that medical attention and a hospital were only hours away. The Flying Doctors and their pilots have always had to be ready for anything and one trip about this time was for the wife of a Turkey Creek policeman. Maggie said "She had a twisted bowel and she screamed in agony all the way. Hours later they got her to hospital but she died and the pilot said however long he lived he'd never be able to get the sound out of his memory."

"There was one year before the runway was built when Sam was very sick with pneumonia and we couldn't have moved him hundreds of miles over the track into hospital by car. We were just lucky that Norma Buchanan, Bobby Buchanan's mother, came out to nurse him and stayed with him for ten days." It was before the advent of antibiotics, and pneumonia was a very serious illness. Norma Buchanan, another pioneer woman of the Kimberley, had nursed some of the survivors of the *Koolama* disaster and her daughter Bobbie Buchanan wrote the story of her famous pioneering great grandfather, Nat Buchanan—*In the Tracks of Old Bluey*.

Maggie and Sam had been making arrangements with their neighbour Walter Macale to buy Greenvale. Old Walter lived in the Greenvale homestead—a battered, rusty corrugated iron and bush timber shed. "There was an old clay sort of fireplace that smoked. It you lit it you had to get out. Old Walter slept on a bush timber and greenhide laced bed but he didn't seem to mind." His meat was hung in a bucket in an old Boab tree to keep it away from the dogs. "Old Nancy used to cook for him in a bough shed. She'd make a stew in a huge camp oven with great lumps of corned beef and then throw in a quartered cabbage." Maggie can mimic Walter's delighted anticipation as he surveyed the great sea of bubbling stew. "Oooh, Maaag!" he'd say. "That's good stoo too!" The damper was made in a tin dish. "Old Walter would get down on the ground and mix the damper in an old miner's dish with his dirty hands. When Walter and Nancy were eating, if any of the dogs came close he'd hit them on the nose with the spoon. They were short of forks and old Nancy would clean the dirty ones on her skirt!" It was all too much for Maggie. "Sam and I always had our meal somewhere along the road before we got there!"

Old Walter died aged 78, in Perth in July, 1945 and final negotiations were completed with his executor that year. Maggie and Sam had contract mustered Greenvale in the two previous years and through that time they gained a useful familiarity with the property which covered more than 600,000 acres (about 250 square kilometres).

Maggie speaks with deep feeling of those nine gruelling years prior to 1945. "My husband and I spent the first nine years of our marriage before our first child was born battling away out in the bush with swags to sleep on, no beds, only damper and beef to eat and when we had time, a stew or a curry. No fridges in our time. Anyway you couldn't carry one on a packhorse. We chased wild cattle, branded the calves and cleanskins. Got the bullocks out to sell." It would be safe to say that Maggie loved activity and achievement but it was a hard life and at times a dangerous one.

During Maggie's first pregnancy, Uncle Jack had had a terrible accident. He had been visiting Frank Lacy at Violet Valley and was about to return to Greenvale. He was mounting his horse and had one foot in the stirrup when a dog raced out and frightened the horse. It shied away throwing Jack backwards and onto his neck and shoulder. Maggie and Sam got word of the accident and after some hours travelling reached Frank Lacey's homestead and a seriously injured Uncle Jack. "He nearly broke his neck and he was in the most terrible pain. We had to get him into a truck and drive to Halls Creek." They had to travel over fifty miles on a rough dirt track. "It was a terrible trip; I'll never forget it. He was in agony and I had to try to hold onto him to stop the truck shaking him too much." He was flown to Katherine and put in hospital where his injuries were attended to but he was never quite well again. Sad to say, the much loved uncle and brother never returned to Maggie and Hannah. He went back to the district of his birth and bought a little block near Charters Towers to spend his last days. Here he was fortunate enough to find kindly neighbours who cared for him. One day, whilst pottering around on his block of land, he slipped and fell in shallow water and was not discovered until the next morning. That was the beginning of the end and he died not long after, leaving everything to the good friends who had watched over him in those last years. Hannah who had lost so many of her loved ones mourned deeply for this favourite brother whose kindness had so often come at just the moment when she and Maggie most needed it.

As a mother Maggie had to accept a new role and relinquish the life she had led as Sam's right hand in all matters to do with stock. Although she was not entirely housebound her activities were limited for the time being. It wasn't long before Sam, missing Maggie's presence, paid her the supreme compliment. He admitted that in starting a family he had "done in the best stockman he ever had!"

After ten years of unremitting struggle the young Lillys moved the thirteen miles to their new home, which was a construction built from the iron and timber salvaged from their old Turkey Creek building which they had demolished and carted over to erect on their new property. They chose a site not far from the Bow River. Their new station combined Greenvale previously owned by Walter Macale and Adavale once belonging to Durack and Martin. Bow River Station or "The Bow" as the family affectionately called it, covered one million acres.

They were now the Lillys of The Bow.

CHAPTER VII

Lillys of the Bow

THE BOW RIVER, a wide, sandy, many channeled watercourse, was named by Michael Durack and Tom Kilfoil on one of their exploratory trips in the Kimberley region. They named it after the Irish river that marked the old boundary between the counties of Galway and Clare.

Maggie's new homestead was close to the boundary where there was an old well and an ancient boab tree. Here teamsters, as far back as 1890, had camped and watered their stock on the track between Halls Creek and Wyndham. It was the very same spot where Maggie's father, Tom Sautelle would have camped thirty years previously when driving from Derby to Wyndham. It was still a track but was nevertheless part of the Great Northern Highway, No.1. At the front of the house were two graves. Though lacking a headstone to mark his last resting place, one belonged to a man named Billy O'Donnell. Apart from the cause of his death, Maggie didn't know much about him. "He was killed when his horse dragged him through the river. He must have done something important because they named the main street in Wyndham O'Donnell Street, and there's a creek between Wyndham and Turkey Creek and a range of mountains in the district named after him." Billy O'Donnell was the man who surveyed the road from Anthon's Landing at Wyndham through to Halls Creek where another street bears his name. He was a great horseman and delighted in a wild unmanageable horse named Whiteface. Few could handle this animal and eventually it beat Billy too. It was Whiteface who dragged him through the Bow.

The other grave bore a handsome headstone in memory of the brothers Macale. Walter, who died in 1945 and Dick — Richard James Eyre Macale — who died on the Bow River in 1922 from fever after bringing in a mob of horses.

At the new homestead, Hannah, now in her late seventies, still cooked for the family but her sight was failing and Jessie, Maggie's right hand girl, helped her in the kitchen.

In those days Bedford Downs Station and The Bow had a combined muster driving all the cattle to the big yards on Foal Creek at Springvale for drafting and branding. Musters were always hard work but the families managed to infuse a trying and tiring task with a little humour. Sam loved a practical joke and seeing everyone enjoy a good laugh, knowing how effectively it broke down the tensions and tempers that mounted in the heat, dust and sweat of the yards.

One night after tea when everyone was ready to turn in, the curlews were calling. Basil Quilty of Bedford Downs recalled Sam saying to his younger brother Mick Quilty, "They're ghosts, Mick, I'll

(Lilly collection)

WHEN CYCLONE JOY STRUCK IN 1966 THE BOW RIVER ROSE ENOUGH TO THREATEN THE HOMESTEAD. SHRUBS AND FRUIT TREES IN THE GARDEN WERE SWEPT AWAY. AS THE RIVER ROSE, THE FAMILY PACKED AS MUCH AS POSSIBLE ONTO HIGHER LEVELS AND SHELVES, LOADED SUPPLIES ONTO THE TRUCK AND WITH THE OTHER FAMILIES, MADE FOR THE SAFETY OF MT LOOKOUT. SAM, WHO COULD NOT SWIM WAS CAUGHT ON THE OTHER SIDE AND NOT UNTIL MORNING DID THEY KNOW IF HE WAS SAFE.

bet you're not game to go and sleep up near the cattle yards on your own." Ten year old Mick had no qualms and assured Sam he was perfectly game. The ghosts didn't bother him! He promptly picked up his swag and carried it away towards the yards, which were some distance away in the dark. That was the last they heard of young Mick that night. Sam later told his family what happened. Once he was out of earshot the practical jokers around the fire began planning the evening's fun at Mick's expense. He was to be scared out of his wits by a visit from a "ju-ardie" (ghost). Poles and a sheet were produced and one of the young men stood still while Sam tied one pole vertically to his back and another across his shoulders, forming a cross which they threw the sheet over. When they judged young Mick to be in his swag and everything quiet, the ju-ardie crept to the yards to do his worst. The others stood in the dark and waited gleefully for the results. At the yards the ju-ardie found the swag but disappointingly, no sign of young Mick. He walked around for awhile trying to find his victim and having no success wandered disconsolately back to the fire to tell of his failure.

The only person there was an old Aboriginal stockman squatting by the fire and totally absorbed in the business of rolling his plug of nicky nicky (tobacco) in some ashes which had the same binding effect on the chewed and gradually disintegrating plug of tobacco as flour has on a rissole.

He heard the movement and looked up to see the white form towering over him. The old man leapt to his feet accidentally knocking over the billy sending water sputtering onto the red coals. Clouds of ash and steam rose into the air adding a dramatic touch. With a howl of fear he raced off into the night yelling "Ju-ardie! Oooooooh ju-ardie! Ju-ardie! Ohoooooo!" The figure under the sheet hearing the cry fading far into the distance felt the warm glow of satisfaction. That trick really worked — shame it terrorised the poor old black stockman though! Young Mick had known something was going on when Sam dared him to move his swag. So he climbed a tree and watched the whole entertaining outcome from his vantage point.

The purchase of Greenvale included several thousand head of stock and when the first muster in 1945 took place the cattle ready to be sold were yarded for the stock buyer inspection. He duly arrived and after formalities and smoko had a good look at the penned animals. "Give ya six quid" he said to Sam with a smug grin, meaning six pounds per head. He expected his low offer to be snapped up with some alacrity and gratitude, knowing it was the Lilly's first year on the big new property. He reckoned that they would be bound to owe money and that the cattle, after weeks of mustering could have been brought from anything up to seventy miles distant taking many days to walk them in. The sale was "in the bag".

"Eight" replied Sam.

"Six is the offer. Take it or leave it." The buyer said offhandedly.

Sam lifted an arm in the direction of a couple of the black stockmen. They read his gesture, "Let 'em out!" He knew the value of the cattle and had no intention of being bluffed into an unsatisfactory deal. Principle was always very important to Sam and after the buyer's ultimatum there could be no backing down or compromise.

"What are you doing?" asked the buyer.

"The boys are putting them out" replied Sam.

"You can't do that!" yelled the buyer.

"Watch" replied Sam laconically as the bullocks moved away from the rails and out of the yards in a cloud of dust. The buyer had come a very long way and just could not believe what he was seeing! He thought he was in control of the situation and it was all going wrong. The big mob of prime cattle he was banking on to fill his order was disappearing in a cloud of dust. With an offhand wave indicating it was the end of encounter, the owner swung onto his horse and followed the mob.

A good stock buyer could play his clients like fish on a line. Years of practice told him how far he could go and at what point he could tip the balance for a sale. His success depended not only on his judgment of the stock but of the vendor. This buyer's judgement of the new owner of the Bow River Station had been far wide of the mark. Since it would take him some time to make up the shortfall if other stations had already sold, he'd learnt a costly lesson. That was one bluff he wouldn't try again on Sam Lilly — and he never got another chance.

Obviously Sam's stand caused Maggie some concern at the time. They still had three annual payments to go before the purchase of Greenvale was complete. "That was '45," she says. "The meatworks re-opened in '46 and we got more money for them the next year anyway, so it worked out alright."

(Lilly collection)

TWO OCTOGENARIANS, HANNAH NICHOLSON AND THE CAMEL, RESTING IN FRONT OF THE MEN'S QUATERS AT THE BOW ABOUT 1949. THE OLD CAMEL BELONGED TO A STRING OWNED BY BILL CAMPBELL; CAMELS WERE AN INDISPENSIBLE FORM OF TRANSPORT AT THE TIME.

When the Lillys settled at the homestead, the Aboriginal families from Greenvale including Jackie and Peggie with their little daughter Angeline came down to join the people at the Bow River camp. Sam set about building a ten room brick quarters for them. "They never used them though; only sleep in it if it rained." Maggie recalls with a laugh. "We had a bit of a gully between the quarters and our house and they'd all camp in the gully. It looked terrible with bits of blankets and tin and brush breakwinds. Then they built a gundie out of bush timber and bits of iron. I used to say come on, we've got to clean this up. It looks terrible."

This would be met with cries of consternation. "You can't pullem that one down! 'Im proper good shade!"

Once the Wyndham Meatworks was operating and the port was again operational, life flowed back into the region. Throughout the War the racing had ceased and it was one of Maggie's priorities to get things started again. "We mustered up about eleven horses between us and Moola Bulla and got Wyndham going. We won the cup with a horse called Silver." Everyone had missed that annual excuse for a good get together, and in one centre after another Race Week with its accompanying balls sprang to life.

"Sam bought a mob of horses, about fifty of them and there was one I liked. Sam didn't want to let me have it and I said, for God sakes, you've got fifty there, you're not going to miss one!" Maggie got her way and the animal she named Whitefoot because of his long white stockings was broken in and later began his brief but distinguished racing career.

On the Bow there was never an idle moment. By now Sam had installed a coolroom of his own creation. "We had a coolroom before anyone else thought of them. We also had a 12 volt lighting

KEVIN, MAUREEN AND ALMA AT THE FRONT STEPS OF THE BOW HOMESTEAD ABOUT 1950.

(Lilly collection)

plant he made and I used to curse it if I had to start it! Crank! Crank! Crank! One engine had a great big belt on it and one day when I got it started the belt grabbed my skirt and dragged me right up against it. It took a great lump out of my dress."

The Army began to dispose of equipment and buildings. The Sydney Williams steel framed houses specifically designed for tropical areas were advertised and Sam purchased one of substantial proportions to extend the homestead. These remarkably efficient buildings were assembled like a Meccano set, with nuts and bolts. By undoing the same nuts and bolts they could be easily demolished and transported. They put it up gradually as time allowed. Sam also bought two weapon carriers to make into a vehicle for difficult terrain. Until it was complete, two quiet old camels much loved by Maggie were invaluable for carrying food to the mustering camp. "They'd carry everything in their packs and when we arrived we'd sit them down and it was so easy getting out what we needed and putting it all back afterwards. I'd say to one of them 'Off to sleep now' and the dear old fellow would put his head down and go to sleep!" Unfortunately there came a time when they wandered off and joined wild camels. That was the end of camel power on the Bow.

By 1948 Maggie was a busy young mother with three children. Alma who arrived in 1946 and Kevin in 1948 were both born in Wyndham. Kevin was made much of by his grandmas as the only boy. Grandma Lilly's children had suffered the loss of all the boy babies born to them and now, on his minute shoulders Kevin bore the sole responsibility for carrying on the Lilly name.

There was plenty of help to keep an eye on the little ones. They each had a nurse girl and the little Lillys began their lives as part of a wider community, their own mother and father and grandmother and the people of the Bow.

(Lilly collection)

SOME OF THE BOW RIVER STATION FAMILY WITH ALMA RIDING THE CHILDREN'S PONY, LARNEY. PEGGY, ON THE LEFT MARRIED JACKIE NICHOLSON, THE LITTLE BOY HANNAH RAISED. ON THE RIGHT, CLARA WITH MONA, TIMMY AND LIDDY TIMMS' DAUGHTER.

Maggie put in a lot of time on maintenance and when the children were little she'd take them and her girls out to check floodgates and bores. "The Bow was a terrible place for floodgates. There were so many." The Greenvale portion was 1300 feet (over 400 metres) above the surrounding country, so rain water running into the gullies and watercourses could be in powerful torrents by the time it hit the floodgates. Floodgates are installed where intermittent watercourses have eroded away the ground beneath fences. Without them cattle would get through underneath. Fixed fencing clogs up with debris in a flood, so a floodgate is usually made of fencing wire and netting hanging from a strong wire or cable stretched across the watercourse in line with the fence. This is secured by posts, or by the trunk of a tree if one happens to be in the right spot. The wire and netting reach down to the bed of the watercourse so livestock cannot get through. Exterior boundaries are the most important. It doesn't take long for stock to find breaches in a fence and a whole mob could be through and far away in no time. If already carrying the owner's brand they would be identified at the next muster of the property to which they had strayed and their owner would be notified. If they were cleanskins, they would automatically be branded on the property where they were mustered.

Always after rain floodgates have to be checked and invariably some need repairs. The debris washed down by the water either lifts them up or builds up against the wire barrier and temporarily dams the water. The force of water after heavy rain can take a floodgate out, posts and all. Good management dictates that they be well maintained and on the Bow it was a huge job. "We lost one of our old stockmen, Mickie, when he and his old girl were working one floodgate up behind Turkey Creek. He was standing in all the rubbish and a snake that was caught up in it bit him. He died and the old gin sat there with him all night until first light when she walked in the thirteen miles to the homestead to tell us. The men went up and buried him where he was."

The bores had to be checked regularly and Maggie and her girls would "pull the bores" This

(Lilly collection)

BRANDING TIME AT THE BOW IN 1978. JIM COULTHARD WAITS ON THE BRONCO MULE WHILST THREE STOCKMEN HOLD DOWN A CLEANSKIN. MAGGIE'S GRANDSON, ROD COULTHARD LOOKS ON. THE LOG STRUCTURE IN THE FOREGROUND IS A BRONCO PANEL. ANIMALS WERE DRAWN RIGHT UP TO THE PANEL BY THE MULE FOR BRANDING, CASTRATION AND EAR MARKING. THIS WAS THE TRADITIONAL METHOD UNTIL RACES AND CRUSHES CAME INTO USE.

meant pulling up the bore pipes and checking the intake for blockages. Nothing could be left to chance when it came to stock water. We'd also be "attending". This meant going to where other cattle were being mustered to collect any that were branded with the Bow brand. I'd only go a day's distance to attend."

"When Sam sent in the cleanskins with the men they'd stay and help us with the branding." In the branding yards there was a bronco panel which consisted of three posts, the centre one taller than those either side. The three posts were a few inches apart. From left and right, rails sloped upwards to the shorter posts. This structure had to be very soundly built to stand up to the work required of it. The rider on the bronco horse or mule rode through the yarded cattle and dropped a looped rope around the neck of a beast in the mob and hooked it onto a collar on the horse or a horn if the saddle happened to be in the American style. The bronco horse then proceeded to drag the roped beast toward the panel. The rider took his mount behind the panel and slid the rope up along the sloping rail until it dropped into the space between the uprights. The bronco horse dragged the beast close to the panel and kept the rope taut whilst the ground crew then ran in and threw the beast. In seconds it was earmarked, castrated (if male), branded and then freed so the process could begin on the next animal.

The fire lit to heat the branding irons was well out of the way of the bronco horse's activity and the panel and to achieve a good clear brand the iron had to be applied red hot. "The girls kept the fire going and I ran the brand." Maggie, small and nimble was adept at this fast work. "Running the brand" meant that she would take the red hot brand from the fire and run, judging the very second it was needed and hand it to the man doing the branding. When it was all over, "the girls and I would take the cattle back to another paddock where they could settle down. The men would go back out to Sam who could have been sixty or seventy miles out. It was a long ride back to camp."

THE OLD TRUCK WITH BUSH TIMBER RAILS WHICH BROUGHT IMPROPER BULLS TO THE BOW FROM GO GO. DURING SMOKO AT MISTAKE CREEK, BARNEY AND MAGGIE ARE ON TOP OF THE TRUCK AND MONA IS NURSING YOUNG KEVIN LILLY WHO WAS ABOUT TWO YEARS OLD AT THE TIME.

(Lilly collection)

MAGGIE ON WHITEFOOT AFTER WINNING THE LADIES RACE AT HALLS CREEK CUP MEETING IN 1950. BY THIS TIME MAGGIE WAS THE MOTHER OF THREE YOUNG CHILDREN BUT FOUND TIME TO KEEP UP HER RACING SKILLS. KEN CAMERON IS HOLDING WHITEFOOT'S REIN.

When the mustering was over and all the men came back to the homestead and their families it was always a big night. "There'd be a great corroboree but they were all back at work the next day."

Whilst Sam's first love was not livestock, he knew that the only types of cattle and horses to run were the best obtainable. A quality beast was no more expensive to run than a scrubber but commanded a much higher price across the scales and ultimately lifted the annual profit margin. Bow River cattle needed an infusion of fresh blood and in 1949 Sam purchased some excellent quality bulls from Go Go Station. These were the type which produced the style of beef popular at the time with a selvedge of fat and good marbling of the flesh. They were red and roan shorthorns and when the new blood was introduced to the Greenvale cattle that had bred within the herd for generations, the result was expected to lift the quality of the progeny dramatically. They set out to fetch them in a recently acquired Bedford truck fitted with a homemade cattle crate of bush timber, pulling a trailer full of swags, food, water and other essentials. Sam, Maggie and toddler Kevin, Kevin's nurse girl Mona, and stockman Barney all went for the long drive to Go Go on the Fitzroy River. A modern vehicle on a tarred road would have made the 600 kilometre trip in a day's drive, but as always it was a different matter in the Kimberley. The drive over winding track, stony watercourses and through numerous gates had to be calculated in days not hours and the young bulls had to be yarded and watered each night somewhere on the way home.

Maggie's ability to judge a fast horse was demonstrated when she won the ladies race at Halls Creek in 1950. She won it on Whitefoot, the horse she had cajoled from Sam. To her great sorrow Whitefoot came to a sad end. He was caught on a short lead, slipped into a river and drowned. Maggie was too far off to help him and no-one heeded her warnings in time.

Someone from the Bow who loved going to the races with Sam and Maggie was Tim Timms. Tim's father was a black Afghan and his mother was Nancy from Greenvale. Tall, smiling and always impeccably attired in black trousers and a snowy white shirt, he was always ready at Maggie's or Sam's elbow to lead and tend the horses from the Bow. He took great pride in his responsibilities and was always Sam's right hand man. Billy Flinders who was still in the carrying business had an Aboriginal worker named Paddy and Maureen still remembers the great rivalry between Paddy and Tim Timms. "Dad would let Tim ride Malwood and Billy Flinders used to borrow a good horse from one of his mates for Paddy to ride in the blackfellas' race." The bookies did a roaring trade and the Lilly nomination was always favourite when Tim was astride the "mighty Malwood".

Race Week at Wyndham brought the ball at the meatworks. Maggie recalls one occasion when she and Sam and Charlie Schultz and his wife Hessie from Humbert River were present. Someone came to their table and asked Sam and Charlie to judge the Belle of the Ball. "For God sakes!" laughed Maggie, "Why would anyone ask those two to judge? Sam might have had some idea because he had sisters but Charlie! He wouldn't have had a clue; he was just a bush boy. You should have heard them! 'Aw, cut it out Sam! She's no good. Can't pick her. She's got legs like a billiards table!' and on it went… 'Dress is too short… too long… hair's a funny colour. That one's not bad… Nah. She's a couple of axehandles across the rump!… What about her? Gawd no! Look, she's walkin' all over that poor bastard she's dancin' with! Can't have a belle of the ball that can't bloody dance, can ya?' " The discussion raged on and on. "Hessie and I were in fits!" says Maggie. "They picked someone in the end." But there is no record of their being invited to officiate as judges the following year.

After Maggie tried her hand at educating the little Lillys, she decided a governess would be a much better idea. She employed a young woman named Rosemarie Richardson. When she went out to do a job, Maggie would take the children and Rosemary in the vehicle with her and leave them under a nearby tree with rugs, Kevin's box of toys and the girls' schoolbooks.

Rosemary had an uphill battle. As Alma remembers it, "We wouldn't stay put. We'd be going in all directions to look at this or that and Rosemary had to keep chasing us. One day she locked me in the tool room." At her wit's end, Rosemary had overlooked the fact that between the roof and the top of the walls in the tool room there was wire netting. Alma found a pair of wire cutters, climbed up the shelves, snipped a hole and wriggled out. The poor governess would just get one child back and the others would be gone. Alma remembered how she hated being stuck in one spot, "It must have been awful for her. We were terrible kids! We wanted to pick flowers and do things, not sit down looking at books! Mum and Dad didn't know what to do with us." Eventually, the two girls were sent in to the new Halls Creek township to board at the Australian Inland Mission Hostel and attend the local school.

Walkabout for the Aboriginal people began in the wet about Christmas time. Where possible, Sam — or "Cham" as the Bow River people pronounced it — tried to arrange for half of them to go and return before the other half left. They went supplied with tea, sugar, flour, rice, curry, jam and tobacco and tall square bottles of Bushells coffee and chicory, an essential part of a station order in those days. This concentrate — which was poured into a cup and mixed with hot water — was almost everyone's favourite. Sam let them take the donkeys to carry their supplies. Initiation ceremonies took place at Turkey Creek but the walkabout usually took them as far as Bedford Downs. "Not all of them came back," Maggie discovered. "Now and then we'd lose one or two."

In those months largely confined to the homestead and sheds, Sam tackled harness repairs, mended all the saddles, made greenhide straps to carry the hobbles and had everything in working order for when muster started. Engines were high on the maintenance list and as the Bow became more mechanized he had more to attend to. The Sydney Williams house frame was now bricked and completed. Instead of using the corrugated iron skin Sam, helped by Kevin, made bricks from the creek sand. They gave old Brickie Stewart the job of brick laying. "We came back from somewhere to find the walls curving outwards. He never told us he was nearly blind!"

Locals followed the building of the homestead with great interest. One character called Grease Gun commented "The house at the Bow is goin' pretty good. They're even puttin' lubras in the winders!" It was the same Grease Gun who, when asked to clarify the spelling of his name over the Flying Doctor Radio spelt it out "Gun. G for Jesus, U for onion and N for pneumonia."

The homestead ended up with six bedrooms, a loungeroom and twenty six doors. At the front was a big room with several tables and lots of chairs for the family and a place to sit down and have smoko. Time and again someone would go in for a quiet cup of tea and be disconcerted to find a whole party of strangers sitting at one of the tables. Passers-by on Highway No.1 mistook the homestead for some sort of roadhouse and finding this big room decorated by pots of colourful flowers and greenery took it as a dining area where they sat waiting for service. Sam took practical steps to stop the invasion of their privacy. His next "improvement" to the Bow was to reroute the road around the bottom of the hill, well away from the house.

Sam built Maggie a very large aviary, which gave her enormous pleasure. She loved her birds and had a splendid collection of corellas, finches, doves, galahs, pigeons, quarrians and parrots. Unfortunately the snakes that abounded in the area shared her love for the inhabitants of her aviary. Huge pythons spent a lot of time working their way around the wire looking for a space in the wire or the iron sheeting on the roof to get through. Maureen recalled the scene. "You'd hear Mum yelling for someone to bring a gun," Maureen recalls. "She'd have found a big snake caught in the cage with a big lump in it. Once they'd swallowed something they couldn't get back out. The swelling in their belly would stop them escaping. Sometimes there were several lumps. She was very proud of one pair. The hen had two eggs she was sitting on in a great big milk tin. A python had found its way in through the wire and took the eggs but the two parents died of fright."

Maggie had a pair of beautiful birds she referred to as Blue Mountains parrots with blue head, orange chest and dark green wings that came every year and built their nest in the ceiling above the big front room. One of the old blacks said to Maggie, "You pullem off roof. You findem big snake." Investigation through the manhole proved him right. There was a very big snake who'd taken the Blue Muntains parrots' eggs and then swallowed the female. "When we opened her up there they all were, two eggs first and then the mother. The male came back for a couple of years after that and then we never saw him again. It was very sad."

Pythons and king browns were part of life. The pythons rarely tackled Maggie's fowls. Most had the sense to realise they were just too big to engulf. Maggie caught one trying to swallow one of her hens, it's skin stretched to transparency around the fowl's body. "It was a funny sight," she says. "There was this big snake with the chook half in and its yellow legs sticking straight out of its mouth." The snake disgorged it soon after. Having killed the prey they begin the swallowing process from the head so that the feathers lie flat and the quarry doesn't become caught half way down their gullet.

"One time a family came to Halls Creek to work for a bit and they lived on the back of a truck. There were the parents, and a couple of small children and a baby. One day when the parents came back to the truck they found marks on the baby's forehead where a python had had a go at swallowing it but it must have decided it was just too big to get its jaw stretched around. That child will probably carry those scars all her life."

In the wet of 1951 the Lilly family had its first holiday. By then they had acquired one of the early post-war American Jeeps. These wonderful little four wheel drive vehicles were rough to ride in but tough and reliable, so with a trailer on the back to carry the luggage they headed south and spent a couple of months touring. "Mum and Dad sat in the front," Maureen remembers, "and they filled the back with rugs and cushions. We kids could sit up or sleep whenever we wanted."

The journey took many weeks and covered thousands of miles. Sam finally managed to see some of the places he'd planned to visit all those years ago before his round Australia trip came to a full stop in Wyndham. The intrepid family covered huge distances over bush tracks. Three thousand kilometres got them to Perth. Then they crossed the Nullabour in the baking heat of high summer — but accustomed to living near the hottest town in Australia they took that in their stride.

In their absence Joe Summerfield, manager of Dunham River Station, kept an eye on the Bow and when they got back he reported to Sam and Maggie on his caretaking. "Maggie, all those pots and baskets of flowers you've got in that front room…I watered them every day for you. Can't say the bloody things have grown or look any better now than they did when you left."

"No" said Maggie, "they wouldn't. They're all plastic, but thanks anyway."

Attention had to be given to the road on Greenvale. "It was seventy five miles round Frog Hollow, twelve miles from Mable Downs and then back over Frog Hollow Creek crossing it God knows how many times, then to Violet Valley and back to Greenvale." Maggie had good reason to complain about the distance. She and the Bow River girls spent a lot of time on maintenance.

Eventually it was partially rerouted. "We got it back to forty two miles (67.5 km) but there were still a couple of jump-ups and gullys to get up to Greenvale." Saving thirty miles certainly reduced the road maintenance which was a laborious process. The seventy strong donkey team pulled the dray with the heavy welded steel V frame hitched on behind to smooth and clear the stones and rocks off the track. With the point of the V toward the donkeys' tails, the steel arms fanned the rubble off to each side. Most stations used a similar implement in those days and the lubras and children walked behind pitching the loosened rocks to the sides or gathering them up to fill holes. There was never an end to such work. It went on year in and year out.

When Kevin was old enough for school in Halls Creek he wasn't interested. He knew he'd been on a good thing and wanted to stick to it! The Lilly children were raised on goats' milk, fresh vegetables from the garden, eggs from the fowls and homegrown beef richly augmented by bush tucker. They each had a nurse girl who carried and cuddled them, cared for them and played with them. Maureen's nurse girl was the diminutive Cuppatea, a bright affectionate companion, Alma's was Mona, and Jessie looked after Kevin. Maggie and Sam took a siesta in the hottest part of each day. "Mum and Dad had a rest from noon until four every day and we kids all went off down to the creek with the families." The men were expected to be back on the job by two and the girls had another couple of hour's grace. It was a wonderful arrangement for the children and they still cherish the memories of those childhood years.

In the dry all the station children spent their days romping in the river waterholes and when the wet came they floated in the channels in old inner tubes that Sam kept mended and inflated. On Sundays their nurse girls, accompanied by all the other youngsters and anyone else who wanted to go, went "sugar bagging." Small black stingless bush bees build their hives in the hollow limbs of trees and with every eye alert for the tiny creatures and the directions in which they flew or congregated, the search was on. Everyone would listen for the sound of bees working inside the limbs and once located, a lump was cut out of the limb and the honey they made was scooped into a tin to be shared by all. The only rule that applied to these glorious days of fun was that, everyone had to be back by four to shower, water the vegetable garden and clean up around the area. What little six year old in his right mind would want to exchange all this for school?

So Kevin was taken into Halls Creek under protest, carrying a white ant in a matchbox. When his white ant took too long to eat the school down he decided to run away; to go home under his own steam. He and two other little friends absconded. When they were discovered missing a police search began. Home for Kevin was two hundred kilometres away with a lot of wild country in between. As a bush kid he knew that following a cattle pad eventually led to water so the three small runaways picked a likely looking cattle pad and started on their journey. What they overlooked in their haste to escape was that it was their parents who'd taught them survival tactics and the first thing the parents did was to follow the cattle pads! The police found them, none the worse for wear but very put out by their ignominious return to the hated school.

Two sons of the Turkey Creek postmistress Nan Langridge and her husband Ron, who was the linesman, were about the same age as Alma and Kevin. Roy and John Langridge and the Lilly children were inseparable throughout all the years they boarded at the A.I.M. Hostel at Halls Creek, and the friendships have never waned.

It wasn't long before a small pony made an appearance and the Lilly children learnt to ride. They'd always been sat on donkeys and horses but this one, called Larney, was theirs. Maureen and Kevin were natural horsemen loving every minute of it but for Alma it was just part of life and not her favourite occupation. The Bow was still very dependent on horses and donkeys and if you wanted to get around you had to either walk or ride. Alma, in spite of the idyllic early years on the station, knew very early in her young life that her future lay elsewhere.

From their earliest days the Lilly children heard and learnt the language of the Bow River people but they were not permitted to speak it. Kevin completely ignored this and being a boy got away with it. He was fluent in the language and was eventually honoured by being given "a blackfella name" by which the Bow River family still addresses him. They learnt how to find bush tucker with the other children, delving in the damp river banks for freshwater mussels, gathering the black plums and exploring their own private Eden.

There were green and black plums but only the black ones grew at the Bow. They favour the higher country whilst the green variety which Maggie describes as "a bit tarty" grow as far inland as Dunham River and like flat sandy country. Maggie loved the plums and ate them fresh, or stewed them like conventional plums—but the women used to make a long lasting dehydrated cake from them. By hours of patient crushing and bashing they formed a solid mass of fruit which could be carried and eaten when needed.

The indigenous people knew how and where to find wild food but they had to cover a lot of distance to achieve it. "Goannas were easy to find; they taste a bit like fish. The blacks used to heat stones and bake echidnas and emu eggs with the chicks in them." Maggie hated that. "You could hear them squeaking in the shells! Echidna was very greasy; didn't like that at all."

With so many people to feed and clothe there had to be some sort of structure to the days. Sunday was a day for fun and treats and going sugarbagging, and there was always a heap of boiled lollies on the table. Maggie's homemade soap was heaped up beside the boiled lollies. "Nobody worked on Sunday. All the kids on the station got lollies including us," according to Alma. "Everyone got a handful. The men each got a tin of Log Cabin tobacco and a packet of cigarette papers and the ones who liked to chew tobacco got a block of nicki nicki. They also got tobacco on Wednesday. Besides Mum's homemade soap there was always a cake of toilet soap for everyone, and hair oil. Both the men and women liked to use hair oil." Alma went on, "There was no such thing as soft drinks in those days so we kids made our own by dissolving the boiled lollies in a glass." Grandma Nicholson frowned on this practice as messy and forbade the manufacture of illicit soft drink — but the free roaming Lilly kids could always find a spot far away from their grandmother "to brew their own".

Homemade soap was part of station life and made from any fat available, resin, water, borax, caustic soda and kerosene boiled in a kerosene tin for a few hours and poured into large trays to set. Later it was cut into small blocks. If the soap maker felt inclined, a bottle of citronella poured in at the last gave it a fresh smell. In buying soap, the choice was limited. Bars of Sunlight, packets of Lux Flakes and Rinso were about all that was available and always a relatively expensive item. Dishwashing liquid was unheard of. A lump of Maggie's soap in a wire holder swished around in the washing up water until it lathered was all there was.

The homestead had a big kitchen with a girl who cooked for all the families and a big laundry with a copper, two sets of double tubs and wash boards where everyone's clothes were washed. Monday was wash day. "They all wanted to do something and I was flat out finding a job for everyone. There were always a couple left sitting down." These unfortunates were treated with great scorn and derision by the ones in the laundry who had some sort of a task to perform. Maggie mimicked the constantly uttered insult "look 'um there! Lazy fella sittin' on his haarse!"

PROUD OWNERS. MAGGIE AND SAM LILLY WITH MALWOOD JUST AFTER A WIN. THE GROUND MAY BE BARE AND THE GRANDSTAND ONLY A BOUGH SHELTER BUT THE LADIES ARE ALL DRESSED UP FOR THE DAY.

Much to her delight Maggie eventually saw the last of the old gundie in the gully: "Anyway there was one old boy who used to be out in the bush. He was the last real bush black that I remember. We used to call him Bush Paddy. He never worked. He just stayed out in the bush. He had a couple of old girls and a lot of dogs." Bush Paddy eventually came in to the station and for some reason wanted a whitefella burial when his time came. "If we went anywhere he'd say 'Yummun [a word meaning woman or mother]. You hurry up and come back y'know. You got to bury'em me.' And we did!" He died in the old gundie so after that they did burn it. In the old days the blacks would dispose of bodies in a crevasse in the rocks and then push rocks in all around it." The Bow River people began to prefer the white man's way and from then on the Lillys saw to their wishes. "We buried five of them over the years."

"We had about twenty babies born at the Bow and only one died. They didn't want to go to town. They'd go down to the creek and make a hole in the sand with a bit of brush around it and sit in it. One other woman would go with them and I'd go down every so often and take them food and hot tea and see how things were going. When it came to naming time the mother would ask me 'What we gonna call um?' I'd bring out a lot of names and say, well that's a nice one. 'Oh yes,' they'd say, 'that's a nice one.' They'd already given it an Aboriginal one. I had to register the births in Halls Creek and named them after the father. If he was Henry, then the kids would be Johnny Henry and so on. There's still a big Henry family and a big Ramsay family around."

Sam's top man Tim Timms and his wife Liddy had a family of six. The eldest girl Mona was

Kevin's nurse girl, then later helped in the house and married Rammie, a very successful horsebreaker. Next was Jessie who was Maggie's right hand girl in all the work they did when the men were away mustering." Also there was Linda, Alan and Timmie. Liddy had another baby between Linda, and Timmie and for some reason her milk stopped, something that had never happened before or again and the baby would have died if Maggie had not kept a supply of goat's milk up to him. Nature had known better. The boy, Kimberley, was mentally impaired. "At the races he would drink a lot and then he'd come up and sit at my feet," said Maggie "and if anyone tried to shift him he wouldn't budge. He'd say no, I'm talking to my Mummy."

Christmas time at the Bow included everyone. On Christmas Eve all the Bow families had a party. There was a great spread of cakes and party food and everyone received a present. Alma recalled the fun, "All the kids got toys, the women and girls all got something nice like perfume, a dress and other personal items and the men something they would appreciate. Christmas Eve was for all the people and then on Christmas Day we had our family Christmas. Everyone else did what they wanted to."

In spite of all the work on the Bow the Lillys found time to enjoy their deep involvement with their race horses. Sam bought in some promising youngsters. One of them, Malwood, won the Wyndham Cup two years in a row, 1952 and 1953, and went on to many other triumphs in the North. At the time they had several good horses and all in top form so Sam and Maggie decided to enter them in the Derby Cup meeting of 1953. Instead of trucking the horses they chartered a Bristol Freighter from Glenroy Air Beef at the cost of one hundred and eighty pounds to fly from Wyndham to Derby. Three Bow River horses, Malwood, Beau Arran and Devil's Own were on the flight, as well as a horse named Desert Dust owned by Brian Moore, brother of their trainer, Joe.

On the banks of the Bow, the laconic Sam Lilly with the ever present cigarette in his mouth leaning against his little Jeep four wheel drive. Although Sam worked as hard as anyone with the livestock his leaning was towards things mechanical.

(Lilly collection)

THE FIRST AND ONLY AIR LIFT OF RACE HORSES FROM WYNDHAM TO DERBY. THE BRISTOL FREIGHTER WAS CHARTERED FOR £180. IT TOOK FOUR HORSES OWNED BY MAGGIE AND SAM LILLY AND BRIAN MOORE TO DERBY IN 1953.

They were all winners and justified the exercise. No one had ever done this prior to the Lillys' experiment and successful though it was, no one has ever done it since.

Bush racing was a family affair and all the children went. They had plenty of playmates, black and white. Everyone set up their camps and the fun began. All the old friends came to town from enormous distances. The Underwoods from down at Inverway, the Quilties from Bedford Downs, the Schultzes from Humbert River, the Duracks; the list was long. It was an exciting time and on the race course emotions and tempers boiled over now and then. "We kids had a great time," says Alma. "We were always given two shillings to bet with. We'd go up to an old bookie named Sam Thomas and he'd write us out our card. We loved to bet on Malwood or our other horses but it didn't matter whether we won or lost, we'd take our tickets back and he'd give us our money. He was a dear old man, one of the real old timers."

The Lilly kids were regarded as tearaways and were known as The Tiger Lillys. "People thought we were very spoilt children although we were very shy with strangers. We were always encouraged to speak out and be independent. To be seen and not heard wasn't us. We were always heard! Debate was encouraged. Then after we'd spoken out and aired our views we were told what was acceptable and what was not. It was carefully explained so we understood." Sam was always teaching concepts; tolerance, learning, striving. He reminded them from time to time of the speech given at the opening of the Halls Creek School. It referred to the Cannas and Cantas, frogs that were thrown in a bucket of water. The Cannas struggled and got out and the Cantas stayed there and drowned. It was all about achievement.

There was plenty of grog at the race meetings and as always some made more use of it than others. One old chap after a lifetime of dedicated drinking thought he'd finally gone too far. He'd been outside the Six Mile pub and saw a lot of white rabbits hopping about. The Kimberley did not have a rabbit population. He stood and watched the little creatures and decided this must be a mild dose of the horrors. He'd always expected to see pink elephants and wrything serpents, but white rabbits! He wandered off and sat down. Perhaps a little rest and no more grog for a while. Jack Bourke who was taking a couple of the Lilly's horses to water stopped for a word or two. After a few pleasantries Jack said, "I just got a bit of a shock. I notice Woodlands over at the pub have got white rabbits; must belong to the kids." An expression of sublime relief passed over the old man's face. "So you've seen them too? Oh Gawd, Jack, I'm so relieved!"

When the children were away at school, Maggie would go out to help with the muster. "Sam and the horse tailer would be away mustering in very wild rough country under the Durack Ranges." Bush Paddy's son Stormy, who was a good horseman, and a couple of black girls, the husband of one of the girls and I would collect the mustered mob of wild bullocks, a few hundred at a time and work them towards a big set of steel yards. They were real big rail yards, proper branding yards built by Gene French who used to work on the Bow. One of us would ride in the lead, saying all the time, 'Keep goin', keep goin'' and one on each wing to keep the mob bunched and leave Stormy behind in case some broke." Stormy was the best for this position as it demanded at times all the skill of a top horseman. "I used to be real worried that if some broke the rest would go before we got them yarded. And wasn't I ever relieved when I saw the last tail go in and closed the gate!"

Once cattle find they can break away they will keep on trying so the best idea is not to give them a chance in the first place. Keeping them moving at a good pace means they have to concentrate on where they are walking and being bunched up doesn't allow much opportunity for a breakaway. It also requires constant alertness on the part of the riders and a horse with good stock sense. Both have to be one jump ahead of the cattle. An old droving acquaintance of Maggie's, Jackie Charlton spoke of the cure for breakaways, "You'd flog 'em off the camp for a mile and flog 'em back. They soon learnt!" However effective that may be in training rebels to settle in and stick with the mob on a long drive, it was no option for Maggie. There was no time for that. There would be another mob waiting to be collected by the time they'd got back from yarding the ones they already had.

Converting his two Weapon Carriers to one vehicle was a wet season project for Sam. "It used to follow the stock camps around and he had one old blackfella, Rammie who always drove it. It would go over anything and carried everything but it only went about one mile an hour." Maureen laughs at the memory of Rammie's dogged patience. "It could go a bit faster, depending where you were but Rammie was a very careful slow driver."

About the mid-fifties Sam imported a tractor, much to the hilarity of the other Kimberley station owners. Nobody ever had a tractor on a station up in the North and soon amid hoots of mirth from his neighbours, Sam was given a new title, "Farmer Sam". He took no notice whatsoever of the derision and proceeded to put the little tractor through its paces. Of British manufacture and known as a Ferguson TEA, the tractor was equipped with threepoint linkage and power take off from which it ran a huge range of implements specially designed by the manufacturer for Ferguson tractors. Sam whose innovative brain was seldom at rest could see the time and trouble it would save. Instead of mustering and harnessing a team of donkeys to grade the road, he could use the blade on the Ferguson for much of the work. The carry-all could take drums of fuel, fence posts and machinery anywhere at a moment's notice. The post hole digger made the tedious job of fencing faster and easier. The jib could lift and drag items and if a carcass needed moving it was a matter of moments with the little "Fergy". Before very long all the other station owners had stifled their merriment and also became proud possessors of little grey Ferguson tractors.

At the age of nine, Kevin was a seasoned rider. While he and a couple of the boys were mustering some horses, his mare threw him. He broke his leg just above the knee and was knocked unconscious as well. Bill Hall, the head stockman, carried him down to the road and left a boy with him until Sam could drive over to Turkey Creek thirteen miles away. It was a painful ride for the now conscious Kevin; it was impossible to keep the vehicle from bumping over ruts and across creeks and watercourses. At the Post Office, Kevin lay on a table while the postmaster, Ron Langridge, contacted the Royal Flying Doctor Service in Wyndham. The doctor gave instructions to Ron who relayed them to Sam who proceeded to set Kevin's leg. Afterwards he was flown to Wyndham where they had no facilities to treat him. He spent a night there, then flew to Derby where he spent another night. Because they also had no facilities the next stop was Perth and the Princess Margaret Hospital. The fracture was considered unusual and difficult. A large fragment of bone had broken away and remained in the flesh until it was slowly absorbed during the body's natural healing process. The Perth Hospital agreed that Sam had done a good job setting the bone, and after six weeks in plaster and traction Kevin was sent back to home and his horses. Kevin was lucky compared with Maggie's friend Jimmy Darcy. The Halls Creek postmaster operated on him taking his instructions one letter at a time in Morse code.

Anyone who uses horses on a regular basis is bound to suffer injuries one way and another over the years and Sam had his share; in one instance he was lucky to escape death and serious injury. Sam rode a horse named Barney in gymkhana events. Educated to such things as barrel races, tent pegging, flag races etc., Barney was quick on his feet and a fast learner, so Sam taught him to chase and kill dingoes by running them down and trampling them. Barney became most adept and the Sam and Barney act accounted for many a dingo, which in those days were present in enormous numbers causing heavy stock losses. One day Barney spotted a dingo and took off full pelt after it when Sam's attention was elsewhere. Before Sam had time to gather the reins or duck, Barney went under a big branch wiping Sam off in the process. Slamming into a branch at high speed has killed or maimed many a horseman. Sam hit the ground badly bruised, winded and with a permanent injury to his back but he escaped death, broken bones and a trip with the Flying Doctor.

At the Bow, Hannah was still cooking for the family. She was eighty nine and undiminished in spirit but her sight was nearly gone. One day towards the end of 1957 she tripped and fell, breaking her hip. She was taken to Darwin, and although Maggie spent as much time as she could going back and forth, Hannah was desperately unhappy. After several weeks Maggie decided what to do. "I made a bed in the back of the car and brought Mum home." It was a thousand kilometres on rough dirt road to Wyndham, but Hannah was going back to her own territory and was much happier. She seemed to be progressing and was stimulated by all the visits from old friends in the town to which she had come with her beloved Tom Sautelle and little Maggie forty five years before. However, her condition suddenly began to deteriorate; pneumonia set in and the old lady slipped away.

Hannah Nicholson died on 1 February, 1958. She was laid to rest the following day in the Wyndham Cemetery that lies in the valley to the north of the Bastion, not so very far from where she first stepped ashore in 1915 to begin her life in the town. The writer of Hannah's obituary in *The Northern Times* said "The Spirit of the Kimberleys and Mrs Nicholson's life story are synonymous, and have been equally enriched one by the other."

Maggie was bereft. The two women had never been parted for more than a matter of weeks in nearly fifty years; not even when Sam and Maggie were first married. "I always tried to look after Mum. She'd had such a dreadful life and I never left her."

Chapter VIII

How the Lillys Grew

The first months of 1958 were ones of great emotional upheaval. Hannah's death left a huge void. "Mrs Nicholson retained all the energy and forcefulness of her vigorous personality," her obituary had said. For forty five years Maggie had lived in close communion with this strong, stoic pioneer woman who had experienced so much tragedy. Maggie has never ceased to mourn her passing.

Hannah's funeral took place at the start of February and this was also the time for the girls to return to Perth to go to school. Maureen had begun senior studies the previous year and it was now time for Alma to begin first year at high school. Sam and Maggie drove them in to Wyndham to board the 8.00 am DC3 flight next morning. The plane refuelled en route and the journey ended in Perth very late that night. The DC3s still hold a world record in safety but the noise level in the cabin was very high and they shuddered and shook in flight. Nervous passengers watching the movement in the wings would wonder if they would at any minute part company with the rest of the plane.

Sam's youngest sister, Violet Lovell, lived in Perth and was prepared to care for the children while they attended Belmont High School. She already had Grandma Lilly living with her. Some years previously Carl and Elizabeth Lilly had retired from Derby where they had both spent many years working at the hospital and leprosarium. They took up residence with Violet. Sadly Carl had died in 1951. Elizabeth who lived to the age of 97 remained with the Lovells and consequently the Lilly children able to enjoy a close relationship with their paternal grandmother which had been impossible previously. "Grandma Lily was a lovely old lady," Alma remembers. "She used to sit in the room with Aunt Violet and do all sorts of beautiful fancywork all day. She could still see to embroider until she died." There is no doubt that whilst Maureen and Kevin inherited Maggie's love and ability with horses, Alma took after the Lilly women, Elizabeth and her daughter Violet.

Maureen found her aunt a demanding woman. "She used to order these huge piles of wood and when I came home from school and I had to be back by a certain time, I had to split the wood, fill the wood shed, pile up the kitchen fire wood and enough for the lounge room. I had to do the garden and water it and she treated me like a slave." Alma on the other hand had a different relationship with Violet. "She was more like a mother"; but when Maureen went home Alma inherited all the duties. Violet was a professional seamstress and Alma who admits to being a more indoors person, thoroughly enjoyed her time there. "I did stand up for myself but I used diplomacy, but Maureen, being the eldest did as she was told. She was very good to me and used to make my dresses but I never thought they were quite right so Dad bought me a sewing machine so I could make my own." With her flair for fashion Alma had great fun with the new machine. It was one less job for Violet who with five people in the household and her professional dressmaking had her days fully taken up. Sam always saw to it that the Lovell home was up to date with domestic labour saving devices to at least ease some of the burden of housekeeping.

Maggie and Sam began preparation for the arrival of the dry season and with it, the start of the annual muster. Horses had to be brought in and shod, supplies sorted and packed and everyone equipped with what they would need whilst out in the camp. Twice a year Maggie ordered the station supplies from various business houses. "I'd order in April/May and November before the wet. J. & W. Bateman, Fremantle, sent the general supplies and Good, Durant & Murray of Perth sent clothing. Medical supplies came from Fauldings, Southern Cross was the place for windmill parts and pipes and Coventry Motors supplied motor parts. Flour came in fifty pound bags and sugar in seventy five pound bags. Tea came in a chest. I always ordered a roll of Berkmeyer for the swags. I'd make a list of what I wanted and then see what Sam needed; hardware, nuts, bolts, horseshoes and nails, fencing supplies, tools etc. It was always written out and mailed. It all came by ship and a carrier would bring it out to the station." For years pack animals delivered the orders two weeks or so after they had been collected at the jetty in Wyndham but when motor transport took over in later years it cut delivery time to a day or so.

"If something was needed urgently we used the flying doctor or telegrams. Some of the places had pedal wireless and if messages were hard to get through others would relay them." Maggie tells the well known story of the station boss communicating by pedal wireless and the signal kept fading because the old black fellow doing the pedalling kept slowing right down. Every so often the frustrated communicator would turn and shout at the old fellow 'Pedal you bastard, *pedal!!*'"

A PEDAL TRANSCEIVER OF THE TYPE USED BY THE LILLYS AT THE BOW AS LATE AS THE 1950S. THIS MACHINE IS IN THE POSSESSION OF THE WYNDHAM HISTORICAL MUSEUM.

(Ingham collection)

The Royal Flying Doctor Service had a base in Wyndham and this was a wonderful communication service for the station people. Telephones were decades away but the radio provided a wide variety of services and at times much hilarity. There were daily "skeds" for regular services. At 6 pm the 6 to 6 rainfall figures were collected followed by telegrams. The operator would ask for 9 Oscar November which was the Bow's call sign. At the Bow whoever was at the radio would respond "This is 9 Oscar November — over." "Good evening Maggie — we have two telegrams for you" He would proceed to read these out, sign off and go on to the next. Each morning at 9 am was the medical session. Anyone with problems would call in and jostle to get their problem attended to. One by one the doctor would work his way through the radio queue. With the individual's call sign identified, the Doctor would ask the patient to describe the problem. "Do you have your medical kit there? — over." All stations had the standard Royal Flying Doctor Medical Kit with every item numbered. "Yes — over." "Have you got bottle No. 22? What is on the label? — over." "Penicillin — over." The doctor might reply "Yes that is correct. Give the patient..." and prescribe the dose, then move on to the next call. Everyone who was tuned in to the Flying Doctor base's frequency could hear the session — a ship in the Cambridge Gulf, an aircraft pilot, people on the stations. From hives to haemorrhoids, all the Kimberley knew who had what.

"We held our gymkhana meetings and I.C.P.A [Isolated Children and Parents Association] meetings over the radio. We had Cockatoo Galah sessions." Maureen recalled. These were the free and easy skeds when people in the far flung homesteads could join in general conversations and catch up on news and gossip. When the telephone finally came to the Kimberley it offered privacy, speed and efficiency but compared with the R.F.D.S. radio network, it was a sterile alternative.

Apart from their day to day needs, all the Aboriginal families were supplied with goods. "The gins got a single blanket if they weren't married and those with kids a double blanket. Next thing I'd see the piccaninnies dragging them around; one pulling the blanket and another sitting on the end!" Maggie rolled her eyes at the state in which the lovely new blankets ended up. "In late March when the boys went out on muster each one got new R.M. Williams boots, a hat, trousers, shirt, single blanket and three yards of Berkmeyer for a new swag or ground sheet. The men got ten pounds a week and the girls got a bit less. We always gave them money for the races too." Maggie always made sure the storeroom held extra of everything. There was no such thing as a quick trip to the shops.

Maggie always made the girls clothes on her treadle sewing machine. Alma commented, "People thought we were rich because we always had a nice dress to wear when we went anywhere and we did, but we also had to wear hand me downs. I remember one hideous red dress of Maureen's and it came to me. I had to wear it. I said to Mum, I'm not wearing that horrible dress. I hate it! And Mum said 'Yes you will. There'll be no new dress until that one is worn out.'" Alma would not be beaten. "I wasn't going to wear it so I went down to Dad's workshop and got a lump of sandpaper and I did wear that dress out — I wore holes all over it!"

The muster continued for months and Sam worked his heart out. "You know," says Maureen, "when Dad was out mustering he'd work all day, cook for the men and there'd be a dozen or more to feed and if anything went wrong at the homestead, he'd leave the blackfellas in charge and go back to fix it. He'd ride all bloody day and all bloody night, fix the generator or whatever it was and then go back out and get on with the next day's mustering."

The Bow River stockmen were a good team but Timmy Timms filled a special place in the life of the Lillys. When Sam was out in the stock camp and the day's mustering was over a small ritual began. As Sam finished his meal and lit another cigarette Timmy would come up, quietly seat himself on Sam's swag and give a long and detailed account of the day's happenings. Sam was held in deep affection by his stockmen but it was Timmy Timms alone who accorded himself the honour of a seat on Sam's unrolled swag and a long man to man talk.

It was Timmy who always saw to Maureen's welfare during muster. "He'd make me have a big long drink before we started. He'd say 'Long time, no water.'" It was a long time between feeds too, so Maureen would cut a couple of slices of corned beef and slip them into her shirt pocket. The young members on the muster could not turn for home when they'd had enough, get a drink when they were thirsty or a feed when it suited them. They could be two days' ride from the homestead and if they went out on muster they worked all day every day, ate at night at the camp and slept in their swags under the same conditions as the seasoned stockmen.

Each year a mob was sent to the Wyndham Meatworks and the numbers increased as the breeding stock on the Bow built up. The long walk into Wyndham after the weeks of muster was unavoidable in those days and took a heavy toll of the condition of the cattle. No matter how good the season, walking cattle always lost condition. It took the best part of a fortnight on the road by the time they were counted over to the Meatworks men at Chimooly. Here there were quarters for the five stockmen whose job it was to take charge of the mobs as they came in and move them to the big yards en route to the killing floor. The Lillys would be present in town for the kill but Maggie only went onto the killing floor once. The children were with her that day and they stood watching the animals coming up the race and into the "knocking box" where a man hit each beast on the head with a heavy hammer. The second it fell it was dragged out and the next one came in. Unfortunately the very next animal to come in was a big brown and white beast. "There's Sunshine!!" the kids yelled in unison, only to see the animal stunned, drop and be dragged away. The bullock had been a motherless calf the family reared on Sunshine milk, hence the name. In time he was big enough to join his fellow weaners out in the hills on the Bow. Over the years he grew into a big bullock and was mustered with the rest of his kind destined for the works but the children never forgot Sunshine. Poor Maggie — "Didn't I have a bawling match on my hands then! I never ever went up there again after that!"

It is when the carcasses are on the hook that the quality of the stock, their dressing out percentages and level of management are revealed. Seasons and bloodlines play their part in the outcome but no matter how good the product, the producers were always at the mercy of market forces. The Bow carcasses were headed for the Smithfield Market in England as chilled beef.

1959 was Maureen's last at school. "I came home and did the cooking. I cooked for everyone, all the blacks and had to make all the bread and cook it in the big old fuel stove in the terrible heat." Few fifteen year olds could handle such a task. Maureen had inherited Grandma Nicholson's job as well as that of cooking for the station people. "I was to do it for two years and when Alma came back I could go on my trip around Australia."

When Kevin finished school at Halls Creek he left to attend High School in Perth, going on to Narrogin Agricultural College. As a son he would be permitted to complete the full five years' secondary schooling, whilst Alma came home to help on the Bow, working with Maureen and the station girls.

Alice Downs Station, between Halls Creek and Turkey Creek, had a new manager, Frank McMahon. He, his wife Dolly and their daughter Patsy came to the Kimberley in 1960. One day they called in at the Bow. Patsy recalled the visit "We went into the big room that was just like a road house; no wonder people kept going in there expecting morning tea! Anyway, three heads popped around the corner to see who was there. It was Maureen, Alma and Kevin. They were shy and sat at another table. I was shy too and sat with the adults and all the time the three Lilly kids were laughing and talking and I wished that I had been sitting with them. Mum and Mrs Lilly got on very well and we've been friends ever since."

Sam was always aware that his children should have some young company. Now that Patsy McMahon was at Alice Downs she was included in Sam's weekend muster. Alma recalls, "On weekends he would try to arrange something for us. He was good with young people and he'd round them all up from the other places and we'd all go fishing or have a picnic." Maureen remembers his thoughtfulness: "Dad never let us forget that we were girls. Just because we worked like men at times, it was no excuse. If we were going anywhere he would ask 'Now what have you girls got to wear? Here's some money, go and buy what you need.' People thought we were privileged but in some ways we certainly were not. Mum didn't believe girls needed education so we had to leave school earlier than others to work on the station."

Years earlier, Sam had built a pit dunny at the back of the house for the station girls. It had a very deep pit and a little house complete with a boarded in bench with a hole cut in it set up over a frame placed over the pit. Galvanised iron nailed on the upper side of the frame fitted neatly against the walls of the building. Earth dug out of the hole was heaped all around and over the iron platform so the cavity was neatly sealed. Often in pit dunnies a ring was placed at the end of the frame and when the site could no longer be used, the whole structure was snigged off by a draft horse or tractor to another location. People used to save wood ash from the stove and copper in a kerosene tin bucket. They used an old jam tin or some such item as a scoop to empty ash into the pit at each use to reduce the offensiveness.

One morning when all the girls were busy doing the chores around the laundry and cookhouse, one of them went off on a visit to the dunny. The door had not been closed more than a few seconds when it was flung open and a terrified girl rushed out and ran down the path, her eyes starting from her head and yelling "Eh! Missus! Missus! That shit'ouse! 'Im bin goin' oink!"

Maureen and the others went to investigate. Indeed by the time they got to the little building the "shit'ouse" was emitting a whole chorus of oinks. An inspection of the rear of the building revealed the problem. Heavy rain had washed the earth away from the iron covering, leaving a gap that the station's family of pigs discovered. The first one had worked his snout into the gap and with much wriggling and rooting enlarged it until his head could fit and it was just a matter of a little more effort and his whole body slid through the slippery muddy aperture. The rest of the inquisitive creatures had to see what their relative had found so interesting and one after the other they all pushed their heads into the gap, lost their footing in the mud and slid in. "It wasn't really so funny," said Maureen. "I was the one who had to get a big lump of wire and hook them all out!"

Alma had matters in hand before long and Maureen was able to leave on her well earned trip to see Australia. The good part of returning home for Alma was that she could spend time with Sam. "Dad had to do all the books, wages and things so I learnt to do that to help him."

After the clearing of a runway at Turkey Creek in 1945, mail day became a weekly event for the locals. "When it was dry we'd go through Mistake Creek. Who went depended on what was happening on the station at the time. You never went anywhere without doing jobs along the way. Keep an eye on everything; maybe throw out some rock salt for the cattle." Rock salt, which in those days came out as ballast in ships, came in great rough lumps and was very heavy to handle. It was cheap but a great dietary supplement for cattle, sheep and horses that would stand and lick the jagged lumps smooth and shiny. Alma sometimes had to go on her own "I'd have to start the pump on the bore at Mistake Creek to fill the tank for the troughs. It was an old Lister Diesel engine and at six and a half stone [about forty kilograms] I couldn't hold the handle down and turn the motor over at the same time." The handle on the top of the engine had a spring which when held down released the compression in the engine so it was easy to crank. "So I got a big rock heavy enough to keep the handle down, wind away at the engine with both hands until it kicked over and then quickly tip the rock off." With the stolid old diesel thumping away driving the bore pump Alma would continue on her way to Turkey Creek.

Several hours later, on her way home, she would stop by the bore, turn off the fuel tap on the pump and wait for the engine to thump slowly to a halt. Then topping up the tank from a can of diesel she had packed in along with all the other essentials for travelling, she left the pump in readiness for next time. One travelled at one's peril without extra fuel, water, tools and some food. Turkey Creek was relatively close but breakdowns and lengthy holdups were always a possibility.

"There'd be people from Mabel Downs, Texas Downs and all around and we'd have a great smoko. Nan Langridge would make cakes, everyone would come with something, fresh meat, vegetables from the garden, fruit, whatever they had and share it around. One day Nan made a chocolate cake which hadn't cooked to the centre. When they cut it all the middle was still runny and she never lived it down. The men teased her each time saying they wondered if her chocolate cakes all had a 'mud spring' in them." The hospitable Langridge family often gathered the locals together for a party and Turkey Creek was a lively centre.

In the early 1960s Patsy McMahon who had become firm friends with the Lilly family was engaged to be married and invited Maureen to be her bridesmaid. On the day of their first visit to the Bow, the McMahons had made arrangements to get fuel on their way through Nicholson, one of the string of stations owned by the English Vestey family. The bookkeeper at Nicholson, George Appelbee, had seen to the refuelling. Pasty and he had met several times since that first encounter and decided they were in love. They married in March 1962 at the Catholic church in Halls Creek, with a reception at the Kimberley Goldfields Hotel.

George applied successfully for a new job as Main Roads Board secretary of Halls Creek. Soon after he and Patsy took up residence in Halls Creek, the Main Roads Boards were being converted into shire councils, so George was made shire clerk. Sam Lilly was appointed to the position of shire president. George developed a great respect for him. "I'd known Sam and the family casually but when Sam became president of the Halls Creek shire and we worked together I really got to know him well."

Patsy tells the story of how she and George and the McMahons joined the Lilly camp at the Wyndham Races that year. "We'd all set up camp and Maureen and I had got dressed and gone down to look at the horses on the track. Someone said, ooh, look at that black smoke! Someone must be burning some tyres. We looked and it seemed to be coming from the Lilly camp." The whole camp with everyone's belongings was burnt to a cinder. "Mum and Dad's caravan was alright and so were their clothes but Mum lost her little dog. Mrs Lilly's got away. All we had was what we stood up in. All our ball gowns were gone. We picked through the ashes and found little bits we could recognise as belonging to us."

The meatworks rallied with mattresses and bedding and people in the town gathered clothes for the camp. "We put a big tarpaulin down with the mattresses on it and camped on that." No one ever knew what started the fire. It could have been a live ash from a fire or a cigarette butt carelessly cast away, but it made the Wyndham Cup a big loss for the Lillys and Appelbees that year.

With the main road to Halls Creek passing close by, road works and council matters in general were always part of life at the Bow. Sam's appointment as Shire President of Halls Creek placed him in a position wherein he could try and introduce improvements. "As soon as I was sixteen I used to drive Dad to Halls Creek for his meetings so he could have a few drinks with the men and enjoy himself," says Alma. Two hundred kilometres each way on the old dirt track meant hours of driving and it was in that time that Sam talked and Alma learnt. "Dad talked about politics and the running of councils and all sorts of things. He got me very interested in politics. He never stopped learning and he never stopped teaching us. He used to say, if you want to learn something ask or get them to show you but don't let on you don't know." Alma loved those trips when she could talk one to one with her father with whom she felt a great rapport.

The Halls Creek Shire Council Chambers was a rough tin shed some twenty feet by twenty feet. Three were corrugated iron and the fourth was stacked forty four gallon drums. In one corner was a desk where the council's executive and clerical work was carried out and the rest of the shed was given over to dingo scalps in varying stages of putrefaction. "There were hundreds and hundreds of them for which bounties had been paid to the cattle stations." They were dry salted so they could be preserved for when the local government auditor called on his annual visit.

Sam and Maggie visited the Appelbees one evening and Sam said, "These dingo scalps are starting to get up my nose. I think something should be done about it." That was the night when

The fact that Halls Creek was a remote township with some thirty residents hundreds of miles from anywhere did not lead to any relaxation of formality in the presentation of debutantes in 1962.

new premises were first mooted and with the approval of other Council members the Council borrowed £20,000. "That was a lot of money in those days and we had to do a lot of work ourselves to save what we could. We had to cart in thousands of cubic yards of sand from the river for the foundations." George recalls the community effort. "Sam had a little tractor with a front end loader, and a bucket, and the Civil Aviation had a tip truck they kindly loaned. We had no compacting equipment so Sam's little tractor went backwards and forwards thousands of times to create a pad with a suitably hard surface." The building slowly took shape under the direction of the builder, Vos Volodka.

Sam and Maggie decided to buy Goose Hill, which had once been a Durack holding named Ascot, from another pioneer, Bob Skuthorpe. Goose Hill was not a large station compared with the Bow or others in the region but it was very close to Wyndham and the idea was to use it as a fattening paddock to finish off cattle that walked in from the Bow. When they bought it, it was a going concern with some fifteen hundred head of cattle on it and cost them £32,000 or $64,000. When the Lillys took over, the large dam at the front was nearly dry and as the Ord River is tidal and therefore salty the cattle could not drink it. Sam was obliged to buy two water tanks on trailers and cart the water for the stock from Parry's Lagoon until the dam filled again in the wet. A grown beast will drink on average some 40 litres of water per day so Sam was committed to an all day every day water carting job for months on end. Fencing on the property was poor and the plan to keep Bow cattle there to fatten was not a success. It was strange country to them and without good fences, they simply began to head home towards the Kimberley Hills.

Sam at this time was extremely busy. He and George had to attend a meeting of Shire Council heads in Perth. While in Perth George bought a Ford Utility. It so happened that Patsy was in hospital in Perth awaiting the birth of their first child and Sam was most entertained by George's solicitude. "Everywhere we went we had to stop when George saw a telephone box so he could ring the hospital and see how Patsy was going." Patsy was delivered of a son whom the Applebees named Mark.

George drove home from Perth with Sam: "We couldn't see any point in going home with an empty vehicle so we filled the back with stuff for the new shire office. We were up driving on the old, old road from Port Hedland to Broome only a few hundred yards from the ocean. It was only one lane and terrible condition. About midnight we saw lights coming. We couldn't pass and nor could they. Sam knew the man, a local pastoralist, so we unrolled our swags between the cars, lit a fire and got out a bottle of scotch." Sam and the man talked for hours but George nodded off. "I was first up and when I went to roll my swag there were thousands of centipedes underneath. I let out a yakkai and woke the others. When they rolled their swags there were thousands under theirs too. They must have come up for the warmth but there was not one in any of the swags!"

Sam's appointment as President of the largest shire in Australia meant the Lillys found themselves involved in hitherto unthought of activities. They entertained overseas dignitaries interested in the problems of local government and in 1962, the Governor of Western Australia when he and his party visited. The Bow joined their fellow stations in hosting the Vice Regal visitors to meals and overnight stays.

At the Halls Creek Race Club Ball in September 1962 Maureen and Alma made their debut. It was carried out with as much attention to detail and protocol as a similar event in a large city. The girls in their glamorous white dresses were presented to the Bishop of the Kimberleys, by the matron of honour. Eight young men, sons of Kimberley pioneers, were their gallant partners. In spite of the isolation, the parents made sure that the young people of the region were not deprived of events that youth in other parts of Australia took for granted.

Alma laughingly recalls the fashions at one Halls Creek ball. "We bought our dresses from Boan's catalogue. On the front of the catalogue was a ball frock with a round neck, no sleeves and nipped in at the waist and flared out at the knee. It was available in pink or white. Eight women rocked up wearing the same dress and there weren't more than fifty people there. Most were white but I remember Mum's was pink." There would have been a preponderance of men at the gathering so out of perhaps twenty women nearly half wore the identical style. Few of those big hearted women of the outback would have given it a second thought. Exclusiveness had never been a feature of catalogue shopping and it was the get together and the fun that counted. "Dad and Tom Quilty were great mates and they'd sit together and talk. Tom played the musical saw. There was always some trickery going on and Tom used to invite the girls to sit on a chair beside him." Great was the men's mirth when the young women, feeling so ladylike in their ball gowns gracefully accepted the gallant Tom's invitation and sank with a swirl of taffeta and lace into the proffered chair to the accompaniment of a long and loud rude noise for which they appeared to be responsible. "He had one of those fart cushions on the seat. I remember when he caught Lurline Norton!" It would be highly likely that Lurline remembers it too.

Maggie speaks nostalgically of the days when all the stations in the Kimberley functioned as working units supporting families both white and black. "Halls Creek was a gay little place at race time and Christmas time in those days. There were families on the stations and lots of people around the town."

Although the gold rush at Halls Creek was almost a "flash in the pan" Maggie also speaks of the gold fossicking in the area. "The Aborigines did a lot of fossicking with pack donkeys out around the Willy Willy and the Mary out towards the desert and they used to get a lot of gold. One woman even picked up a nugget in the street in town."

Maggie often went to Halls Creek with Sam, taking the opportunity to visit Patsy while George and Sam worked on the new premises. On one homeward journey they were almost half way back to the Bow only to find the Ord River was up. "We sat down for about three days waiting for it to go down. We had one old blackfella and Maureen's old nurse girl Cuppatea with us. They'd come for the ride and a visit to their people." Maggie was fed up with sitting around getting nowhere and tempers started to fray. "We were all starting to starve. Sam got out his rifle and tried to shoot a turkey. The place was all green after all the rain and there was a big flock of them. He banged away with his Army issue .303 and didn't hit one. The noise was terrible. In the end I said to him 'Why don't you throw the bloody thing at them!'" Maggie didn't have a lot of faith in Sam's marksmanship.

Intense hunger led to intense thinking about a way to get across the river and home. To drive through the water without drowning the engine was impossible. If only the car was just a little higher in the water they could make it. An idea was born. "Sam, the old blackfella, Cuppatea and I cut a lot of logs and pushed them up under the car body and stretched the springs as high as we could. This lifted it up just high enough to get across without stalling the engine."

In 1963 Queen Elizabeth was to visit Kununurra to open the diversion dam for the Ord River Scheme. The new township of Kununurra was created to serve the scheme and as Sam was president of the shire the Lillys were guests at all important functions. The site for the salubrious occasion was a bare patch of ground that would one day become the palm lined entrance to the country club.

To have the Honour of Meeting
His Excellency The Governor - General
The Right Honourable Viscount De L'Isle
V.C., P.C., G.C.M.G., G.C.V.O.

His Excellency The Governor
and Lady Kendrew
request the pleasure of the company of
MR. AND MRS. E.J. LILLY
at a Garden Party
at
Government House, Perth
Wednesday, 3rd March, 1965, at 4 p.m.

Lounge Suit

...cretary, Government House, Perth

Cr. S. LILLY.
President.
HALLS CREEK SHIRE COUNCIL.

The President and Councillors
OF THE
Shire of West Kimberley
DESIRE THE PLEASURE OF THE COMPANY OF
Mr. & Mrs. S. Lilley
at the official opening of the
"Civic Centre"
by the Honourable Leslie Logan, M.L.C.
Minister for Local Government
on Saturday afternoon, 3rd October, 1964
at 3.00 o'clock.

GOVERNOR-GENERAL'S VISIT, 1965
№ 4381
ADMIT MRS. E.J. LILLY
(One only)
to the
GARDEN PARTY
at Government House, Perth, on Wednesday,
3rd March, 1965, at 4.00 p.m.

ROYAL VISIT, 1963 № 3730
ADMIT
MRS. E. J. LILLY
(One only)
to the
EVENING GARDEN PARTY
at Government House, Perth, on Monday
25th March, 1963, at 8.30 p.m.
66240/12/62—500

On the occasion of the opening of the completed Parliament House by
His Excellency the Governor of Western Australia
Major General Sir Douglas Kendrew
K.C.M.G., C.B., C.B.E., D.S.O.
WESTERN AUSTRALIA
The President of the Legislative Council
and
The Speaker of the Legislative Assembly
request the pleasure of the company of
E.J. LILLY, ESQ. AND MRS. LILLY
at Parliament House, Perth,
on Monday, 23rd March, 1964, at 3.15 p.m.
R.S.V.P. TO THE CLERK OF THE PARLIAMENTS
BY 9TH MARCH, 1964.

To have the Honour of Meeting
Her Majesty The Queen
and
His Royal Highness The Duke of Edinburgh
His Excellency The Governor
and The Honourable Lady Gairdner
request the pleasure of the company of
MR. AND MRS. E.J. LILLY
at an Evening Garden Party
on Monday, 25th March, 1963, at 8.30 p.m., at
Government House, Perth
R.S.V.P. to
The Private Secretary, Government House, Perth
Dinner Jacket
Lounge Suit
Long or Short Dress

The modicum of accommodation in tiny Kununurra was taken up by visiting dignitaries. The Shire President and his lady came in from Bow River, a day's drive over dirt track and met The Shire Clerk, George Applebee and his wife Patsy at the Denham River Bridge. The Lillys and the Applebees carried their swags and other items down under the bridge and set up camp. The only difference from the usual requirements for a stock camp was that formal attire to meet the queen was packed instead of spare pants and shirts. They had a fire going in no time, the billy was on the boil and life in the shade under the bridge was very pleasant. "Nobody could see us," Maggie says, "and we had our bath in the river." George remembers that at the time the river water was as clear as crystal. When the time came to dress, formal frocks and suits were removed from the dust proof wrappings and soon the Lillys and the Applebees emerged from under the bridge attired in all their finery. They climbed up the bank to the road and walked to their cars parked in the shade under a tree. In minutes they joined their fellow V.I.P.s to meet the Queen. "Then," says Maggie, "we drove over to meet her again in Broome a couple of days' later. It was terribly hot." Maggie was fascinated by the Queen, not for her Royal Status but by her comments. "She was so concerned about the country people and the problems they were having at the time. She knew all about it and was genuinely upset by it."

In 1962 when the Wyndham Races came round again Sam was becoming disillusioned with the sport. He had endeavoured to improve the quality of racing by bringing in professional jockeys from the South. It may well have lifted the standard of race riding but unfortunately this also attracted bigger money and professional tricks of the trade. Sadly for Sam the bush race meetings lost the priceless element of fun and he ceased to take part in the game. It made no difference to Maggie for whom horse racing was a passion. Over the years her horses had left a trail of triumphs in Wyndham, Derby, Broome, Fitzroy Crossing and Halls Creek with cups, trophies and bracelets filling every cabinet and shelf in the homestead. At the Wyndham Meeting, Alma and Maureen were introduced to a couple of attractive young men in town from the stations for Race Week. They were two friends from South Australia working in the Northern Territory, Bob Lowe and Jim Coulthard. Bob Lowe and Alma Lilly were attracted to each other and it wasn't very long before they decided to marry. In August, 1965 when Alma was nineteen, Sam and Maggie had the first of their children's weddings to plan. Patsy Appelbee was matron of honour and Maureen the bridesmaid with Bob's old mate Jim Coulthard as best man. At that stage Sam had a part share in the historic Six Mile Hotel where the wedding reception was held. The young couple was offered the management of Goose Hill. Romance was in the air and at the wedding a new courtship began when Maureen and Jim decided to keep company.

The newlyweds set up a camp at Goose Hill while a new homestead was built for them.

Sam and George and their fellow councillors had the intense satisfaction of seeing the Halls Creek Shire Chambers become a reality and in 1965 the Minister for the North West, Charles Court, later Sir Charles, and his entourage of officials visited the town. George recalled their concern, "We still had very little money and our biggest worry when we received word that the Minister and his party were coming was how to pay for their travel expenses. There was a big sigh of relief when we found out the Government was footing the bill for everything!" There was a big gathering of district people to attend the official opening, followed by a gala ball. Mr Court unveiled a plaque containing the names of Sam and George and the council members to commemorate the occasion. During the evening George received a signal from Sam, "Sam gave me the nod so I went outside and we sat on an old grader tyre in the middle of the yard. Sam was a proud man at that moment. It was a big milestone for Halls Creek. Sam said 'George it's a terrific thing the Council has done and I'm proud of them. It doesn't matter what the future brings they can't take away the names on that plaque.'"

George and Sam had formed a friendship and respect that lasted through the years. "When Sam spoke at council meetings in the Kimberley he never blew things out of proportion and whatever he said came straight from the heart. It made people sit up and take notice of whatever he was saying. He was a very sincere, honest and down to earth basic man. As the shire clerk I used to get very frustrated and Sam would talk to me in cool calm sensible language and in the end it always worked out. I respected him as a man and as shire president he was a gentleman."

In 1966, Cyclone Joy struck the region and dumped heavy rain on the area surrounding the Bow. There was no doubt that the Bow River would flood and in the homestead feverish activity took place with Maggie and Maureen stacking goods as high as possible. "We then loaded up the truck and took it across the watercourse to high ground." Two grader men were working on the road and were caught by the rising water. From their vantage point everyone watched until darkness fell, wondering what the fate of the two men would be. The sound of the rushing water dominated the night hours. The families huddled on the hill watched the flickering light of a hurricane lamp that the grader men had hung on the branch of a bottle tree. It went out and the roar of water indicated the continuing rise of the river.

Weary worrying hours dragged by but finally the sky began to lighten. Through the gloom they could see that the river had gone right down. The sound had diminished in the early hours and what they hoped was happening was now revealed. Maureen organised a fording party. "We took a rope and tied it around each one of us and crossed the watercourse."

The grader was still in place but the boab with the hurricane lamp had been washed away. To everyone's relief the men were still clinging on to the top of the grader where a sheet had been stretched to provide shade for the driver. Their gaunt faces attested to the night of terror they had endured. Both had climbed as high as they could on the vehicle and clung like limpets to the steel frame through the hours of darkness. They could see nothing and as the river rose beneath them they had no way of knowing how much higher it would get. At any moment they could have been torn from their steel frame and carried away in the roaring torrent. They did not know if they would survive the night. Their terror increased from time to time as every so often gravel would be eroded from under the grader by the rushing water and the big machine would settle to one side or the other as the tyres sank into the space. Then they sensed a drop in the level but could still see nothing in the pitch dark and they simply clung on doggedly. The sounds of voices coming towards the grader was music to their ears. The two men could hardly move after their taut muscles had spent hours in almost the one position. With painful movements they eventually climbed down to the driver's platform and then slowly into the water where proffered hands both black and white steadied their descent.

With the grader men safe, it was time for the family to investigate what damage had been done to the homestead. It was with enormous relief Maggie and Maureen found the water had stopped just short of the homestead, but a great deal of Maggie's garden had gone down the river. Many shrubs, fruit trees and vegetables had disappeared but the worst loss in the garden was her precious lemon trees. As they walked around surveying the damage they realised that all the pigs were gone; all except one lonely little orphan who had survived the flood and came trotting to greet them, grunting and oinking his relief and welcome.

Chapter IX

Back to the Six Mile

Life on Bow River Station returned to normal after the flood. Sam turned up a couple of days later having failed reach to the Greenvale stock camp. The homestead was a hive of activity restoring articles to their rightful place in the store room, righting fences and filling washaways in the vegetable garden.

Preparations were in hand for another wedding celebration in August 1966. The Lilly's elder daughter, Maureen and Jim Coulthard were to be married. By August each year the muster was over and people on the stations could contemplate some social life in town. The weather was at its best and after the months out in muster camps, people were ready for a well earned break. The Six Mile Hotel was again the scene of the celebrations and after the wedding reception the bride and groom went off for their honeymoon, a brief trip before they settled in to manage Lilla Creek, a property that had been in the Coulthard family for many years.

With both daughters gone the big Bow River homestead would seem empty indeed. Sam would miss Maureen, his wonderfully competent offsider on the station and for two years he'd deeply felt the absence of Alma who had helped with the big load of clerical work involved with running the station. Quite apart from the practical considerations, he sorely missed their company. The years when all the family surrounded him were the happiest times but Sam was the first to acknowledge they had to have a life of their own and as long as they were happy, so was he.

The Bow underwent some form of improvement every year and at this point it had over twenty sets of cattle yards, fences, dams and bores. Maggie's childhood friend, Sandy Cole had become a much sought after bore sinker working wherever he was needed in the Top End and it was he who came to the Bow whenever another bore needed to be sunk. From his first visit when he put down the bore up behind the old homestead to replace the ancient one that had been in use since the 1890s, he had watched the Bow change. It had evolved from the fenceless miles of country made up of Turkey Creek, Greenvale and Adavale to the first class operation it was in the late 1960s. Maggie and Sam had every reason to be proud of their achievements over thirty years. "In the early years we never wasted money. If we went into Wyndham we didn't stay at a hotel. We took our swags and camped at the Marsh." Almost everything they earned went back into improvements and by this time the Bow was carrying well over ten thousand head of cattle.

They had joined the top operators in the cattle industry with an improved marketing strategy of

(Lilly collection)

MINE HOSTS, SAM AND MAGGIE LILLY SHARING A CONVIVIAL MOMENT WITH MEMBERS OF THE BAND AT THE SIX MILE IN 1975.

turning off cattle in peak condition at short notice. The station had purchased its own road train which they named "Belle of the Bow". Most of the big stations had their own road trains to move cattle. It would only carry 150 to 170 head per time rather than a mob of a thousand or fifteen hundred walking bullocks which could take the road at once, but delivery now took a matter of hours and the train could return in short order for another load. No longer was it necessary for the owners to send cattle to market or meatworks, leaving their station of origin in the best condition the management could achieve only to arrive at their destination weary from the long trip and often wasted even further by lameness and hard conditions. In the old times the mobs had the time and opportunity to come in contact the highly contagious tick fever and pleuro which could decimated them. It was an uphill battle even at the best of times. Breath taking as the sight of a huge mob of cattle on the stock route may have been, it was almost a thing of the past. On the road train any loss of condition was negligible, so there were more kilos across the scales, losses if any were minimal, wages for many men over weeks and months were saved and the cheque in payment to the vendor came in the mail in days instead of months.

Kevin who was now helping on the station was coming up to the age of nineteen. He was a good stockman, and Maggie found he shared her love for racing. Maggie was always proud to describe her son's skills as a horseman; "Kevin was never a rough rider; not interested in riding the buckjumpers but he never let a beast get the better of him in the muster. He'd go over anything and everything to get it. I had a couple of horses trained up for him that were older but still had a year's racing in them, Panto Boy and Zamie. He did alright and won a lot of races."

He was doing all right elsewhere too. Kevin had met Georgina, a girl from Perth who was staying with relatives and working in Wyndham. Kevin and his young sweetheart were married in June the year Kevin was twenty two. Maggie, Sam, Alma and Alma's two year old daughter Jodie went to Perth for the wedding. "They had the reception at a big old place called the Palace Hotel where all the Kimberley people used to stay when they went to Perth. It isn't there any more." Maggie's tone is regretful. So many of the places that held happy memories of old times and friends have vanished from the scene.

Sam had recently been honoured by his appointment as a justice of the peace and with this came more community commitment. The Bow was in good heart at the time but always demanding and Sam was wearying of it. He was ready to hand over to a younger generation and move into Wyndham to the Six Mile Hotel in which he now had full ownership having purchased his partner Conlan's portion.

For all the Lillys the 1970s were years of change and upheaval. About the time they took over the Six Mile, Alma found she was again in the early stages of pregnancy. It was at this point that her husband Bob left her for the sixteen year old German girl employed to help in the house. Without a husband, Goose Hill was no joy to Alma. Station life for the sake of it was not for her and she was greatly relieved to be free of it when Kevin and his bride Georgina took over the property.

Maureen and Jim with their two small children came home and assumed management of the Bow and Sam and Maggie went south to Adelaide to be with Alma following the birth of her second child. Alma had bought a house and was planning to stay, but not long after her son Todd was born, she sold the house and came back to her family and her old home town.

Maggie and Sam had taken up fulltime residence at the Six Mile and that gave Maggie no pleasure whatsoever. However, they had good staff and both Sam and Maggie still spent a great deal of time moving between Goose Hill and the Bow giving a hand wherever they were needed.

Alma tells a story of Sam when he was out on the Bow keeping an eye on things. The only contact was by radio and Maggie and Sam had a "sked" at midday. A sked is a prearranged time for contact. During these sessions Maggie and Sam would discuss the day's happenings. Everyone on the same frequency heard the conversations and privacy was non-existent. The discussion for a particular day continued, "Maggie, what do you want to do about these ducks that are getting out? — Over." Maggie's reply: "Well, go around and fill up all the holes and tie up the wire... [Maggie fussed on and on] — over." Sam, very frustrated by now "I've already done all that — over." Maggie made a few more suggestions. Thoroughly annoyed by now Sam shouted "For Christ's-sake, Woman", (he always called her that when he was angry) "For Christ's-sake, Woman, has it ever occurred to you that the bloody birds might become airborne? — OVER!" Maggie's management of the fowl yard was a always source of exasperation to him. He maintained she had some turkeys that were so old he'd have to make walking sticks for them.

Maggie and Sam had always worked together but had many a difference of opinion over the years. Maureen recalls that the greatest bone of contention was the Bow. "Mum always wanted to have a station and never wanted to leave it but by the time they did Dad absolutely hated it. He said it had taken the best years of his life." It worried the girls to see how frustrated and downhearted their father had become and they knew he yearned for a change.

Maggie in spite of her personal disappointments made the best of things and took a substantial share in caring for her two small grandchildren, Jodie and Todd. It was a time of close family involvement and Sam made sure that the little boy had a father figure from the very beginning. Alma said "Mum was marvellous really. She was there for me and at night she'd have the children

bathed and fed." Alma was working at the meatworks for a brief while and Maggie's care of the children was a blessing for the young single mother whose life had been so unexpectedly fragmented.

Now living at the Bow, Jim and Maureen worked as a team and maintained a high level of management with all the station people as it had always been since Maggie and Sam first formed the station. For some five years there was little change but in 1975 the situation altered in regard to the Aborigines' status and Pastoral Awards and the people on the Bow moved in to town. From then on Maureen and Jim ran it single handed and when they needed help Jim went in to Kununurra or Wyndham, 200 kilometres distant, to pick up a few men, paid them the appropriate award wage and took them back to town when the job was finished. It was very different from the old days on the Bow when all the workers, men or women, received a small wage all the year and everyone on the station was cared for.

When Maureen's children, Sonya and Rod, reached school age they were taught by the School of the Air, that wonderful institution by which countless isolated children were educated and learnt to communicate with the outside world. Maureen would take the radio which was hitched to a car battery out to the stock camp where they were working. The children sat in the shade on a rug with

Bird life abounds on Parry's Lagoon (Marglu Lagoon), near Wyndham. "It's a string of about three 'billy bongs' where we used to water the mob and camp when we drove cattle in to Wyndham," explains Maggie.

their school books and responded to a teacher giving lessons over a transceiver hundreds of miles away. The Coulthard children must have enjoyed one of the most spectacular and remote classrooms in the world; the wild and beautiful hills of the Kimberley. Everyone listened in to the lessons enjoying the stories and the children's interaction with the teacher, including their news items from home. These could be harmless or hilarious and some needed censoring. Maureen describes how Sonya attended meetings of the Brownies on School of the Air. "Sonya dressed in her Brownie uniform and sat in front of the radio. When Sonya called in, the Brownie leader would say "Good morning Sonya, how are you today? — Over," and she would reply "Good morning Brown Owl. I'm well thankyou — over." Brown Owl would ask "Are your shoes and belt polished, finger nails clean?" The children could have worn anything and their Leader Brown Owl would have been none the wiser, but that was not the point. The lone Brownies took it all very seriously and proudly followed rules to the letter. They were instructed on all sorts of crafts and were told what to have ready for the next meeting; maybe wild flowers for a collage which would be assembled by instruction from Brown Owl with the whole troop chatting with the teacher throughout the session. Although these children may not have had the same interaction as children in classrooms they became articulate and confident in expressing themselves. They became accustomed to

PRIME MINISTER, MALCOLM FRAZER SWAPPING YARNS WITH THE LOCALS. LEFT TO RIGHT: MAGGIE, UNKNOWN, MALCOLM FRAZER AND ALMA.

(Lilly collection)

forming mental images from instructions given by a disembodied voice and their imaginations were well developed at a very early age.

School of the Air still works in exactly the same way today and countless outback children on stations tune in for their lessons with specially trained teachers who lead them through the curriculum including subjects as ephemeral as painting classes.

To begin with Maggie and Sam ran the pub when the manager was on holidays and learnt something of the trade before it became a full time job. Sam enjoyed the pub life and Alma discovered she loved it too. "Dad was a very positive man. He would not have any trouble makers or shit stirrers around undermining things. He had very strong principles and a great tolerance." This must have been an enormous help in running a pub. "He would curl up one fist and bang it down on his other hand saying 'The principle of the matter is…' That's what drove him. Many times people took advantage of Dad as he was non-confrontational. He'd just walk away. He used to say 'don't waste your breath on such people because they won't listen to you.' "

"Dad always gave us great encouragement. He was the first one to tell us if we'd done a good job but also the first one to tell you if you'd stepped out of line. One night I had the 'flu and after working all day I was buggered. I got someone else to close the pub for me. Well, did I get a serve for that! It didn't matter how sick I was, it was my responsibility." Another father might have left a grown daughter angry and resentful but Sam always explained his reasons and if there were tears there was every chance he would cry too. "He was a very emotional man and not afraid to show it."

However, in spite of the close Father and daughter rapport, after a couple of years working together she and Sam discovered they had very different views on how an hotel should be run. "Right," said Sam "you take over." Sam made the lease over to Alma who became at twenty six one of the youngest female licensees in the state. "I loved the work and the activity."

Everything went well until one night when the pub was very busy and Alma was in the kitchen. Maggie called little Jodie and Todd over to have their bath. A friend heard Jodie yelling and ran to find her. "Lucky she ran in the right direction" said Alma. "She'd been grabbed from behind a tree by a young blackfellow. He was only in his teens but was over six feet tall. He'd grabbed Jodie and had her knickers off when my friend caught him. He'd been raised by a missionary but already had a long record for molestation of small white girls. That was when I realised that I could not carry on. A pub was no place to raise kids."

It was back to work at the pub for Sam who was kept busy thinking up new ideas to attract the patrons. One ploy was to import a band from Perth. The boys of the band were quite agreeable to the terms Sam presented. On several nights a week they would work as the band and the rest of the time they worked around the pub. This was very successful and the band that went by the name of "Shouse" was a great hit.

"We had a lot of fun at times and one time Dad put a notice out the front, "Topless Barmaids". This brought a great crowd. Everyone came to see. Wyndham had never had or expected to see "topless barmaids." At a certain point in the night "all the barmaids disappeared and the bar service was taken over by the men who'd removed their shirts! The men all played it up for all it was worth and the patrons took it all in good part."

"There was one dear old man, a bookie named Apples and his wife was named Ivy. Anyway, one night another bookie and Apples got into a fight in the bar. Apples had a great big tummy and when he got ready to throw a few punches, up came the fists, in came the tummy and down went his pants." Alma said "from then on, old Ivy had to shop very carefully for Apples' underpants just in case of a fight. She always bought ones with pink elephants and other designs just in case they'd be put on show. She wanted to be sure everyone would have something to look at when Apples pulled his belly in."

Alma decided on her first step in a new career that was destined to become a great success. With a friend named Vickie Sargeant she bought a shop in Wyndham called Molly's and they renamed it VA Agencies. "I mortgaged an insurance policy I had to start off and Mum and Dad were horrified. What experience had I had to start a dress shop? What experience did I have to be licensee of a pub? I asked them." Horrified though they might have been they backed her up in every way they could especially helping with the two children.

The long tradition of the Six Mile Pub was drawing to an end with the intrusion of bureaucracy. In the early days of the settlement The Six Mile Hotel was little more than a tin shed and a favourite "watering hole" for the drovers on their return from delivering their mobs of Kimberley cattle into the Port. In catering for its lusty, hard working, hard drinking clientele it was a much loved and well supported institution and a real blood house. In time a larger building was put up to cope with the increasingly heavy trade and but later it was partially destroyed by fire. Like the Phoenix, it rose from the ashes and during the rebuilding the loyal clients hardly noticed any reduction in the dispensation of grog. The building was rough and battered but no one worried about that. There were six cash registers for the six barmaids so they could keep up with the trade and it was said that the truckies always had terrible trouble "jumping the hurdle" at the Six Mile. There were no dress rules and Yakka singlets and shorts were common attire for the patrons. Humour was always welcome, bawdiness encouraged; some cartoonist drew a picture on the wall of a frowsy old tart with the caption "Take me, you fool — I'm yours!" For the lusty drinkers of the North, fights, hangovers and visits from the police were all part of the ambience.

The accommodation was made up of a number of portable buildings located at the rear. The Bureaucracy of the time decided to condemn the old Six Mile building and the Lillys were obliged

(Photo courtesy of Western Australian Newspapers Ltd)

WHEN KEVIN LILLY TOOK OVER GOOSE HILL THERE WERE MANY BULLS ON THE PROPERTY. THESE WERE SALEABLE TO THE MEATWORKS. BULL CATCHING IS A WILD AND RISKY BUSINESS BUT WELL WORTH THE EFFORT. WHERE POSSIBLE THE BULLS ARE MUSTERED AND YARDED USING FOUR WHEEL DRIVE VEHICLES. WHERE THIS IS NOT POSSIBLE THEY ARE CHASED, KNOCKED DOWN AND SECURED AND LATER PICKED UP BY TRUCK.

to demolish the old structure that had served its patrons so well for so long and put up a new one on the site. This was the fourth Six Mile Hotel built on the same spot and a far cry from the one where Maggie had begun her working life as a fourteen year old.

Sadly, the newly built pub was not a great success. Patronage fell away. The lusty workers' "watering hole" was replaced with something that had to conform with modern regulations. The old atmosphere, redolent of fights, booze ups, and the camaraderie of the cattle train drivers who succeeded the old time drovers was sanitised away. In 1979 the Wyndham Council bought it and it became a private club.

Maggie absolutely hated hotel work and when that was finished Sam impressed her even less by purchasing a house in Wyndham; town life did nothing for Maggie. Her heart was back at the Bow.

Sam was free of what had become yet another millstone and in spite of his obvious decline in health gave whatever help he could to all his family. Especially he welcomed the opportunity to give his grandson Todd more attention which time proved to be of lasting benefit in the boy's development. "He was wonderful to me in the business" said Alma. "He'd come over and see what needed to be done. He built shelves and all sorts of things and I really think he enjoyed it all. He had time to talk to people and having grown up in Derby in the town, he'd been used to company."

In 1980 Alma went to the Kununurra Races and was the victim of some fond matchmaking by her brother in law Jim Coulthard. "Jim introduced me to Ian Petherick who he said wanted to take me to the ball that night. I looked at Ian who had a big smile on his face and said 'yes'. Then I spent the rest of the day trying to work out how to get out of it. Anyway, Jim made sure I didn't and eight months later we had the wedding and it's been a very happy marriage."

Ian was a helicopter pilot who had done a lot of mustering on the Bow and became great friends with Maureen and Jim. He knew Maureen had a sister but until they met at the races had no idea that Alma's interest lay not in the land but in commerce and she was deeply involved with what was rapidly becoming a flourishing fashion business.

When Ian was a teenager, his father managed the East Kimberley properties of Carlton and Legune and then he took the position of Assistant Manager of Victoria River Downs in the Northern Territory. When his father went back to their home in Queensland at the bayside suburb of Redcliffe, Ian stayed on at "the Big Run", as Victoria River Downs is known, as a ringer in 1969-70. Then with a friend Wayne Browne, he went contract bull catching on the station. There were thousands of bulls on all the big stations that had eluded the musters for years and while cattle prices were good it was a worthwhile but risky occupation. Ian met with a serious accident and lost his leg. By the time he was flown to Darwin Hospital gangrene had set in and the amputation was more drastic than expected. However, Ian bounced back and back became head stockman at Pidgeon Hole, a Victoria River Downs out station. He then acquired a private helicopter license and mustered for the Hooker Corporation which owned Victoria River Downs in 1976. Ian already knew the huge run well from his experience as a ringer and could anticipate the likely behaviour and favourite haunts of the cattle. He was a most successful pilot and particularly proud of one achievement in bringing well over 1000 cattle in from Mt Sanford single-handed; no mean feat!

John Weymouth, who owned Helimuster, the world's biggest aerial mustering company based at V.R.D. approached Ian to fly for him. Ian and four other men went to Los Angeles in the U.S.A. to gain their commercial helicopter licenses. In the late seventies he was transferred to the Kimberley section of Helimuster, managed by his friend and colleague, Kerry Slingsby. When Ian and Alma were engaged, Kerry was asked to be best man.

Ian inherited a ready made family in the form of Jodie and Todd and later Alma presented him with a daughter they named Merrilie. Todd found a kindred soul in Ian who encouraged him in his passion for aircraft and flying.

Every year the Lilly family made an effort to get together on Christmas Day — in Wyndham or wherever they could best manage it. Sam was Father Christmas, as Maureen relates. "Alma had a boat and one year we met halfway at Dunham River. We'd covered the boat with water weed and Dad dressed up and came in to the shore in the boat and handed out presents." For the grand-children it was a most exciting event full of gifts, games and fun but it was a special day for everyone now and a part of very precious family recollections.

"Dad was a wonderful, funny grandfather. When any of the kids threw a tantrum, he would get down on the floor and throw one too. In no time they'd forgotten theirs they were so busy laughing at him!"

The Bow was in the capable hands of Maureen and Jim but not all station business can be conducted on the station itself so if they needed to go away at any time, Maggie would take over. The same applied to Goose Hill where Sam would step in as caretaker for Kevin and Georgina who by now had produced four children, three sons and a daughter Samantha. Great Grandma Elizabeth Lilly would have been very gratified to know that her little pride and joy, Kevin, the one and only male heir in the Lilly family perpetuated the male line through to the following generation.

Kevin was making a name for himself in bush racing circles. He won the first Kununurra Cup. The family were still at Goose Hill and Maggie used to go out and help Kevin with the bull catching but in general things were not turning out so well. Too many problems were arising. The cattle were running on the bird sanctuary area and that was not looked on with favour by the wild life authorities. A great many things conspired towards the Lillys leaving Goose Hill and in the end it proved a very costly business for the family. There was a great deal of cattle shooting and the property was badly infected with the noxious plant Parkensonia which spreads easily. Because it was a fishing area people tended to walk anywhere they pleased instead of using the weed free tracks and this exacerbated the wild proliferation of the prickly menace.

There were always so many animals and jobs around the stations, which could not be neglected, even for a day so Maggie's and Sam's willing assistance made for some welcome and necessary flexibility.

For years the cattle breeders of Australia were exhorted to produce more cattle. They were led to believe there was a bottomless market for beef but in 1978 it all came to a grinding halt. Talk then was of the "mountain of beef" in Europe. The cattle market collapsed almost overnight. Producers who may have received eighty cents a kilo were lucky to get eight cents, but costs remained the same. It broke many cattle breeders and those who managed to stay in the industry took years to recover. With the drought that followed in various parts of the country even more lost the battle. The Bow River Station was no exception. The Coulthards worked at picking up the pieces and in 1980 the Bow was sold. Maureen and Jim stayed as managers for a couple of months to start the new owners off and then left for Perth. It was time to see to the higher education of their children. They had no intention depriving their children of any opportunities to further themselves in life. They bought a block of land out of Perth and named it Bow Park, remaining there for some years whilst Sonya and Rod went to college.

Sam had always suffered from haemochromatosis, a genetic mutation that confuses the body's iron controls. Nicknamed "rust disease" it can cause many serious problems if left untreated. These include heart disease, arthritis, loss of energy, cirrhosis of the liver and liver cancer. Arthritis and loss of energy were two which afflicted Sam. Relief from the condition is achieved by giving frequent donations of blood to deplete the body's store of iron. His brother Toby had succumbed to the disease in his fifties. Maureen and Alma have both inherited the condition but the problem is better understood and managed now. People put Sam's condition down to his heavy smoking but Alma believes that like her own mild asthmatic condition causing a breathlessness, Sam had always suffered similarly and it took a toll on his heart. Arthritis in the hands causing constant pain added to his affliction.

Alma didn't know what to make of it. "People, including the doctor used to ask me 'what is wrong with Sam? He's not well.' And he wasn't, but he never said a thing to anyone except sometimes he'd say to me 'I'd just like to lie down and die.' All the years on the Bow had worn him out we knew, but later I discovered when helping with the housework that he was suffering haemorrhages."

Sam put off going to a doctor and undergoing tests as long as he could. Finally he and Maggie went to Darwin where it was discovered he had bowel cancer and an operation was the only option. "Dad rang me and although he didn't say it was life or death, he said I've been told it's a risk. It's something I have to do. I have to take that risk." Alma left Todd and with her six month old baby Merrilie flew to Darwin and arrived ten minutes before he was wheeled in to theatre. "Mum was crying, Dad was crying and he just hugged me." Sam knew it was possible he may not survive the surgery but after an operation taking much longer than expected, he did come through. A wondrous feeling of relief swept over Maggie and Alma who had sat waiting and watching a clock that hardly seemed to move; neither had spoken of it but both knew what a slim hope it was that Sam would survive the surgery. Sam was put in the intensive care ward and began to improve.

A boab tree typical of the Kimberly region.

Alma decided to fly home. Jodie was home from boarding school with Ian and she was anxious to see Sam so Alma put her straight on a plane to visit him in Darwin before she went back to school. Jodie was on the telephone to Alma almost immediately after arriving at the hospital. "Mum," her tone was urgent, "Pop's not in intensive care! They say he's got golden staph and he's not allowed to stay there. He's been put down in another ward and he's saying crazy things." Alma asked her to put Grandma on. "What's going on, Mum?" Maggie replied she didn't know; she didn't understand any of it.

"Ian was working for Helimuster at the time." As an aircraft hire firm it could charter fixed wing aircraft as well as helicopters. "So I rang and said I wanted to charter a plane. Couldn't afford it. Mum and I sat there for two days." Jodie, who was due back at boarding school in a few days, flew out of Darwin as Alma was flying in. "When I got there he was back in intensive care. He'd rallied a little at that point and sometimes he would wake up and talk to us. Kevin came up to visit and Dad, knowing Kevin would have cigarettes, asked for one. It took a bit to convince him he couldn't smoke in the intensive care ward." As a heavy smoker of long duration it was no wonder poor Sam took some convincing! "Mum and I had to laugh one day when he asked 'Are you keeping an eye on me, you two?' We assured him we were and off to sleep he went." A couple of days later Sam took a turn. "It was in the evening and it was terrible. He was pulling off his oxygen mask and I was trying to put it back on, thrashing around in the bed. I was so upset I asked the nurse couldn't they give him something to settle him. They explained with the golden staph which he had contracted from the intensive care ward after his operation and his bad heart that it was not advisable. I eventually made the decision that the state he was in would be equally dangerous so requested they give him something. He settled and went to sleep so Mum and I went away for the night."

When we came back the next morning a nurse came to the waiting women and said, "You're not to feed him anymore. Just leave him alone."

To Alma, this was as "red rag to a bull!" "Are you telling me we've just got to leave him to lie there and die?" Alma tracked down the doctor "whom we knew well from his Wyndham days, Dr. Tony Noonan who was wonderful to Dad." Sam had come through the operation so well that Dr. Noonan went to visit friends at Lissadel and handed his patient over to the care of another doctor. "It was then that they discovered Dad had golden staph." By the time Dr Noonan returned to the hospital Sam was sinking. It seemed there were two people in the hospital with the infection, Sam and a younger patient but there was only enough medication in Darwin for one. Alma went again to the doctor asking for medication to be obtained "but it was too late. I was so upset I could not stay and watch him die, nor could I say goodbye. My last words to him were 'See you later, Dad'. Mum stayed all through. She just sat with him until the end which came on the 7th of June, 1983. Maggie never left Sam's bedside for the six weeks of his hospitalisation, apart from brief breaks to eat and sleep. When he died she rang and said 'I'm coming home'".

Alma wanted to see her father once more so Ian took both her and Maggie back to see Sam. Alma has always been glad she made that last visit. It left her with a memory of a man who had relinquished his burden in life and was at last free of those final days of torment when fever racked his exhausted body and his mind was distorted by delirium. "He was so much at peace. He looked twenty years younger." Earlier Dr Noonan had explained to Alma the urgency of the operation. "Dad's bowel cancer had gone too far and he would have died a painful death within six months. He knew the risk but reckoned Dad was too nice a person to suffer an end like that."

Sam has been dead seventeen years but his daughters' grief lives on and tears flow freely as they talk of their loss.

Sam's body was brought back to Wyndham for burial and the service was held at the church. At the back of the church behind all the other mourners stood the tall dark silently grieving Tim Timms, Sam's head man, immaculate in his white shirt and black trousers paying his own special respects.

The cortege moved to the cemetery where it was met by the people of the Bow River Station accompanied by their children and joined by many others from Kimberley stations. They carried plastic bags full of wild flowers that they'd spent hours gathering in the hills. No sooner had the minister begun his quiet graveside service than the Aboriginal people began their own mourning. The noise was overwhelming with cries of "Our Boss is gone! Our poor Boss is dead! With the wailing and weeping not a word the minister uttered could be heard. "Some people at the service wanted us to tell them to shut up and go away." Maggie would not hear of it. She understood the honour that they were bestowing on their beloved "Cham" and that, deafening and unnerving though it may have been for the other mourners, they must be allowed to voice their grief and respect in their own way. For them to attend the funeral of a white man was almost unheard of. "Just leave them alone, I told them" she said. In the words of Sam's obituary in the newspaper, *The Kimberley Echo*, "It was a fitting tribute to a man who gave so much and took so little in his seventy one years in the Kimberley."

CHAPTER X

The Long and Winding Road

AFTER FORTY EIGHT YEARS of married life Maggie was once more alone. She had never been so alone. Before she knew Sam there had always been the strong loving presence of her mother Hannah. A huge and frightening void stretched before her. From the time of their marriage in 1935 Sam had always been there. They had struggled through the years to achieve their goals and in spite of their differing opinions it was a close relationship. For ten years before the birth of their children, they'd worked together day in and day out in the isolation of the bush, cooked by a campfire and slept under the stars in their swags with the minimum of creature comforts, in love and in harmony. When they brought their children into the world they raised them to respect honesty, decency and integrity.

These children were adults now with children of their own and Maggie had every reason to be proud of them. They were all at probably the most demanding phase of their own lives, helping growing children through school, college and university, building businesses and security for the future. She could only hope to have a small share in each of their lives and keep on trying to achieve the impossible: fill the empty space that Sam once occupied.

Maggie had to take stock of what remained. The inestimable attributes of courage, spirit, good health and energy were hers in abundance. Her children and grandchildren were close and she had countless friends. Good friends, some she had grown up with and others who came later but there was a priceless continuity and loyalty involved. With their loving support life regained its momentum.

Alma, now living in Kununurra, decided to sell VA Fashions in Wyndham and concentrate on her recently acquired shop in Kununurra. With Todd at school, a young baby, Merrilie, and Ian occupied with his trucking business, the regular trips from Kununurra out to the old town consumed hours each day and proved too much to handle. As it was, local demand and tourism were increasing every year in Kununurra. Alma and Ian built a home at Packsaddle, a few kilometres out of the town and invited Maggie to move from Wyndham and take up residence in the nearby cottage they had lived in during the new home's construction. It was just a matter of time before Alma expanded her enterprise to encompass several other businesses and was busier than ever.

(Petheric collection)

Back, Left to Right: Elder daughter, Jodie Young, Merrilie Petherick and Todd Petherick. Front: Ian and Alma Petherick. The Pethericks in Kununurra are involved in several businesses including Alma's V & A Fashions, which has gone from strength to strength since she began it with a partner in Wyndham years ago.

(Lilly collection)

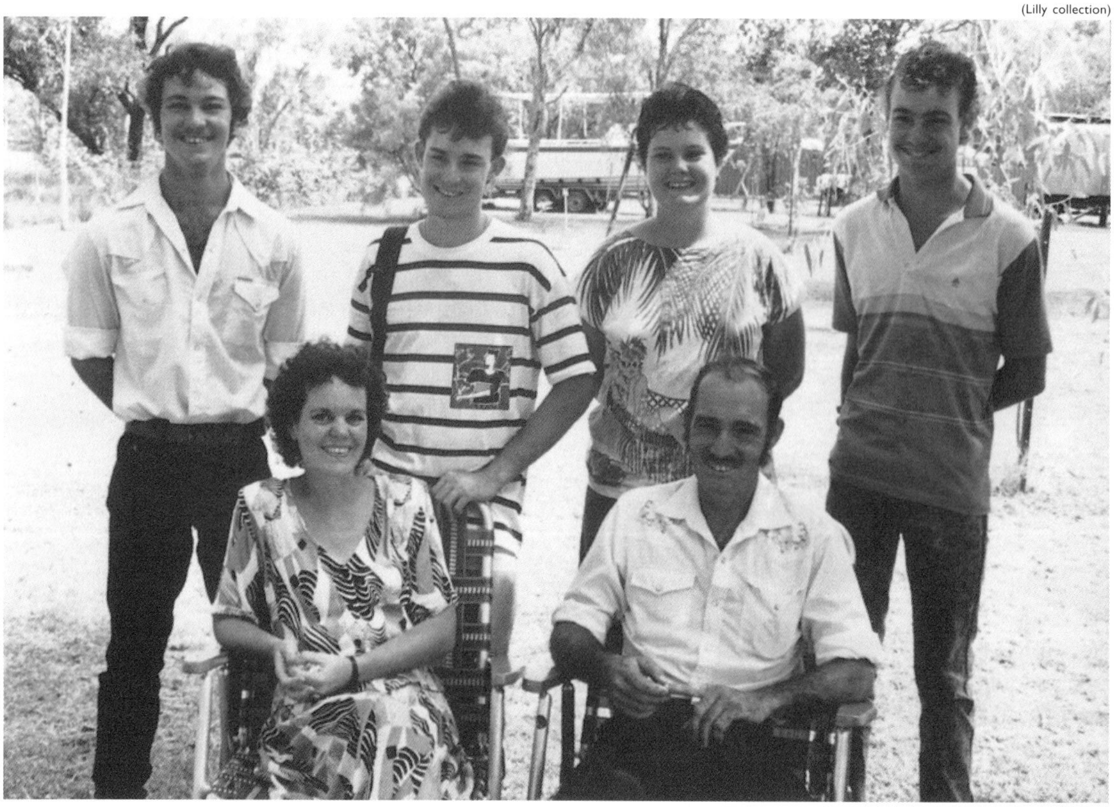

Kevin and Georgina Lilly with their family of four, the three boys Anthony, Shayne and Jason and daughter Samantha.

The Bow River Station was again for sale and Alma and Kevin tried to repurchase it. The lease on Goose Hill was nearly at an end and Kevin and his family would have to be gone in twelve months. There would be no further tenancy permitted to cattle enterprises. There were 3000 cattle on the station and somewhere would have to be found for them. Alma was prepared to put up her businesses as security and money to the tune of $420,000 to buy back the Bow. What actually happened was quite different, as Alma describes. "The Government had given the Bow River family of Tim Timms a loan of $250,000 loan and a $200,000 grant with which to purchase the Bow River Station. At this stage the families, after living in town for nearly a decade and not working, were ill equipped to run a station. They employed a white contractor to muster cattle on the property and he sold everything he could with no consideration for the future of the herd. Today, Tim Timms and his son Rammie still live on the property along with a few others but the bulk of the family spend most of their time in town on the grog. What was once a profitable business and cattle station is now subsidised by ATSIC in the form of grants and by the Commonwealth Development Employment Programme. Tim and some of the others have taken to joining Tony Oliver in Darwin to do dot painting." Kevin was desperately disappointed. The land is now the home of the Warmun people.

Following Alma's suggestion that Maggie come to Kununurra, Maggie sold the house in Wyndham at a huge loss and moved to the thriving young town fed by the new irrigation areas on the Ord River Scheme. "It was a nice house and Sam and I spent a fair bit on it in improvements but houses in Wyndham aren't worth much any more."

For some years the meatworks — which had sustained the town of Wyndham since 1915 — had been undergoing great difficulties in maintaining production, not helped in the least by the 1978 beef crisis. Union strikes in the late seventies and the eighties finally broke the back of the struggling business. In 1985 the meatworks ceased to operate and the little town almost died with it, so there is very little demand for housing. A crocodile farm now exists on part of the site of the old Meatworks but where once the mighty multi-floored building stood is a half burnt out shell surrounded by the debris of collapsed sheds and piles of rubble. In the charred hulk of the main site sits the huge engine that drove the machinery, an indication of the immensity of the operation that once existed.

Wyndham now has a circular jetty and it is once more a port for live cattle export. No longer do the cattle run down the hill into a race near the site of the old Wyndham Hotel and on to Anthons Landing to board the ships as they did prior to 1919. Now they arrive in the giant road trains that rumble past the derelict buildings, past the decaying yards and down to the jetty, driving on one end and then off the other after disgorging their loads onto the waiting ships.

What is left of the Meatworks only fifteen years since operations ceased is a desperately depressing sight, made more so when Maggie points to clumps of vegetation and bare patches of ground and says, "That's where the Theatre Garden was and here's where the basketball court was,... and the bunk house... and the ballroom where we had the dances and concerts... and the cafeteria... and the two up school... and the White House where they had parties for all the important visitors." Maggie gives no indication of sorrow when showing visitors the ruins where so much pertained to her own youth and happy times but the very sight of it all must evoke heartaches and memories of incidents and people who dwelt in that lively past .

Once the decision to sell the house was reached, Maggie set about packing up the furniture and setting up in her new residence in Kununurra. Wyndham was a few hours drive from there but that was nothing to Maggie and if she wanted to visit old friends it was no problem. Once she settled in

(Sonja Tece collection)

THE GIRLS' CAMP AT VICTORIA RIVER DOWNS. LEFT TO RIGHT: SONJA COULTHARD, LIZ GRAHAM, MARY QUILTY, HEIDI ARMSTRONG, GEMMA CLAPIN AND MERAN HIGGINS. THE SIX GIRLS LED BY SONJA MADE UP ONE MUSTER CAMP. THE GROUP UNDERTOOK EXACTLY THE SAME WORK AS THE MEN'S MUSTERING CAMPS AND THEIR RECORD OF ACHIEVEMENT WAS AHEAD OF THE BOYS. SONJA WENT ON TO MANAGE OTHER STATIONS AND IS NOW WORKING WITH HER HUSBAND AT NICHOLSON STATION IN THE KIMBERLEY.

to Kununurra she became involved in many things, especially where the family needed her help. Alma speaks of the whole-hearted support Maggie was able to offer her at a most difficult time in business "In 1989 they built a row of new shops in Kununurra and Ian and I negotiated a loan to buy a new shop, when the interest skyrocketed. It was an additional $2200 per month fixed for two years. I had to think hard and I decided to take the business out to the Aboriginal communities." They'd load up the vehicle with whatever they thought was inviting to their clientele and drive the long distances to the various communities. "Mum used to come with me and help sell. She was very adventurous really and hated to sit down. She hated things like housework but she'd always help us do something." It was during one of these visits, to the Wave Hill community, that Maggie, who had lost touch with her childhood Aboriginal "brother" Jackie some years before caught, up with two of his grown children, Rosina and Rosita, both women retaining the name of Nicholson and their relationship to their aunt, Maggie. Jacky and his first wife Peggie had separated many years earlier and he had returned to Turner Station south of the Bungle Bungles close to the region of his birth, where he had remarried.

Alma did get through the bank squeeze with hard work augmented by the regular trips out to the communities to increase the turnover. Maggie, who threw herself wholeheartedly into the work, had been an immense help and enjoyed every minute of it. She was involved in doing something enjoyable and productive and by using up some her remarkable energy she was tired enough to sleep at night and subdue the harshness of her loss.

At the Pethericks home at Packsaddle are many magnificent mango trees. They were a small commercial proposition but the women had a better idea for distribution of some of the crop. Each

(Lilly collection)

A line up of Lillys. Left to Right: Jason Lilly, his father Kevin, Maureen Coulthard and Maggie. The occasion was the Centenary of Wyndham in 1986 and at seventy four, Maggie was back in the saddle at ease as ever with her beloved horses.

year when the fruit ripened Alma and Maggie would pack a vehicle with all the fruit it could hold and take it out to the communities at Turkey Creek, Frog Hollow and the Bow where an affectionate welcome awaited them. "Mum had a ball. She'd catch up with all the families and they'd bring out all the young ones to show to Yummun." Whilst Maggie was Yummun or Mother the old people referred to Alma as Gunou — "young one" — and tell her happily "We help grow em you all up."

Maggie began regular stays of two or three months in Perth every year. So many of her friends were living there and she spent many happy times with them, including their erstwhile horse trainer Joe Moore and his wife Margaret. Les and Maisie Wilde were there too. Les was the stepson of the Burts from the old Turkey Creek Police station. Patsy Appelbee who also missed her old Kimberley friends would take Maggie on a round of visiting and the irrepressible Maggie always had a riotously happy time.

In 1986 Maggie, Maureen, Kevin and his son Jason rode in the float parade to celebrate the Centenary of Wyndham. Maggie now 74 sat a horse with as much pride and style as ever. For this auspicious occasion the baker, Frank Cruttenden baked an enormous cake that Maureen described as "the size of a car trailer" and it was the subject of many a photograph. It had green and yellow candles and all the oldest residents were invited to cut the cake. These were Maggie, Cissie Leetong, Blue Lloyd and Joe Sommerfield. No one had more fun and memories to swap than the four senior citizens from the Kimberley township.

Jim and Maureen Coulthard were back in the North and after a time at Go Go Station, they moved to Victoria River Downs where they have remained. Jim is now general manager of production for Heytsbury's, which owns the station. Both the Coulthard children went to university before returning to station work and have inherited their grandmother's passion for horses and stock work. Rod, a champion rodeo rider, specialises in bareback bronc riding with considerable success attending fixtures on the Rodeo circuit on weekends and running the family property during the week.

After university, Sonya spent two years contract mustering at Go Go Station prior to working at Victoria River Downs. Jim Coulthard, one of Australia's leading cattlemen, instituted the Girls' Camp in which the young women carried out the same work as the men, mustering, castrating, branding etc. There was a great competitive spirit between the camps. Sonya was in charge of the girls' muster camp. It need not be supposed that the young women lost their femininity in the process; coarseness and rough behaviour were not accepted. Like Maggie, like her daughters and like her grandaughter Sonya, they were all able and efficient in anything their job, always considered a male province, demanded — but they kept their femininity and richly earned the respect and admiration of their fellow workers.

Both the girls' camp and the men's camp had a penalty box into which they paid fines. In the girls' case it was $1 for swearing and $5 for falling or being thrown from their horse. The men waived the swearing fine but paid their $5 for every fall. The girls had boyfriends in the men's camp but as everyone on muster worked from before dawn to well after dark every day for several weeks at a stretch, romance had to be put on hold until the regular break between camps. Then, complete with proceeds from the penalty boxes to subsidise the revelry, they were all off amid clouds of dust to Top Springs or Timber Creek, the latter about 140 kilometres away, for some serious partying. Sixty years ago when it was known as The Depot, Sonya's grandmother Maggie had partied on there too.

Sonya went on to overseeing on one of the Heytesbury stations, and to other projects but now she is married. With her husband and baby daughter she has returned to the Kimberley, and lives on Nicholson Station.

Maggie was enjoying her life now and began to travel even more often in company with her friend Greta, Jim Coulthard's mother. Maggie is very good company and will join in whatever is going just as readily as she always did, with good humour and a willingness to fit in. The two friends managed several trips all over Australia including a spectacular wildflower trip in their own state and another across Australia to Cairns during which she was able to visit Pentland, her mother Hannah's birthplace and nearby, the lovely old town of Charters Towers. Maggie, to whom distance is of no consequence after a lifetime in the outback, thoroughly enjoyed the journeys. After all, 400 kilometre round trip just to do some shopping soon teaches patience on the long miles.

In 1990 Maggie first became a great grandmother when Alma's daughter Jodie produced a daughter, Rachael. Young Todd had grown into a fine young man reinforcing the value of Sam's loving investment of time and care in his grandson. Constantly encouraged by his stepfather Ian, Todd became a licensed aircraft engineer, specialising in helicopters. Needless to say the two men are the best of mates and have never been known to run out of absorbing topics to discuss.

There were several occasions for celebration in the Durack households in Perth and Maggie went down to join them each time. The years were flying by and the straight limbed young Durack men of her youth were now showing their years, but none of them had forgotten how to laugh or how to enjoy friendship and good memories.

Every spring Patsy Appelbee came up from the home near Perth where she and George now lived, to help Alma at Packsaddle. Maggie always looked forward to Patsy's visit. In spite of the difference in years the two women have always been very close friends and frequently Patsy would

(Ingham collection)

PORTRAIT OF MAUREEN AND JIM COULTHARD'S SON ROD AND DAUGHTER SONJA — TWO OF MAGGIE'S GRANDCHILDREN — WITH THEIR FAVOURITE HORSES AT VICTORIA RIVER DOWNS STATION, N.T. PAINTED BY THE AUTHOR IN 1993.

accompany Maggie on a trip when the work at Kununurra was completed. In 1991 they went to the Ringers' Muster at the Stockman's Hall of Fame in Longreach, Queensland where Maggie was in her element. Assembled there for the Muster were old ringers, stockmen and station managers many of whom were known to both Maggie and Patsy. Roger Steele who was closely associated with the Stockman's Hall of Fame at the time made sure the two women quickly caught up with mates from the past. After half a century Maggie caught up with boss drover Jackie Charlton, one of the legendary Murrunji drovers. They talked and laughed until the tears ran down their faces about incidents that happened when Jack was lifting a mob in the 1940s and Maggie was present for the "lift". Such encounters brought her close once more to the precious days when she and Sam were young and they were at Turkey Creek, building the foundations of what would one day become the mighty Bow River Station.

Local government honoured Maggie when the Highway was rerouted to pass through the valley where Maggie and Violet had driven on the bird catching trips so long ago. Maggie was surprised to find there was a Maggie Jump-up, a Maggie Bridge and a Maggie Valley. She enquired here and there and discovered that "an old fellow named Edgar Birch working on the road knew that I was the first person to drive a motor car into that area." Maggie regards it all as a great bit of fun, especially as she loves that valley with its thousands of boab trees where so long ago two teenage girls laughed and talked, shared their dreams and spent much time digging the little Chev 4 out of sand bogs.

A few years ago Maggie began to have trouble with her sight and after driving about seventy years she was obliged to relinquish her licence. This really was a severe blow to a woman who had never questioned her capability to come and go as she wished. Having to be dependent on others has presented Maggie with a cruel restriction. Her son in law Ian Petherick understood her frustration and although very busy with his trucking business always took time to see to Maggie's wellbeing. Whenever possible he would take Maggie with him on trips so she could see the country and catch up with events and people in the district. Ian's other drivers were also a source of interest and information. Joining them for smoko when the trucks came in gave her immense pleasure and a link with the outside world somewhat compensating for her present limited mobility.

The Pethericks' full attention is now centred on their town business commitments that have snowballed. Tim Timms comes in to visit whenever he can. "Tim remains the same proud dear old man he always was; he keeps contract with the whole family through me at the shop. When they need a loan they still see us as family. Thirty five years of living together in isolation makes people a family regardless of race." Alma goes on to say "They don't all get help as I am not happy with the way some of the younger ones bludge off the old people and have become so irresponsible and unreliable." Maureen had not seen Tim for a few years and recently she was with Alma when Tim appeared. "You should have seen it. Maureen broke down and they ran to each other with arms out." Maureen now in her mid-fifties and Tim somewhere in his eighties tearfully embraced. The family bond was as deep as it had ever been.

(Coulthard collection)

BACK ROW: JIM AND ROD COULTHARD. FRONT: MAUREEN, DAUGHTER SONJA TEACE HOLDING COURTNEY AND RUSSELL TEACE. COURTNEY — MAGGIE'S GREAT GRANDDAUGHTER — LOVES HORSES. AS THE SIXTH GENERATION FROM SARAH BEASLEY SHE IS MAINTAINING THE TRADITION. ROD AND SONJA BOTH WENT ON TO MANAGE LARGE STATIONS IN THE NORTHERN TERRITORY AND SONJA IS NOW BACK IN THE KIMBERLEY WORKING WITH HUSBAND RUSSELL.

(Sonja Teace collection)

ABOVE: THERE'S NOTHING TO BEAT A GOOD DIP AFTER A LONG HARD DAY IN THE SADDLE. IN THE SOFT LIGHT OF EVENING THREE OF THE GIRLS FROM THE MUSTER CAMP WASH OFF THE DUST IN A CATTLE TROUGH, COMPLETE WITH PRETTY PINK TOWELS, SHAMPOO AND PERFUMED SOAP. GEORGIE FIRTH ON LEFT, MARY QUILTY CENTRE AND SONJA COULTHARD ON THE FAR RIGHT.

(Anne Ingham collection)

ABOVE: MURRUNJI DROVER, JACKIE CHARLTON AND MAGGIE LILLY MET AGAIN AFTER MANY YEARS AT THE 1991 DROVERS REUNION IN THE STOCKMANS' HALL OF FAME, LONGREACH. RECALLING INCIDENTS FROM DROVING IN THE LATE FORTIES, THE TWO OLD TIMERS SAT AND TALKED AND LAUGHED UNTIL THE TEARS RAN DOWN THEIR CHEEKS.

Maggie has now moved into a delightful new home in the town of Kununurra, with distant views of her beloved hills which she can see and delight in. Her near sight has been a problem but fortunately she still has good vision for distant objects. At first the prospect of moving to closer settlement daunted her. At Packsaddle she could still roam over the acres and care for her flock of goats and take an interest in the agricultural goings on around her. Confinement to a small area did not beckon in the least. Filled with doubts Maggie made the move and settled in fully prepared to hate every minute of it, but activity and involvement have begun to fill every day. She began to plan a garden but that is going to take much longer then she expected with all the cups of tea she dispenses to the endless stream of people popping in to visit. There have always been the regular interests of the racing season; "Mum has hardly ever missed a Wyndham Cup Meeting and is a Life Member of the Wyndham Turf Club," says Maureen. "There is always someone, Ian or the Hackett boys up the road, to pick her up and take her home from the races or the rodeo and the local Home and Community Care takes all the pensioners off for outings." Any misgivings Maggie may have had have been swallowed up in an endless round of activity and she's still the same Maggie of long ago. She was settled into the new home in time for her eighty eighth birthday in February 2000.

BACK LEFT TO RIGHT: JOHN PATRICK, JOE THOMAS, TIM TIMMS. FRONT: PEGGIE PATRICK, MAGGIE, PHYUS THOMAS, LIDDY TIMMS. MAGGIE LILLY SURROUNDED BY HER FAMILY FROM BOW RIVER. SHE BELONGS TO THEM AND THEY TO HER AND THE RELATIONSHIP SPANS OVER FIFTY YEARS WHEN MAGGIE AND SAM FIRST FOUNDED THE BOW RIVER STATION AND THEIR CHILDREN WERE BORN AND ALL PLAYED TOGETHER. IT WAS TIMMY TIMMS, NOW WELL INTO HIS EIGHTIES, WHO OVERSAW THE CHILDREN DURING MUSTER AND TAUGHT THEM SO MUCH.

Now she is the oldest white woman in the Kimberley. Wherever she goes she is welcomed and revered and the people of Bow River still regard her as family. She is still "Yummun". Recently Yummun was told of another success story among her Bow River family. Some of the Worman community have been working in the Aboriginal art world and doing very well but the latest to take up a successful career is Tim Timms who has been launched into the art market with a most impressive four figure sum for the sale of one of his works.

Maggie, on the other hand, lives very carefully on a limited income. Ironically, all around the Bow are scattered the Kimberley diamonds, the beautiful coffee coloured gems that have washed down the rivers from the pipes in the hills for countless millions of years. According to Maggie, "People here reckon that if you could get some sort of a dredging plant going at the place where the five rivers meet you'd make a fortune." Diamonds have not yet been discovered on the Bow itself. However one of the places where they were discovered is a neighbouring station, Lissadel which Patsy Appelbee's father used to manage. "Just think of it!" Patsy said to Maggie. "All those years we were driving over the things and we never knew it!"

Having lived in the Kimberley since her birth and being possessed of an excellent memory Maggie retains an amazing continuity of historical detail of the area. People, places and races are her favourite recollections and she is a popular and valued member of the Historical Society.

Few are left of Maggie's contemporaries and in the old days not one of them would have realised that they would one day be revered as pioneers. They took things as they found them and strove to achieve in spite of the monumental difficulties and dangers that surrounded them; even surviving was problematical. To succeeding generations, their names and achievements are becoming legendary. There were the Duracks, the Quilties, the MacDonalds, the Underwoods, the Skuthorpes, Charlie and Hessie Schultz, Tom Ronan, the Fitzers, Kate Rhatigan, Maggie's own beloved Sam, great pioneers all. Some departed for other regions and settled further south and many have died but Maggie Lilly, who never strayed for long from her beloved Kimberley, is unique. Revered by both races, the ancient people of the land and her own of more recent origin she ranks among the great pioneer women of Australia.

WHEN THE ARGYLE DAM WAS PLANNED, THE ARGLE STATION HOMESTEAD WAS MOVED STONE BY STONE TO HIGHER GROUND. THE DURACK FAMILY GRAVES WOULD HAVE BEEN INUNDATED BUT WERE MOVED AND ARE PART OF THE HOMESTEAD GARDEN. MEMBERS OF THE DURACK FAMILY AND FRIENDS GATHERED ON 10 JULY, 1999 FOR A MEMORIAL CEREMONY FOR REG DURACK WHO DIED EARLIER IN THE YEAR. SEATED FROM LEFT TO RIGHT ARE ELIZABETH DURACK, HER DAUGHTER PERPETUA, ENID DURACK, REG'S WIDOW, HER DAUGHTER ANNE, AND MAGGIE LILLY. DIRECTLY BEHIND ANNE IS MAGGIE'S DAUGHTER ALMA.

WHEN THE NEW ROAD WAS PUT THROUGH TO WYNDHAM AND NAMES WERE GIVEN TO FEATURES ALONG THE WAY MAGGIE LILLY WAS HONORED WITH MAGGIE CREEK, MAGGIE VALLEY AND MAGGIE JUMP UP BEING NAMED AFTER HER. "SOME OLD CHAP REMEMBERED THAT A GIRL NAMED MAGGIE NICHOLSON FIRST EXPLORED AROUND THERE AND WENT BIRD CATCHING WAY BACK IN THE 1920S LONG BEFORE ANYONE ELSE IN WYNDHAM, SO THEY CALLED IT AFTER ME!"

The Sting in the Tale!

MAGGIE LILLY HAS LIVED through many changes in her eighty odd years and didn't really expect there was much left that could surprise her. However, one day she received a telephone call and a young man said "Hello Aunt, I'm your nephew, Garry Cook."

Maggie was nonplussed to say the least. Who could this be? The voice continued, "I'm the son of George Cook, your mother's son."

Maggie felt he'd made a mistake and explained to the caller that their George Cook, Hannah's son, had drowned when he was eight. She told him about the letter from George's elderly aunt Caroline Lane which brought the news to Hannah some years after the tragedy. Surely he must have made a mistake and got her family mixed up with someone else's.

"No. George Cook did not die. He was not drowned." Garry assured her. Caroline Lane had lied in her letter and Gary proceeded to enlighten Maggie on the sequence of events that had taken place nearly one hundred years earlier. He promised to substantiate his claims by mail and later posted copies of official documents tracing events in little George Cook's sad childhood.

Having been left by his mother to be raised by Caroline, little George would have experienced a lonely and somewhat unnatural existence compared with other children of his own age who each had a mother, father, siblings and a normal family life. He was isolated much of the time with only the company of an elderly person past the age and inclination to bother or care for a small child and totally out of touch with the needs of a high spirited healthy little boy. As time went by and no communications came from his mother he would have assumed his mother didn't want him, love him or care about him. It may be that Caroline unwittingly reinforced the idea whenever she had occasion to scold him. He totally lacked reassurance; if one's own mother abandons one, who else is there in the world who really cares? Such thoughts must have tortured the little boy and by the time he was eight he was rebelling against his aunt's discipline. He played truant from school for a month and slept out in the open for a couple of nights. It was more than his Aunt was prepared to tolerate or try to understand. She obtained a warrant for his arrest and he was picked up by the police sleeping out at a place called Smedmore near Newcastle.

Eight year old George Cook was committed on 13th September, 1898 to two months' sentence aboard the reformatory ship *Sobraon* moored in Sydney Harbour at Rose Bay.

The entrance book gives the sad details of his commital:

Health: Good. ***Education***: Indifferent. ***Appearance:*** Dirty and Neglected. ***Friends:*** Bad. ***Father:*** Dead. ***Whereabouts of Mother:*** Unknown.

It was probably an easier option for Caroline to write to Hannah announcing her son's death by drowning than to admit that she'd been unable to raise him properly and had had him arrested and sent to a reform institution. Caroline's lie was destined to cause tragic reverberations that lasted for nearly a century and especially throughout George Cook's lifetime.

Having finally received Caroline's letter, Hannah could only accept that her son was dead. It would not have crossed even the most questioning mind that the boy's aunt was lying.

People by the name of Mappin who owned a farm on the Hawkesbury River near Wiseman's Ferry eventually fostered little George. The Mappins cared for children without families and George grew to manhood regarding them as his family. He married the daughter of a neighbour, a half Spanish girl named Catherine Therese Deas and they had a large family of six sons and one daughter. The eldest son, George Edward became an internationally famous oarsman, later coaching young rowers to Olympic level.

Towards his family, George was uncommunicative and all his life carried the hurt of his mother's apparent rejection. He never knew of his aunt's letter to Hannah telling her her son had drowned. The lonely young man tried many times to locate Hannah and his sister Annie, even putting advertisements in the Darwin newspaper, but Hannah was in Western Australia. Had he had access to electoral rolls he may have had more luck but tragically time, distance and primitive communications of the day proved too difficult. George Cook died in 1959, convinced that his mother had abandoned him.

Maggie found the whole story too amazing for words. In eighty four years she had never questioned the information that her half brother met his death by drowning. Now she had to assimilate the fact that she had a half brother until her late forties. He had reached his "three score years and ten" and he had left behind for her a large number of nephews, their wives, a niece and her husband who between them had produced twenty five children! For Maggie it was a most exciting revelation but for Hannah she grieved deeply. "Poor Mum went to her death never knowing that Caroline's letter was a lie and her little son George Cook had lived and tried so hard to find her."

Water lilies growing on Marglu Lagoon (Parry's Lagoon) — a picturesque watering place for cattle being driven in to Wyndham.

Acknowledgements

- **Roger Steele.** Good mate and a constant source of encouragement and information. "Steelo" is a lifetime resident of the Top End who has honoured me once again by writing the foreword for my story.
- **Len Hill** of Charters Towers, Queensland, who generously gave permission to reproduce remarkable historic photographs of Wyndham taken by his grandfather, Thomas Charles White (1864–1931) in 1916. Len Hill spent many years managing Kimberley stations, including Nicholson, and has known Maggie and her late husband since The Bow River Station began.
- **Patsy and George Appelbee,** longtime friends of the Lillys. My sincere thanks for their warm and affectionate contribution.
- **Lance MacSmith** and family for information on The Depot (Timber Creek), N.T.
- **John Hughes** of the Wyndham Museum for generous provision of information.
- **Heather Foote** of the Derby Library who kindly took time to research material pertaining to Derby.
- **Derby Council,** for town maps and information.
- Broome Council.
- **Shire of Wyndham, East Kimberley. Denise Hansen.** Information on Chimooly.
- **Bob Sextant** of Ports Corp. South Australia for his expert assistance in tracing Carl Helmuth's shipping activities.
- **Dulcie Sommers** (granddaughter of Carl and Elizabeth Lilljenqvist.)
- **Nancy Wethersten and son Paul.** For kind permission to use the Mark Twain quote from "W. Folster's Articles". Nancy's father and Paul's grandfather, W. Folster, was a prolific, dedicatedly accurate recorder of the history of the Orange region of N.S.W. His "Articles", as he called them, now compiled and published in book form by Paul, were stored in voluminous scrapbooks along with favourite quotes.
- **Stephen McCallum and the Cook family.** Maggie's nephew Stephen McCallum, son of Hannah's first child Annie Cook, who provided Maggie with papers pertaining to births, deaths and marriages and other material relating to the life of Hannah Nicholson, her family and children. Gary and Suzanne Cook have also provided information from their own research, which has been most valuable in the recording of Hannah Nicholson's background and movements in the 19th century; also for the details of Hannah Nicholson's baby son George.
- **Steve Howell** – Senior Librarian, Reference Services, J S Battye Library of Western Australia.
- **The Staff of the Orange City Library.** I thank them all most sincerely for their great help and cheerful response to all my requests for assistance.

Above: Hannah Nicholson's T-Model taxi in front of the Nine Mile Store and Boarding House near Wyndham. All that remains to mark the site is the well from which Maggie used to draw their water, and a round stone tank stand.

Clockwise from above: Reg Durack's 80th birthday, at his Perth home in 1991, left to right: Eric Durack, Mary Durack, Pat Ryle, Enid and Reg Durack, Eileen Fitzer (a Territorian born in Pine Creek in 1903), Patsy Appelbee and Maggie Lilly; Maggie's mother, Hannah Nicholson. Her life included many heartbreaks and tragedies. She was first widowed at 22, and the baby son of a second marriage died at remote Oobergooma Station. With her husband away, Hannah had to bury him herself; Friends since youth, Charlie Schultz and Maggie Lilly at the Kununurra home of Maggie's daughter Alma, in 1990. Charlie Schultz's life's recorded in *Beyond the Big Run*, by Darryl Lewis..